P9-DEG-774

On Being a Bishop

Papers on Episcopacy from the Moscow Consultation 1992

Edited by J. Robert Wright

THE CHURCH HYMNAL CORPORATION • NEW YORK

Copyright © 1993, The Church Pension Fund.
All Rights Reserved.

Grateful acknowledgement is made to the following for
permission to use their previously published materials:

To The Central Board of Finance of the Church of England for
permission to use pages 5-10, 39-45, and 119-133 from *Episcopal
Ministry: The Report of the Archbishops' Group on the Episcopate*,
copyright © The Central Board of Finance of the Church of
England 1990.

To Augsburg Fortress Publishers for permission to reproduce
pages 59-71 and pages 91-92 from *"Toward Full Communion"
and "Concordat of Agreement"* by Norgren and Rusch,
copyright © 1991 Augsburg Fortress.

The Church Hymnal Corporation
800 Second Avenue
New York, New York 10017

Table of Contents

Preface

There is much interest today, both in the Episcopal Church and among its ecumenical friends in other churches, about bishops—why have them, what are they, are they necessary or just desirable (or even undesirable), what should they do, how should they spend their time, how did they originate, have they always been like they are today, ...??? The questions seem basic and simple, but others are rather more complex: What qualifications should a diocese look for when choosing a new bishop? Must a bishop always be "the husband of one wife" (I Timothy 3:2)? What are the proper grounds for withholding consent from the election of a new bishop? Are the Holy Orders of a bishop indelible? Must the Holy Orders of a bishop be cumulative (including diaconate and priesthood)? What are the essentials of the "historic" episcopate?

Other questions are more practical: Must a bishop have a cathedral? always be styled "The Rt. Rev."? necessarily be chosen by popular vote? have the highest salary of all the clergy in the diocese? have a special chair in every parish church? be the immediate pastor and spiritual advisor of every priest in the diocese? How much authority should the bishop have in the filling of parish vacancies within the diocese? How should the church discipline a bishop who clearly seems to be teaching doctrine contrary to what the church seems to think it believes? What are the grounds for deposing a bishop? Can two dioceses still be in communion with one another, if the jurisdiction of one overlaps the other? Can the existence, can the very consecrations or ordinations, of some bishops but not of others, be described as merely "provisional"?

Readers of this volume will not find the answers to all these questions contained herein! Many of the same questions, though, so common to the American church at present, are also being asked right now in the Russian Orthodox Church as well, the Episcopal Church's delegation to the Moscow consultation of June 1992 discovered. "The old Church in the new Russia," as some lovingly call it, is very much alive and is now experiencing a process of reawakening and renewal that is leading it to ask, for perhaps different reasons, many of those same probing questions about bishops at this critical juncture now that its seventy and more years of Communist domination have ended.

The Moscow consultation of June 22-27, 1992, was only a start to the topic at hand, but most of the foregoing questions were at least raised there, and the participants certainly left with the conviction that the ministry of bishops is both central and critical to the proper renewal, indeed to the worship, witness, teaching and evangelism, that is so necessary in both our churches now as always. In August of 1989 Presiding Bishop Edmond Browning, during a visit to the Russian Church on the occasion of its Millennium celebrations, and in view of the emerging new reality of East-West relations, established together with the Moscow Patriarchate a Joint Coordinating Committee for practical cooperation and bilateral relations between the Episcopal Church and the Orthodox Church in Russia, and this was the fourth—and the most theological—of its meetings that have followed. The first was held in New York City from 12-13 September of 1990, the second in Moscow from 20-27 April of 1991, and the third from 14-20 October of 1991 in Washington, D.C. Many projects of practical cooperation have been initiated through the meetings and activities of this committee, which is chaired for the Episcopal Church by The Rt. Rev. Roger J. White, Bishop of Milwaukee and currently the president of the Episcopal Church's Province of the Midwest. This is not the place to enumerate all these practical steps that are underway, since there are agencies, offices, and institutions within the Episcopal Church, both official and unofficial, whose responsibility it is to publicize and communicate such news and developments.

For the Moscow consultation in June of 1992 the agreed subject was "bishops"—both in theory and in practice—and it was decided that from the Episcopal side there would be seven papers offered, and they are presented here. A word of explanation is necessary, however, concerning the last of these. This paper was intended to be a response by Professor Kortright Davis to the previous paper from the Episcopal side, but it was not actually delivered in Moscow because the previous paper, to which he was supposed to respond, was not ready in time and then at the last moment Professor Davis himself was prevented by an emergency from attending the consultation. He did eventually prepare his paper, though, for the same purpose and context as the others that had been given in Moscow, and therefore, it is included here.

Not only were the first six of the papers themselves translated into Russian ahead of time for the consultation by the Russian Orthodox Church's highly capable Department of External Church Relations, but advance translations as well were made of the five pieces of supplementary material about bishops also submitted from the Episcopal side. These included three chapters taken out of the extensive new study from the Church of England, *Episcopal Ministry: The Report of the Archbishops' Group on the Episcopate* (London, 1990), which form chapters 3, 9, and 13 (the first, third, and fifth supplements) in the present volume. Of the two other supplements from the Episcopal side presented and translated for the Moscow discussions, one was *The Ministry of Bishops: A Study Document Authorized by the House of Bishops of the Episcopal Church* (from the Phoenix General Convention of July 1991), which appears here as chapter 7 (the second supplement) and which was introduced in Moscow (chapter 6, the fourth paper) by the Rt. Rev. Richard F. Grein, Bishop of New York, who had chaired the bishops' committee that sponsored the study document. The other was the essay on "The Episcopal Church and the Ministry of the Historic Episcopate" (chapter 10, the fourth supplement), which was taken from the final report of the third round of the official Lutheran-Episcopal Dialogue in the United States (Augsburg, 1991). These, together with the six papers actually delivered in person at Moscow, under the topics and by the authors as they are listed in the table of contents here, form all together a quite comprehensive survey of the ministry of bishops as that ministry is received and understood in the Episcopal Church today.[1]

The entire collection at the first is set in context by Dr. Suzanne Massie, Episcopalian laywoman and Fellow of the Russian Research Center of Harvard University, author of several noted books on Russia and its culture, and a member of the Joint Coordinating Committee who was herself an active participant in the discussions at Moscow. The actual papers are presented here in the order in which they were given at Moscow, moving from the "historical" and "theological" through the "liturgical" and towards the "practical," although, of course, such divisions are somewhat artificial and, of course, the papers can be read in any order that may be desired. The Official Communiqué and Joint Working Document conclude the volume, the latter giving summaries of all the papers including those offered from the Russian Orthodox delegation. It would have been impossible from these papers alone to give an adequate picture to the Episcopal Church of how the Russian Orthodox understand the ministry of bishops in this one volume, but I am confident that the reader will find herein a picture of the Episcopal Church's understanding, as it was presented to them at Moscow in June of 1992, that is both competent and reliable as well as timely.

• • •

---

[1] It was agreed in advance that the ordination of women to the episcopate and the "truly episcopal" ministry of the bishop of Rome would not be considered in the context of the 1992 consultation, since these topics had already received some preliminary attention in the discussions of August 1989 and since it was agreed that they deserve much fuller treatment at a later date.

Finally, it is with great pleasure that I dedicate this volume to

HIS HOLINESS, ALEKSY II, PATRIARCH OF MOSCOW AND ALL RUSSIA,

the host and patron of these conversations, whose ministry as bishop and now also patriarch of a church and nation in transition exemplifies the highest ideals of which these papers speak. Of him and his church the words of Scripture can appropriately be paraphrased: "We were treated as dying, and behold, we live!" (2 Cor. 6:8-9). May his spiritual leadership of the largest national church in the world stimulate also the bishops of the Episcopal Church to look beyond the local boundaries of our own church and nation to those pastoral principles of episcopal ministry that are constant and enduring across time and in every place.

J. Robert Wright, D.Phil. (Oxon.), D.D., F.R.Hist.S.,
St. Mark's Professor of Ecclesiastical History
The General Theological Seminary
New York City

I

Setting the Context for the Papers that Follow

by Dr. Suzanne Massie
Fellow of the Russian Research Center of
Harvard University

Russia is a country where the ordinary rarely happens. This is part of the great fascination of this nation for those who love and study her as I have for the past twenty-five years. During these years I have had varied and extraordinary experiences with Russians in all walks of life—old and young, poets and artists, politicians and bureaucrats, actors and movie directors, scientists and doctors, military officers and policemen, journalists, writers, museum directors and restorers, students, professors, diplomats, priests and hierarchs of the Orthodox Church, the mighty and the humble. During these years I have written books on Russian cultural history, organized art exhibitions, founded an international group which helped to finish the restoration of a great palace, been the subject of a Russian film, participated in meetings between U.S. senators and high members of the former Soviet government, and been a witness of many historic occasions including the historic celebration of the Millennium of the Russian Church in 1988. Now, as the only woman and a lay member of the first permanent Coordinating Committee between the Episcopal Church and the Russian Orthodox Church, I have been given the rare opportunity to participate more closely than ever before in the reemergence of the Orthodox Church after its long years of persecution.

Patriarch Aleksy II has warned of the danger that "for the first time a society of competitive economy will be built in conditions of spiritual devastation in a society devoid of universal national values." As Russia emerges from its long agony of totalitarianism, attempting to define itself anew, nothing is more important than the questions of morality and national values which the church is being called on once again to define. The outcome of this search for a new moral base will, I am convinced, determine the direction and ultimate fate of the nation.

The most recent meeting of our committee, the fourth in our two-year series of biannual meetings—two in the United States and two in Moscow—took place from June 22-27, 1992. This was the first meeting to deal with purely theological issues; specifically, the role of bishops ("The Episcopal Ministry in the Church"). Each of the American participants, among them three bishops and three professors of theology, presented papers on the topic, which are reproduced in this volume along with summaries of those presented by the Russian side. I will confess that when I first learned that this—"Bishops"—was to be the topic of our meeting, I thought it was a little esoteric for this time of great social suffering and economic difficulty in Russia. I was wrong. For as it turned out, this subject was of great import both theoretical and practical for the current problems faced by the Orthodox Church. It elicited what my long experience in Russia leads me to appreciate as a remarkably frank and often touchingly open response from the Russian side about some of the most painful and immediate problems now being faced by their church. As always, Russia surprises.

Our meetings were held at the St. Daniel (Danilov) Monastery, located in what is now central Moscow. This monastery in itself is a startling testimony to the resurrection and revitalization of religious life and the Orthodox Church in Russia in recent years: old and yet new, restored and yet only just emerging from long dark years of near extinction. When I first saw the monastery barely eight years ago, it was in ruins. Today, where only a short time ago there was only rubble, a profusion of roses bloom, their fragile beauty celebrating the return of spiritual life.

Founded in 1282 by Prince Daniel, the youngest son of the great Russian hero and saint, Alexander Nevsky, the Danilov Monastery has profound historical resonance for the Russian people. Daniel was only two years old when his father, on his deathbed, willed him the small and then quite unimportant principality of Moscow. Prince Daniel grew up to become a peaceful and religious ruler of exemplary character; the monastery he founded became the first center of spiritual resistance in Moscow to Mongol domination. Before his death in 1303 at age 42, Daniel became a monk and was later canonized. Daniel's son, the new ruler of Moscow, moved the monastery into the Kremlin to have its brothers closer to himself. It was moved again in the late fifteenth century. However, the tradition of the former cloister lived on among the new generations of monks and the Rule adopted at the time of Prince (St.) Daniel never lost its importance. In 1560, Ivan the Terrible ordered the St. Daniel Monastery to be restored in its original location and also the building of a stone church dedicated to the Holy Fathers of the Seven Ecumenical Councils and stone cells for the monks. From the seventeenth to the nineteenth century the large fortified architectural complex of the monastery spread over sixteen acres and included three churches and many smaller churches and chapels. Although it was never the favorite monastery of the tsars and the court, because its founder was the humble Prince (St.) Daniel the Danilov Monastery remained a shrine beloved by the people.

In 1721 Peter the Great, who was determined to Westernize his country, mounted a severe campaign against Russian Orthodox ways and the church. Among many acts he abolished the Patriarchate. For almost two hundred years Russia was to have no Patriarch. The church, ruled by the Holy Synod, headed by the Metropolitan of St. Petersburg, had its seat in the new capital. Under Tsar Nicholas II the Patriarchate was restored and a new Church Council convened which elected in 1917 a new Patriarch, Tikhon, shortly before the revolution. However, immediately after Lenin took power, he and the new Bolshevik regime moved swiftly and brutally to destroy the church. The new regime set out to erase religion entirely. From 1918 on, it conducted a ferocious anti-religious campaign of death and destruction, rarely, if ever, equaled in history. Churches, seminaries and monasteries were closed and turned into warehouses, cattle barns, movie houses, and swimming pools. Church property was seized, desecrated, and destroyed: icons sold, bells silenced and melted down. Thousands of priests, monks, and nuns were brutally murdered. Patriarch Tikhon became a refugee in his own land, living in a small monastery in Moscow connected to the famous Holy Trinity St. Sergius Monastery of Zagorsk and later the Donskoy Monastery where, in 1921, he was arrested. He died in mysterious circumstances shortly after.

The Danilov Monastery was closed in 1930, its monks, like thousands of others, murdered or imprisoned, its famous bells melted down. For Americans it is moving to know that the relics of St. Daniel and a few of the sixteenth century monastery bells found their way to our country. The bells were saved by an American businessman who, in the thirties, saw them being melted down on the banks of the Moscow river and managed to buy those that were left. He gave the huge bells to his alma mater, Harvard University, where they are rung today in the bell tower especially constructed to house them in Lowell House. The relics of St. Daniel which disappeared for many years were rediscovered in America and returned to the monastery in 1986.

During all the years of Communist domination the campaign against the church continued unabated. Under Stalin the monastery was turned into a dismal prison for children of the "enemies of the people" and later into a car repair shop. It was not until 1982, after long and secret negotiations by a church commission led by Aleksy, then Bishop of Talinn and today the Patriarch, that Leonid Brezhnev as he died, for reasons we can only surmise, signed papers returning the Danilov Monastery to the church to become the new spiritual and administrative center of the Patriarch and the Holy Synod. After seven centuries, the Danilov Monastery, the first monastery to be built in Moscow, became the first monastery in Moscow to be returned to the church by the Communist regime. This was the first of many signs to follow that the government was beginning to accept defeat in its unrelenting 70-year attempt to kill the church and the religious spirit of the Russian people.

In 1983 the statue of Lenin at the Danilov Monastery was taken down and removed from the courtyard—an early harbinger of the dramatic changes soon to come. That year, under the direction of the Commission headed by Bishop Aleksy, the restoration work began in earnest. The recovery and rebuilding of the monastery aroused enormous interest in Russia. Thousands of pilgrims from all over the Soviet Union came to Moscow, many voluntarily offering to work without pay in the restoration effort. When I first visited the monastery in 1983, I had to pick my way through the courtyard filled with mud and debris. When I came again I witnessed the enthusiastic and devoted work that continued all day and far into the night. Three churches and several buildings were erected, frescoes and icons painted, an impressive new conference building (where our meetings were held) was constructed for the Patriarch, the massive seventeenth century walls surrounding the complex were restored and whitewashed, and new bells hung in the bell tower. This enormous work was accomplished in five short years, in time to celebrate the Millennium of the Russian Orthodox Church in 1988. At the Millennium, I attended outdoor services celebrating the Baptism of Russia in the monastery courtyards packed with thousands of people. As part of this great ceremony, the Patriarch (Pimen) arrived and was officially transferred from the Holy Trinity/St. Sergius Monastery at Zagorsk (now Sergiev Posad) 72 kilometers away to his new headquarters at the Danilov Monastery in the center of the city.

Today the reconstructed complex of the Danilov includes three churches, many individual chapels, and office buildings which house the administration of the Patriarchate. Just outside the walls a new hotel, where we stayed, has been built for guests of the church. The Danilov is an active monastery with forty monks and many novices. The work of reconstruction continues unabated. Gardens are being landscaped and planted and every day the new bells of the monastery peal triumphantly. These are still a new and thrilling sound, for it was only at the time of the Millennium four years ago that the government permitted the church bells of Moscow to be rung again. Only this year were church bells joyously pealed at midnight, as they had been in the past, all over the city in celebration of Easter.

We have just met in this historic place—at a time of great triumph, challenge and stress, of self-examination and searching for the Orthodox Church. The great surge of interest in spiritual matters and the return to religion of people of all ages all over Russia, which has grown at a steadily rising tempo over the past twenty years, is a source of joy and hope but also poses many problems. Much is being demanded of the church—nothing less than the moral regeneration of the nation—by a disheartened, betrayed and discouraged people at a time when the church, still weakened from its ordeal of persecution, is facing multiple problems both economic and spiritual. Grave financial problems are severely aggravated by the need to rebuild thousands of ruined churches. There are schisms; currently, there are five branches of the Orthodox Church, three in Russia and two in the United States. There are public accusations and acrimonious discussion about the degree of collaboration of certain Russian hierarchs with the Communist authorities. The Orthodox Church feels itself beset by onslaughts of Western evangelism backed with plenty of money. It is beginning to face the great questions of reform and the need for greater democratization and revitalization. Unyielding conservatism and unswerving adherence to tradition has been the rock of the church in its long period of adversity. Although forced into subservience, it remained unabsorbable, the only non-Marixist-Leninist institution permitted to exist at all. Today as it faces the demands of a new, younger generation of believers, the unyielding conservatism that was its strength may now be its weakness. The great question for the church is: Has the time come to bend tradition a little? And if so, how and how much? The Russian people are trying to find their way back to the national values and morality destroyed under the Communist regime, searching through the rubble looking for their lost soul... . They are looking to the church to provide answers—and quickly.

It is against this charged atmosphere that the Russians can learn much from the experience of the Episcopal Church in coping with a diversity of opinion in our own changing society while maintaining a firm grounding in tradition. One of the Russian theologians (who had been told, he said, before our meeting that he would be "defending the Orthodox position against a group of Protestants") seemed startled to find that we shared common historical roots. Indeed as the days went by, I noticed a visible growth of trust among the Russians, which I attribute to the tact, sensitivity and compassionate understanding exhibited by our bishops and theologians. Hesitantly at first, then with growing confidence, they began to touch on some of their most sensitive problems: The stressful question of the possible deposing of unworthy bishops, how to bring a wider participation in the choice of bishops in parishes, how to encourage still wary and dispirited priests to become more confident and active? One of the Russian theologians inquired, "People are expecting prophetic words from the church at a time when cults are growing. What are the ways in which you are trying to reach people's hearts?" A lively discussion took place on the question of bishops being chosen by the people, one of the Russians exclaiming heatedly, "The *true voice* of the people must be heard as it was in old Russia!" The level of discussion was always cordial, there was a warm and sometimes even electric contact between the two delegations.

On a personal note: for myself, an Episcopal laywoman and the mother of an Episcopal priest, it was a deepening experience. To tell the truth, I had not up to then thought very much about the role of bishops. For me, they were rather distant and remote figures who appeared, grandly attired in miters, robes and staffs, for confirmations and ordinations. This was a precious opportunity to learn more about not only the essential roots and the central leadership role of bishops in my own church, but to explore the differences of approach and emphasis of the three bishops present within the unity of the church. Each was very different in personality and style, and I asked each what they saw as their primary goal in their ministries as bishops. One answered that he wanted all his people "to become saints"—that is to be infused with the spirit of the living Trinity in their lives. Another answered that he wanted his flock "to sing praises continually,"—that is to exhibit Christian enthusiasm and witness in the community. The last said that he hoped to "forge unity in diversity." I left our meetings very proud of my church and more than ever convinced that we have an essential experience which gives us the possibility of providing support for our Orthodox brothers and sisters as they try to find their way back to their spiritual roots.

The survival of the Orthodox Church and now the growing hunger for spiritual life among millions of Russians is a great miracle of our time. During the past three years more than 12,000 churches have been re-opened, along with many monasteries and convents and several new seminaries. Sunday schools are now functioning regularly. The church is beginning to found its own hospitals and schools. It has begun its charitable work again, and in these difficult days with the government bankrupt, it is virtually the only source of help and comfort for the poor, the old, and the dying. Millions of Russians have been baptized; Patriarch Aleksy has told us that he is faced with the problem of training 14,000 new priests. Public interest is so high that for every television program on the economic situation, there are at least ten evocative documentaries on the church. The church bells which peal again announce this renewal. In my view nothing is more important for Russia today than the eventual outcome of the current reexamination and reorganization of the church.

When one reflects on the primordial role that the Orthodox Church has played in the development of Russian culture and the identity of the nation, it becomes clear that any effort to understand what is happening in Russia today only through the prism of economics and politics, overlooking the profound yearning for a new spiritual content that animates the Russian people today, is bound to be woefully lacking, misleading, and incomplete.

A Russian priest said: "Our people have lost all faith and all hope. If the church cannot give it to them, we shall have failed." May God help them and grant them success.

2

First Paper

The Origins of the Episcopate and Episcopal Ministry in the Early Church

by The Rev. Canon Professor J. Robert Wright
St. Mark's Professor of Ecclesiastical History
General Theological Seminary, New York City

1. Pre-Christian Antecedents: a) Jewish and b) Gentile

The word "Bishop" itself comes from the Greek words "*epi*" meaning "over" and "*skopos*" meaning "seer," and so an "*episkopos*" is literally an "over-seer" or a "superintendent" or even an "inspector" (or, in medieval Latin sources, a "speculator"). Attempts have often been made to find prototypes of the Christian "Bishop" in the Jewish or Gentile backgrounds of Christianity.

We consider first the Jewish, where we find that some have derived the office from that of the ruler of the Jewish synagogue, who presided over the synagogue worship and selected those who took part in its services. In the Septuagint, or Greek, version of the Old Testament (cf. Job 20:29, Wisdom of Solomon 1:6), as also commonly in Philo the Hellenized Jew of Alexandria, the term *episkopos* is used of God, but also in a number of instances of ordinary "overseers," and yet never of cultic persons. Philo gives the title once to Moses, and in First Maccabees the word is used of the inspectors set over the Jews by Antiochus Epiphanes to carry out his religious policy. More recently, the discoveries of the Qumran manuscripts near the Dead Sea have raised again the possible Jewish origin of such an officer, known by the Hebrew word *"mebaqqer."* The Damascus Document describes such an overseer or inspector of the camp, who taught the works of God to the members of the covenant community, looked after them "as does a shepherd his flock," and supervised the admission of new members, the discipline of offenders, and all financial transactions. Likewise in the Manual of Discipline from Qumran, the same sort of officer appears, comparable to the "steward" of the Essene community that is noted by Josephus. Whether or not there is any direct relationship between the overseer of these communities and the office of bishop in the early Christian church cannot be determined for certain. It does seem the case, however, that the *"mebaqqer"* of the Dead Sea documents is, if anything, even more "monarchical" than the *"episkopos"* of the New Testament texts, and for this reason, if for no other, the connection seems remote.

Any possible connections with a Gentile background, though, are even more remote than the Jewish ones. The term *"episkopos"* is fairly common in Greek literature, papyri, and inscriptions, both in its general meaning of "oversight" and as a technical name for officials, both civil and religious. In the works of Homer and others after him, it is applied to the gods. Stoic philosophers used the term to describe their own mission as messengers and heralds of the gods. Syrian inscriptions record *"episkopoi"* as overseers of buildings, provisions and coinage, and cultic associations of Greece and the Aegean isles record the term in reference to directors and cashiers.

I think one must say in concluding this first section that the pre-Christian evidence, both Jewish and Gentile, although enlightening, is not determinative for the early Christian understanding.

2. The New Testament Evidence

Turning next to the New Testament evidence, and following lines of interpretation established by the late Professor Massey H.

Shepherd[1], we find seven key references, generally dating from the turn of the first century: I Timothy 3:1-7, Titus 1:7-9, I Peter 2:25, Philippians 1:1, Acts 20:28, Acts 1:20, and I Peter 5:2-4. We now look at these passages in detail, citing the translations of the Revised Standard Version:

1. I Timothy 3:1-7: "If anyone aspires to the office of a bishop ("the office of oversight"), he desires a noble task. Now a bishop must be above reproach, married only once (*"mias gunaikos andra"*= "the husband of one wife"), temperate, sensible, dignified, hospitable, an apt teacher, no drunkard, not violent but gentle, not quarrelsome, and no lover of money. He must manage his own household well, keeping his children submissive and respectful in every way; for if a man does not know how to manage his own household, how can he care for God's church? He must not be a recent convert, or he may be puffed up with conceit and fall into the condemnation of the devil; moreover, he must be well thought of by outsiders, or he may fall into reproach and the snare of the devil."

This passage is followed by a parallel statement of diaconal qualifications and duties in I Timothy 3:8-13, which repeats some qualifications but not others and treats deacons in the plural although the bishop was referenced in the singular.

St. Augustine of Hippo in the early fifth century, commenting on the author's meaning in this passage, says: "He wanted to explain what 'episcopate' means: it is the name of a task, not an honor. It is, in fact, a Greek word, derived from the fact that a man who is put in authority over others 'superintends' them, that is, he has responsibility for them. For the Greek 'skopos' means 'intention' (in the sense of 'direction of the intention'); and so we may, if we wish, translate 'epi-skopein' as 'super-intend'. Hence a 'bishop' who has set his heart on a position of eminence rather than an opportunity for service should realize that he is no bishop." (*City of God* 19:19).

---

[1] *The Interpreter's Dictionary of the Bible* (New York and Nashville, Abingdon Press: 1962), volume 1, pp. 441-443, s.v. "Bishop."

2. Titus 1:7-9: "A bishop, as God's steward, must be blameless; he must not be arrogant or quick-tempered or a drunkard or violent or greedy for gain, but hospitable, a lover of goodness, master of himself, upright, holy, and self-controlled; he must hold firm to the sure word as taught, so that he may be able to give instruction in sound doctrine and also to confront those who contradict it."

We note that both these passages from the Pastoral Letters are statements of the qualifications and duties of a bishop, in doctrinal and moral terms but with no mention of any sacramental duties. The former passage, from I Timothy, assumes that the bishop will be a man, and one who is married. Mandatory celibacy is clearly ruled out, although one might stretch the meaning of the passage to allow optional celibacy in some instances.

3. In I Peter 2:25, the term *"episkopos"* is used as a title of Christ: "You were straying like sheep, but now you have returned to the shepherd and guardian (the King James Version translates this literally as "bishop") of your souls." This passage may also be compared to the Septuagint Greek translation of Wisdom 1:6, where God is called the *"episkopos* of man's heart."

4. Philippians 1:1: "Paul and Timothy, servants of Christ Jesus. To all the saints in Christ Jesus who are at Philippi, with the bishops and deacons." As in I Timothy 3, we note the close association of bishops with deacons.

5. Acts 20:28, in a speech attributed to Paul: "Take heed to yourselves and to all the flock, in which the Holy Spirit has made you guardians (the King James Version translates this as "overseers"), to feed the church of the Lord which he obtained with his own blood."

We note that this passage is addressed to those who were previously designated as the *"presbyteroi"* of the church of Ephesus; hence, the terms *"presbyteros"* and *"episkopos"* are interchangeable here.

There are also two significant New Testament instances where forms of the word other than the noun are used:

6. Acts 1:20: "It is written in the Book of Psalms [109:8], 'Let his habitation become desolate, and let there be no one to live in it'; and 'His office (King James translates literally as 'bishopric') let another take'." Here the reference is to the 'overseership' forfeited by Judas' treachery and suicide, after which Judas was replaced as a member of the Twelve.

7. I Peter 5:2-4: "Tend the flock of God that is in your charge, [exercising the oversight] (not in the earliest or best manuscripts, but the King James version does include it, translating as 'oversight') not by constraint but willingly, not for shameful gain but eagerly, not as domineering over those in your charge but being examples to the flock. And when the chief shepherd is manifested, you will obtain the unfading crown of glory."

As an exhortation to the elders ("*presbyteroi*"), this passage, as also Acts 20:28, is a second example of the interchangeability of the terms "*episkopos*" and "*presbyteros*" in the New Testament evidence. (The two are also interchangeable in First Clement, written about 96 A.D., for whom the ministerial function of the 'presbyters' is '*episkope*'.)

In terms of recent ecumenical agreements that are related to this New Testament evidence, we note first the Lima Statement from the Faith and Order Commission of the World Council of Churches (BEM, 1982): "A ministry of *episkope* is necessary to express and safeguard the unity of the body. Every church needs this ministry of unity in some form..." (Ministry, para. 23).

Second, we note the Canterbury Statement on Ministry and Ordination from the Anglican-Roman Catholic International Commission (1976): "The early churches may well have had considerable diversity in the structure of pastoral ministry, though it is clear that some churches were headed by ministers who were called '*episcopoi*' and '*presbyteroi*.' While the first missionary churches were not a loose aggregation of autonomous communities, we have no evidence that 'bishops' and 'presbyters' were appointed everywhere in the primitive period. The terms 'bishop' and 'presbyter' could be applied to the same man or to

men with identical or very similar functions. Just as the formation of the canon of the New Testament was a process incomplete until the second half of the second century, so also the full
emergence of the threefold ministry of bishop, presbyter, and
deacon required a longer period than the apostolic age.
Thereafter this threefold structure became universal in the
Church." (Para. 6.)

And in the same statement, we read: "An essential element in
the ordained ministry is its responsibility for 'oversight' ('episcope'). This responsibility involves fidelity to the apostolic faith,
its embodiment in the life of the Church today, and its transmission to the Church of tomorrow. Presbyters are joined with the
bishop in his oversight of the church and in the ministry of the
word and the sacraments; they are given authority to preside at
the Eucharist and to pronounce absolution. Deacons, although
not so empowered, are associated with bishops and presbyters in
the ministry of word and sacrament, and assist in oversight."
(Para 9.)

With the completion of this survey from the evidence of the
New Testament, we shall now turn to the witness of the early
church fathers, and here we shall discern in them, in common
with the study of Bishop Kallistos of Diokleia (formerly Timothy
Ware)[2] and with the address to the bishop-elect on page 517 of
the 1979 Book of Common Prayer of the Episcopal Church,
three separate and complementary, but not contradictory

---

[2] Kallistos Ware, "Patterns of Episcopacy in the Early Church and Today: An
Orthodox View," in *Bishops, but What Kind?*, ed. Peter Moore (London,
SPCK: 1982), pp. 1-24. For the outline of the present essay I am indebted to
the schematic arrangement of this article, which itself parallels that of the
address to the bishop-elect on page 517 of the Ordinal of the 1979 American
Book of Common Prayer (upon which *The Ministry of Bishops: A Study Document
Authorized by the House of Bishops of the Episcopal Church:* 1991, is based). At a
number of significant points I have altered or expanded Ware's schema or its
contents, but in the few instances of verbal dependence I am in complete
agreement and am happy to acknowledge my indebtedness.

emphases in the ministry of bishops in the early church: the bishop as president of the Eucharist (in Sts. Ignatius and Hippolytus), the bishop as teacher of the faith (in St. Irenaeus), and the bishop as leader in the councils of the church (in St. Cyprian).

3. The Witness of St. Ignatius of Antioch and St. Hippolytus of Rome to the Bishop as President of the Eucharist and Provider of the Sacraments

When we come to the writings of St. Ignatius of Antioch, c. 107 A.D., we encounter directly the emergence of the monepiscopate at the head of a threefold ministerial office, a development that can be fully explained by none of the surviving documents of the post-apostolic age. Not only does Ignatius make the presbyters or elders, no less than the deacons, subordinate to the bishop, but he is also the first clear witness to the monepiscopate (also called, perhaps misleadingly, the "monarchical" episcopate), that is, the phenomenon of a single bishop presiding as authoritative leader over the entire Christian community in any given city or place. How far one can generalize from the evidence he presents is certainly a question, and it has been suggested that at Alexandria the collegial system of presbyter-bishops may have survived well into the third century, but he does reflect the situation as it was in Syria and Asia Minor at the beginning of the second Christian century.

Ignatius was only rediscovered in the Christian West, and his letters identified and translated in the seventeenth century, thanks to the work of the Anglican Bishops Ussher and Pearson. Their work on Ignatius, in fact, soon persuaded the Church of England to adopt a "higher" doctrine of the episcopate, that is, no longer as merely "*bene esse*" in a strict parity with the ministries of non-episcopal churches but rather the concept of episcopacy as being even of "divine right" (over against the Puritans). It is not hard to detect their influence in the English Act of Uniformity, 1662, which made episcopal ordination to the priesthood a virtual and invariable necessity for incumbency of all benefices in the Church of England.[3]

With Ignatius, we have the first clear evidence, as we do not have in the New Testament, of a threefold church order of bishops, presbyters, and deacons (in order, 1-2-3), mentioned together no less than twelve times in five of his seven letters. For Ignatius, all three, bishops and presbyters and deacons, are "appointed according to the will of Jesus Christ" (Philadelphians, preface), and the three even seem to have titles of a hierarchical sort: the bishop is "*axiotheos*" (godly), the presbyters "*axioi*" (worthy), and the deacon "*syndoulos*" (fellow servant) (Mag. 2, cf. Smyrn. 12). Ignatius always puts the three in this same order, at times relating them to the unity of the church and its one Eucharist (Phil. 4), and he often portrays the three offices as representatives or antitypes of heavenly realities. His most common analogies, or symbolic correspondences, are between the bishop and God the Father, between presbyters and the apostolic council, and between deacons and Jesus Christ (Mag. 6, Trall. 3). In two other places, though, it is the bishop who is analogous to Jesus Christ (Mag. 3, Eph. 3), and in one place the parallel is of the presbytery with Jesus Christ's "law," to which the deacon must submit (Mag. 2). The presbyters or elders, moreover, function for Ignatius as something of a college under the presidency of the one bishop. There is "one bishop together with the presbyters and the deacons my fellow servants," he remarks (Phil. 4), and elsewhere he likens the relation of the presbyters to the bishop "as the strings to a musical instrument" (Eph. 4).

The bishop is for Ignatius the center of the church's unity in every given place and community, and as such Ignatius expects the bishop to be obeyed. We should "be subject to the bishop as to Jesus Christ," he urges, and "we should look on the bishop as

---

[3] See further Paul F. Bradshaw, *The Anglican Ordinal* (London, SPCK: 1971), esp. chapter 6, and Richard A Norris, "Episcopacy," in *The Study of Anglicanism*, ed. Stephen Sykes and John Booty (Philadelphia, Fortress Press: 1988), pp. 296-309.

the Lord himself" (Trall. 2, Eph. 6). The bishop presides "in God's place" (Mag. 6), and so, without the bishop, there can be no Eucharist and no church. He writes: "Avoid divisions, as the source of evils. Let all of you follow the bishop as Jesus Christ did the Father. ...Let no one do any of the things that concern the church without the bishop. Let that Eucharist be considered valid which is held under the bishop, or under someone whom he appoints. Wherever the bishop appears, there let the people be, just as wherever Jesus Christ is, there is the catholic church. It is not lawful either to baptize or to hold an '*agape*' without the bishop. Whatever he approves is also pleasing to God...He who honors the bishop is honored by God. He who does anything without the bishop's knowledge is serving the devil." (Smyrn. 8).

Insofar as any texts of Ignatius indicate his views of what would later come to be called "apostolic succession," he presents what Metropolitan John Zizioulas has called an "eschatological approach to apostolic continuity," as the future end is anticipated even now in the church's eucharistic structure under episcopal presidency (cf. Mag. 6)[4]. Ignatius says little else about "apostolic succession," which we do find in a rudimentary form in his contemporary Clement of Rome and in a more developed way in Tertullian and St. Irenaeus of Lyons almost a century later. He says nothing about ordination, for which the first clear evidence is Hippolytus nearly a century later, nor does he present Holy Orders as being "sequential" or "cumulative," that is, the "lower" being a prerequisite for the "higher." Overall, for Ignatius the bishop is the one who presides over the eucharistic unity of each

---

[4] John D. Zizioulas, *Being as Communion* (Crestwood, N.Y., St. Vladimir's Seminary Press: 1985), esp. Chapter 5. See further Emmanuel Clapsis, "The Sacramentality of Ordination and Apostolic Succession: An Orthodox-Ecumenical View." *Greek Orthodox Theological Review* 30:4 (1985) 421-432, esp. pp. 430-432.

local church, an emphasis that has been made well known in this century by the Russian theologian Nicolas Afanassieff. [5]

The church, in Ignatius' view, is essentially eucharistic by nature: there is an organic relation between the Body of Christ understood as community, and the Body of Christ understood as sacrament. For Ignatius, then, the bishop is not primarily a teacher or administrator, but the one who presides at, and as "*episkopos*" watches over, the eucharistic liturgy. The presidency of the Eucharist can be designated by the bishop to one or more selected presbyters, although for Ignatius bishops and presbyters are not interchangeable (as they were in the First Epistle of Clement, c. 96 A.D.). In a typical passage Ignatius writes: "Take care to participate in one Eucharist, for there is one flesh of our Lord Jesus Christ, and one cup for union with his blood, one altar, just as there is one bishop together with the presbyters and the deacons my fellow servants" (Phil. 4). His emphasis upon the Eucharist as the focus of the church's unity, and of the centrality of the bishop's eucharistic ministry within the one church, is seen here in his repetition of the word "one," as Ware (p. 4) has observed: "one Eucharist...one flesh...one cup...one altar...one bishop." So there is one bishop, one eucharistic Body, and one church, all three being interdependent. The theme recurs constantly in his writings: "Let there be one prayer in common, one supplication, one mind, one hope in love...Hasten all to come together as to one temple of God, as to one altar, to one Jesus Christ, who came forth from the one Father, is with the one Father, and departed to the one Father" (Mag. 7).

The context of the emphasis on unity in Ignatius, of course, must be kept in mind. Ignatius is writing at a time when there was probably only one bishop for any city and also no more than

---

[5] See, for example, Nicolas Afanassieff, "The Church which Presides in Love," in *The Primacy of Peter*, ed. J. Meyendorff et al. (London, Faith Press: 1963), pp. 57-110.

one eucharistic assembly for any city, a situation which greatly reinforced the bishop's function as the visible focus of unity, not as a distant administrator and occasional visitor but as the local chief pastor whom all the people saw at least every Sunday at the Eucharist. And it was not yet a time of assistant bishops (suffragans, auxiliaries, coadjutors), as are now common in virtually every church that is episcopally ordered, nor of titular bishops, as are frequently encountered in the Orthodox and Roman Catholic Churches, nor of overlapping episcopal jurisdictions, which are found, in contradiction of the eighth canon of the first Ecumenical Council of Nicaea (325 A.D.), in these churches as well as occasionally in the Anglican Communion. Even in the Holy City of Jerusalem, where in March of 1992 this present essay was written, as late as the end of the fourth century the pilgrim woman Egeria found that, despite the large numbers of pilgrims as well as local resident Christians, there was still as a rule only one Eucharist on each Sunday or feast, celebrated by the one bishop of Jerusalem and attended by everyone (*Travels*, 24-43).

• • •

To explain the transition from the earlier evidence, and more especially from the interchangeability of episcopate and presbyterate that we find in Acts 20 and I Peter 5 and in I Clement to the fully developed monepiscopate at the head of a threefold ministerial office that we find in Ignatius and later in Hippolytus, scholars have advanced two contrasting interpretations: 1) that the episcopate arose by elevation from the presbyterate, or 2) that the presbyterate evolved by delegation from the episcopate.

The former interpretation is the classic hypothesis of the Anglican Bishop J.B. Lightfoot: that originally "bishops" and "presbyters" or "elders" were synonymous terms, but that the episcopate arose out of the presbyterate by "elevation" into a distinct and higher order and thus, by implication, the "original" ministry of the church was presbyteral rather than episcopal. Adolf von Harnack and B.H. Streeter also inclined to this interpretation, the former emphasizing a process of localization and the latter suggesting a stage of collective or collegial episcopate in some places before the monepiscopate was fully established. The interpretation that the episcopate arose by elevation from the presbyterate, both offices being originally synonymous and interchangeable, was also, with slightly differing emphasis, the position of St. Jerome, who in the fifth century wrote: "A presbyter...is the same as a bishop, and before ambition entered into religion by the devil's instigation and people began to say 'I belong to Paul, I to Apollos, I to Cephas,' the churches were governed by the council of presbyters, acting together." (Commentary on Titus 1:6-7.)

The other view, that the presbyterate evolved by delegation from the episcopate, maintains that there was an original distinction between the office of bishop and that of presbyter or elder, admitting that (some) bishops may also have been numbered among the presbyterate but stressing that the bishops were presbyters/elders specifically appointed/ordained for liturgical and pastoral functions of oversight and holding that not all presbyters/elders were bishops. In this view, the presbyterate was a position of honor, not of ministerial office, although in time, with the rise of the monepiscopate, presbyters/elders had certain ministerial functions of a liturgical and pastoral nature delegated to them by the bishops. R. Sohm and W. Lowrie, among others, have inclined to this latter interpretation, concluding that the presbyterate as an order of ministry and not merely a title of honor or seniority came into being by delegation from the episcopate.

The Anglican tradition has generally held to the second of these interpretations at least since the mid-seventeenth century, influenced as it has been to a "higher" view of the distinctiveness and necessity of episcopal office, in part, by the rediscoveries of the epistles of Ignatius of Antioch and Clement of Rome in the seventeenth century (and of Hippolytus still later). This transition in understanding of the episcopate can be seen from a very interesting perspective in the changes of Scriptural texts appointed for the ordination rites of the Church of England before and after 1662 and for the Episcopal Church in the U.S.A. before and after its Prayer Book of 1979.[6] Before the revised Ordinal of 1662, the Church of England used the passage we have examined from I Timothy 3, which speaks of the qualifications and duties of a bishop ("*episkopos*"), as the Epistle to be read liturgically in the rites for *both* priesthood and episcopate, thus suggesting no distinction between the two, and allowed the passage from Acts 20, which uses the term "bishops" but implies an interchangeability with presbyters, as the alternative Epistle in the rite for ordination to the priesthood. In the Ordinal of 1662, however, which was revised to show clearly the episcopate as a separate and distinct order, an entirely different passage (Ephesians 4:7-13, which has no mention of bishops) was substituted for I Timothy 3 in the rite for priesthood and the reading from Acts 20 was transferred to the rite for ordination to the episcopate. Even two of the three alternative Gospels in the pre-1662 rite for priesthood, Matthew 28:18-20 and John 20:19-23, both of which contain commissions to the Apostles, were transferred to the rite for the episcopate, presumably to show that bishops and not priests were the successors of the Apostles. And in the 1979 Prayer Book ordinal of the Episcopal Church in the U.S.A., the passage from I Timothy 3 was retained as the Epistle for the episcopate and that from Ephesians 4 for the priesthood, and the ambiguous passage from Acts 20 is gone altogether. The passage from John 20 is now the first choice for the Gospel, and the passage from Matthew 28 is gone altogether, presumably because its text is later and doubtful.

• • •

Nearly a century following St. Ignatius, the next major block of evidence about the episcopate is found in the *Apostolic Tradition* of St. Hippolytus, the conservative/traditional bishop or presbyter of Rome, which is generally dated to about 210 A.D. and is very similar to Ignatius in its emphasis upon the bishop as president of the Eucharist and provider of the sacraments. Hippolytan

---

[6] For the following observations I am indebted, in part, to Paul F. Bradshaw, "Ordinals," in *The Study of Anglicanism*, ed. Stephen Sykes and John Booty (Philadelphia, Fortress Press: 1988), esp. p. 149.

authorship of this treatise, which contains the earliest ordination rites known in church history and is the earliest surviving document to look anything like a book of common prayers, was firmly established by R.H. Connolly in 1916 on the basis of further manuscript discoveries in the late nineteenth century. The definitive text is now that of the Roman Catholic scholar Bernard Botte, although in English the text is best known in translations by Anglicans Gregory Dix (which is overly complicated), B.S. Easton (which is oversimplified) and G.J. Cuming (which is the most helpful).

Comparing Hippolytus to Ignatius, we find certain similarities and other differences. Similar to Ignatius, we find in Hippolytus a full threefold order headed by the monepiscopate, bishops and presbyters not interchangeable, and the three orders not prescribed as cumulative. In contrast to Ignatius, however, we find in Hippolytus the popular election of bishops ("chosen by all the people") and a succession that is established on the basis of ordination by episcopal laying-on-of-hands, as well as the principle that it is the bishop alone who ordains. [Canon 4 of the first ecumenical council, Nicaea I, in 325, will state for the first time that three bishops are necessary for episcopal ordination or consecration.] Hippolytus' stipulation "Let the bishop be ordained after he has been chosen by all the people" clearly excludes any appointment of bishops "from above," such as by secular authority, or by a synod of bishops, or by a patriarch, or by a Pope. For Hippolytus the ordination of a bishop is to take place on a Sunday, the descent of the Spirit is invoked, and the new bishop is described in terms of "high priesthood" with authority to remit sins (which implies, at least possibly, authority to admit to eucharistic communion). The bishop is also shown as presiding at the Eucharist and at Christian initiation, as ordaining presbyters and deacons, as consecrating the three holy oils, as appointing some minor officers, and as taking a lead in daily instruction and in giving various blessings.

The rediscovery and authentication of the text of Hippolytus seems to have been the principal influence leading to the affirmation of the Roman Catholic Church, made at the Second Vatican Council, that the episcopate is the primary order of ministry constituting the fullness of the sacrament of holy orders (a view which Anglicans have generally held since the seventeenth century).[7] By this decision, the Roman Catholic Church in effect moved from the first interpretation of the evidence of St. Ignatius noted above to the second, and in the new (1968) Roman Pontifical, the ordination prayer for a bishop is paraphrased from that of Hippolytus, as is the same prayer in the new (1979) ordinal of The Book of Common Prayer of the Episcopal Church. Both of these recently revised prayers for the ordination of a bishop, therefore (but not that of the Church of England), are now paraphrased from the same Hippolytan prototype, the earliest ordination prayer known in the church's history.

Hippolytus' concept of succession, also, is most clearly stated in his *Refutation of All Heresies* (I, Proemium): "None will refute these [errors], save the Holy Spirit bequeathed unto the Church, which the Apostles, having in the first instance received, have transmitted to those who have rightly believed. But we, as being their successors, and as participators in this grace, high-priesthood, and office of teaching, as well as being reputed guardians of the Church, must not be found deficient in vigilance, or disposed to suppress correct doctrine."

4. The Witness of St. Irenaeus of Lyons to the Bishop as Teacher of the Apostolic Faith

When we turn to St. Irenaeus, Bishop of Lyons c. 185-200 A.D., we find the bishop presented primarily as the link between

---

7 It is worthy of note that the pre-Vatican II position of the Roman Catholic Church, also known as the medieval or "Jeromian" view, which was predicated upon a basic interchangeability of episcopate and presbyterate and did not understand episcopacy as an independent order or sacrament in the church but rather as a granting of ordinary episcopal authority by the bishop of Rome (with whatever grace was necessary for it), was still the prevailing influence upon Roman Catholic doctrine at the time of the papal condemnation of the orders of the Anglican episcopate in 1896.

each local church and the teaching of the apostles. Irenaeus generally echoes the eucharistic teaching of Ignatius, remarking that "Our opinion agrees with the Eucharist and the Eucharist confirms our opinion" (*Adversus Haereses* IV.18.5), but his greater emphasis is upon apostolic doctrine. Because of his confrontation with the Gnostics, Irenaeus attaches particular importance to the continuity of church teaching and its relationship to apostolic tradition and apostolic authority. Whereas the Gnostics had appealed to a secret tradition handed down by a hidden succession of teachers, Irenaeus answered by appealing to an apostolic tradition that had been openly proclaimed in the four canonical gospels and openly taught in the unbroken public succession of bishops seated upon the episcopal throne or chair in each local church, especially in those churches of known apostolic foundation. [The bishop was thus seated, as was still the custom of teachers in that day and on until St. John Chrysostom began the custom of standing to preach.] Irenaeus is thus a contrast to Ignatius, who had very little to say about the bishop as preacher and teacher of the faith and very little to say about the bishop as the link between the church of the apostles and that of his own day. Whereas for Ignatius the bishop's "cathedra" or throne was the chair upon which he sits at the Eucharist, for Irenaeus it is far closer to the chair of a professor: "The throne is the symbol of teaching," he says (*Demonstration*, 2). And while for Ignatius the bishop is primarily the one who unites us around the Eucharist, for Irenaeus the bishop is above all the one who teaches the one truth, by which unity is preserved. "Having received this preaching and this faith," he says, "the church, although scattered in the whole world, carefully preserves it as if living in one house" (*Adv. Haer.* I.10.3).

For Irenaeus, though, as for Clement of Rome before him and for Acts 20 and I Peter 5, the bishop is synonymous or interchangeable with the presbyter, and this is illustrated in a famous statement he makes concerning the bishop's teaching authority as based on a succession from the apostles: "We should obey those presbyters in the church who have their succession from the apostles, and who, together with succession in the episcopate, have received the assured 'charisma' of truth" (*Adv. Haer.* IV.26.2). Apostolic succession for Irenaeus, as Ware emphasizes, is not a mechanical or quasi-magical way of ensuring the preservation of "valid" sacraments, but, rather, its purpose is to preserve the continuity of apostolic doctrine and, understood in this sense, is not something that the bishop enjoys as a personal possession in isolation from the local community and place where he presides. It does seem significant that, when Irenaeus constructs his succession lists, like Hegesippus his contemporary in the mid-second century and like Eusebius of Caesarea in the early fourth century, he does not trace the succession through the consecrators of each bishop, as is often done today, but through the throne or seat or see of each Christian community in each place. Irenaeus says: "We can enumerate those who were established by the apostles as bishops in the churches, and their successors down to our time," and he refers next to "those whom the apostles left as their successors, to whom they handed over their own teaching position" (*Adv. Haer.* III.3). He also says, "We appeal to that tradition which has come down from the apostles and is guarded by the successions of presbyters [here, as before, synonymous with bishops] in the churches" (*Adv. Haer.* II.2). And again, "What if there should be a dispute about some matter of moderate importance? Should we not turn to the oldest churches, where the apostles themselves were known, and find out from them the clear and certain answer to the problem now being raised? Even if the apostles had not left their writings to us, ought we not to follow the rule of the tradition which they handed down to those to whom they committed the churches?" (*Adv. Haer.* IV.1).

The same concept, we may remark, is also found in Tertullian, writing about the same time and also confronting the Gnostic crisis, although he does add the notion of a succession in ordination. He says of the Gnostics: "Let them produce the original records of their churches. Let them unfold the roll of their bishops, running down in due succession from the beginning in such a manner as that first bishop of theirs shall be able to show for his ordainer and predecessor some one of the apostles or of apostolic men" (*De Prescriptione Hereticorum* 3.2).

It is also worth noting that the concept of "succession" in the ministry of bishops comes earliest in the First Epistle of St. Clement of Rome, c. 96 A.D. (rediscovered to the West only in the seventeenth century). There the understanding is the more rudimentary one of a retrospective linear historical succession of persons by appointment, as Zizioulas observes, rather than the succession in teaching first emphasized by Irenaeus and Tertullian or the eschatological approach to succession found in Ignatius of Antioch. Clement writes: "The apostles also knew, through our Lord Jesus Christ, that there would be strife over the question of the bishop's office. Therefore, for this reason,...they appointed the aforesaid persons and later made further provision that if they should fall asleep other approved men should succeed to their ministry" (I Cor. 44). And he further explains his view that the succession is of persons by appointment: "The apostles received the Gospel for us from the Lord Jesus Christ; Jesus the Christ was sent from God, and the apostles from Christ" (I Cor. 42).

5. The Witness of St. Cyprian of Carthage to the Bishop as Leader in the Councils of the Church and the Bond of Administrative Unity between Each Local Church and All the Others

It remains to treat, rather more briefly, the witness of St. Cyprian of Carthage, who died in 258 A.D., which constitutes the third emphasis or model of episcopal ministry from the pre-Nicene period. Cyprian was a bishop who gave such priority to his function of administrative governance that he was even willing to flee persecution and the prospect of martyrdom with his own people around the year 250, and later to re-admit the lapsed, in order to continue from a safe distance his episcopal administration and to preserve the unity of the church under his oversight. For him the offices of bishop and presbyter are distinct and not interchangeable, and he is also the first Christian writer to portray the three orders as sequential or cumulative. Like

Ignatius, he speaks of the local church as assembled around the altar with the bishop as its eucharistic president, and in one respect his concept of apostolicity is even stronger than that of Irenaeus, going so far as to identify the bishops with the apostles (*"apostolos, id est episcopus"*: Letter 3.3.1).

Cyprian's view of episcopal succession is a noteworthy development from those of Ignatius, Clement, Tertullian, and Irenaeus, for it is a succession by means of consecration, or rather, a succession of episcopal authority handed down by means of ordination. In his view bishops were directly instituted and consecrated by the apostles who were themselves consecrated by Christ. "Hence by means of a chain of succession through time (*"per temporum et successionum vices"*) the ordination of bishops and the structure (*"ratio"*) of the church has flowed on so that the church is built upon bishops and every act of the church is controlled by these same superiors" (*"praepositos"*), he writes, even referring to "all those placed in charge who have succeeded to the apostles by delegated ordination" (Letters 33.1.1, 66.4.2). What constitutes a bishop for Cyprian, then, is ordination, followed by occupancy of the episcopal chair (*"cathedra"*) and supervisory responsibility (*"episcopatus"*) over a flock of people (*"plebs"*). (cf. Letters 44.1.1, 45.3.1, 48.4.1). Here we see, clearly, in the way in which he treats both succession and ordination, his emphasis upon the episcopal authority necessary for the administrative governance and good ordering necessary for the church to survive in time. And his stress on the need for unity with one's bishop echoes Ignatius of Antioch: "The church is the people united to the bishop, the flock clinging to its shepherd. From this you should know that the bishop is in the church and the church in the bishop" (*"Episcopus in ecclesia et ecclesia in episcopo"*: Letter 66.8.3). Even more, to be "in communion" with one's bishop is to be "in communion with the Catholic Church" (Letter 55.1.2).

Cyprian's primary emphasis, thus, is upon the bishop as the bond of unity between the local church and the church universal; indeed, he is the author of the earliest surviving treatise on the nature of the church: *De Unitate Ecclesiae*. In this context, he stresses the conciliar or collegial character of the worldwide episcopate, of bishops meeting in council and together reaching a common mind under the Spirit's guidance, and so he calls our attention to this conciliar and collegial feature of any episcopate that would claim to be truly "historic," a feature that has its more recent parallel, for Anglicans, in the worldwide Lambeth Conference of bishops that has met at periodic intervals since the year 1867. And to the question of how bishops should make decisions in such meetings, Cyprian replies that it is not numbers but concord that matters: "the greatest significance is not given to numbers but to the harmony of those who pray" ("Non multitudini sed unanimitati deprecantium plurimum tribui": *De Unitate Ecclesiae* 12). He summarized this principle of the conciliar solidarity of the episcopate in a phrase the meaning of which is much debated: "The episcopate is a single whole, of which each bishop has a right to and a responsibility for the whole" ("Episcopatus unus est, cuius a singulis in solidum pars tenetur": *De Unitate* 5). Each bishop, in other words (Ware suggests, and I agree), shares in the one episcopate, not as having part of the whole but as being an expression of the whole; just as there are many local churches but only one universal church, so there are many individual bishops but only one worldwide episcopate. His meaning is not, however, as simple as a statement that "the whole is made up of the sum of the individual parts." The bishop, though, is the bond of unity between each local church and all the others, and this is his emphasis. He makes his point another way when he says: "There is one church throughout the whole world divided by Christ into many members, also one episcopate diffused in a harmonious multitude of many bishops" (Letter 55.24.2).

As for those bishops who deny this unity by insisting on their own teachings or actions even to the point of schism, Cyprian declares: "He, therefore, who observes neither the unity of the Spirit nor the bond of peace, and separates himself from the bond of the church and from the college of the bishops, can have neither the power nor the honor of a bishop since he has not wished either the unity or the peace of the episcopate" (Letter 55.24.2). And in a way that could not anticipate the questions raised in our time by the existence of suffragan or auxiliary bishops and of overlapping jurisdictions in full communion, Cyprian expounds the Lord's words in John 10:16 "There shall be one flock and one shepherd" by stating his own maxim: "A number of shepherds or of flocks in one place is unthinkable" (*De Unitate* 8). Thus, Cyprian's doctrine of episcopal collegiality is directly linked to his doctrine of the church, as he summarizes: "It is particularly incumbent upon those of us who preside over the church as bishops to uphold this unity firmly and to be its champions, so that we may prove the episcopate also to be itself one and undivided" (*De Unitate* 5).

The bishop's ministry for the good ordering of the church is also related, in Cyprian's letters, to the bishop's personal role as an exemplar and living standard of conduct: "In proportion as the fall of a bishop is an event which tends ruinously to the fall of his followers, so on the other hand it is useful and salutary when a bishop shows himself to the brethren as one to be imitated in the strength of faith" (Letter 9.1.2). "May the Lord who condescends to elect and to appoint for himself bishops in his church protect those chosen and also appointed by his will and assistance, inspiring them in their government and supplying both vigor for restraining the insolence of the wicked and mildness for nourishing the repentance of the lapsed" (Letter 48.4.2). "While the bond of concord remains, and the undivided sacrament of the Catholic Church endures, every bishop disposes and directs his own acts, and will have to give an account of his purposes to the Lord" (Letter 55.21.2).

6. Conclusions

Thus we have seen three complementary, but not contradictory, models or emphases of episcopal ministry in the early Christian church, in the writings of 1) Sts. Ignatius of Antioch and Hippolytus of Rome, 2) St. Irenaeus of Lyons, and 3) St. Cyprian of Carthage. These three models emphasize, respectively, the roles of the bishop as 1) eucharistic president, 2) chief teacher, and 3) administrative leader. They also present three different models of church unity, each focused upon the bishop and again complementary rather than contradictory: 1) eucharistic unity, 2) doctrinal unity, and 3) administrative unity. And, finally, they present three complementary pictures of the primary ministry of a bishop: 1) one who presides over the eucharistic unity of each local church, 2) the link in time between each local church and the teaching of the apostles, and 3) the bond across space for the unity of each local church with all the others. It is also possible that these three models, or emphases, or pictures, bear some relationship to the classical description of the work of Christ as 1) Priest (Ignatius and Hippolytus), 2) Prophet (Irenaeus), and 3) King (Cyprian).

Several questions for discussion arise out of the early evidence, and to list them is, of course, by no means to solve them: 1) Can we place the early patristic development upon a level of authority equal to that of, or even greater than, the evidence of the New Testament (which is admittedly rather sparse)? 2) What weight of authority should we give today to the qualifications for episcopal office established in I Timothy 3:1-7 and in Titus 1:7-9? 3) Do we today regard the emergence of the monepiscopate at the head of the threefold ministerial office in Ignatius and Hippolytus as necessary? as irreversible? 4) Do we regard the distinction of episcopate from presbyterate as essential, in spite of their interchangeability in Acts 20, I Peter 5, I Clement, and Irenaeus? 5) Given the absence of any evidence for the prescription of cumulative orders before the work of Cyprian, do we regard this development as necessary and irreversible, or only as normative or even indifferent? 6) Given the evidence for popular choice of bishops in the earliest ordination rites, those of Hippolytus, what judgment should we make upon other methods for appointment of bishops by rulers, popes, patriarchs, or synods of bishops? 7) Are the five different concepts of episcopal/apostolic succession that we have encountered all complementary and capable of synthesis, or should one or more of them be given a higher weight of authority: eschatological (Ignatius), retrospective/linear/historical (Clement), doctrinal (Irenaeus), ordinational (Tertullian and Hippolytus), and authoritative/administrative (Cyprian)? 8) Is the indelibility of Holy Orders, and in particular the life tenure of episcopal ordination, which does not seem to be mentioned in this early evidence apart from Clement of Rome's remark that the apostles made provision that if those whom they appointed "should fall asleep other approved men should succeed to their ministry," nonetheless an essential and constitutive ingredient of what might be called the "historic" episcopate? 9) To what extent are the three major emphases outlined in this paper, as well as the differing concepts of episcopal/apostolic succession and other differences concerning interchangeability, cumulative orders, indelibility, and the like, mainly attributable to geographical differences, such as Antioch and Asia Minor, Syria, Rome, and North Africa, and thus reflective of an inculturation or cultural differentiation that was perhaps more readily tolerated in this early period than today? 10) What are the emphases, or functions, of episcopal ministry in our current liturgical texts, and how do they correspond to the classical evidence of episcopal ministry that comes from the New Testament and from Ignatius and Hippolytus, Irenaeus, and Cyprian? 11) Are there other functions of bishops today more important than any of the three that have been highlighted in this essay? 12) What are, and what should be, the major emphases or functions in episcopal ministry today?

3

Second Paper
Theological Reflections on the Patristic Development of Episcopal Ministry

by The Rt. Rev. Mark Dyer
Bishop of Bethlehem

Introduction

The theologian is a person of faith who asks questions that seek to understand and discern God's presence and activity among us. The theological reflection of this paper concerns the early patristic development of the episcopate, specifically why the Fathers of the early Church regarded the ministry of bishops as essential to the life of the Church. It is also meant to be a response to Robert Wright's all-important question: "What are, and what should be, the major emphases or functions in episcopal ministry today?"[1] It is also intended to be a corollary, from the aspect of ascetical theology, to *The Ministry of Bishops: A Study Document*, authorized by the House of Bishops of the Episcopal Church, 1991. And finally, it is intended to accompany the foundational essay "The Communion of the Trinity and the Life of the Church" from the recent report on *Episcopal Ministry* from the Church of England.

My understanding is that the Fathers of the Church considered episcopal ministry to be a gift of God for the sake of the holy life,

---

[1] Wright, J. Robert, "The Origins of the Episcopate and Episcopal Ministry in the Early Church," p. 32.

i.e., to serve, preserve and nurture communion (*koinonia*) with God, the Holy Trinity. Therefore, the bishop is called by God from within God's People to serve the mystery of our communion with one another and with God.

The ministry of the episcopate is a series of sacred acts that serve, preserve and nurture communion. As president of the Eucharistic assembly, chief teacher of the Word of God and the Holy Tradition, sign of unity between the local church and the church universal, the bishop is absorbed, by the grace of the Holy Spirit, into a created participation in the uncreated holiness of God. Thus absorbed into the life of God, the bishop leads the people of God in the holy life. The episcopate, faithfully exercised, is a sacred deed where heaven and earth encounter the holiness of God. It is the ancient command of God to Moses: "Speak to all the congregation of the people of Israel and say to them: You shall be holy, for I the Lord your God am holy." (Leviticus 19:1-2)

Communion With God:
The Gifts Of God For The People Of God

Robert Wright tells us that the early Church understood a bishop to be president of the Eucharist and provider of the sacraments, teacher of the apostolic faith, leader in the Councils of the Church and bond of unity.[2] Now we ask what it is that enables a bishop to carry out his ministry with holiness and fidelity? This theological question would have us go beyond what the bishop does to who the bishop is before God.

God and union with God in Christ Jesus is a given reality of the Christian life. Saint Ignatius writes to the Ephesians:

> Let us therefore do all things in the conviction that he (Christ) dwells in us. Thus we shall be his temples and he will be our God within us. And this is the truth, and it will be made manifest before our eyes. Let us, then, love him as he deserves. (15,3)

---

[2] Ibid., p. 30.

This gift of communion with God the Holy Trinity is the principle of unity and source of life for the bishop as he carries out, faithfully, his public ministry.

In the liturgy described by St. Hippolytus after the bishops pause in prayer for the descent of the Holy Spirit on the person to be consecrated a bishop, the consecrator lays on his hand and prays:

> ...now pour forth that Power which is from Thee, of the princely Spirit which Thou didst deliver to Thy beloved Child Jesus Christ, which he bestowed on Thy holy Apostles who established the Church which hallows Thee in every place to the endless glory and praise of Thy name. (*Apostolic Tradition*, 3)

The bishop received that "Power" God the Father gave to Jesus Christ and to the Holy Apostles for the sake of the Church. Therefore, the bishop is called in a special way to union with God, and finds his only source of unity and life in God. There is no way to nurture this mystery of communion without prayer.

The bishop is called, therefore, to seek out prayerfully and to celebrate the mystery of God's love, God's presence, and God's power. The grace of prayer unites the bishop in communion with God and deepens unity within the Church.

St. Paul writes:

> "But when the fullness of time had come, God sent his Son, born of woman, born under the law, in order to redeem those who were under the law, so that we might receive adoption as children. And because you are children, God has sent the Spirit of his Son into our hearts, crying, '*Abba*, Father!' So you are no longer a slave but a child, and if a child, then also an heir, through God." (Galatians 4:4-7)

God has sent the Spirit of his Son into our hearts crying, '*Abba*, Father!' Saint Cyprian speaks of the 'Our Father' as the most excellent prayer. It is most effective because God the Father is pleased to hear the words taught by his Son and because it is a prayer of communion. It is a prayer of mystical union with God and with one another in the Church.

Saint Cyprian writes:

> Before all things, the teacher of peace and the master of unity would not have a prayer to be made single and individually, as for one who prays to pray for himself alone. For we say not 'My Father, who art in heaven;' nor 'Give me this day my daily bread;' nor does each one ask that only his own sins should be forgiven him; nor does he request for himself alone that he may not be led into temptation, and delivered from evil.

> Our prayer is public and common; and when we pray, we pray not for one, but for the whole people, because we the whole people are one. The God of peace and teacher of concord, who taught unity, willed that one thus pray for all, even as He Himself bore us all in one. (*De dominica oratione*, Introduction and 8,5)

Prayer is communion. The Holy Spirit sent by the Father into our hearts establishes us as adopted sisters and brothers of Jesus, God's Son, and we together, in unity, cry "*Abba*, Father," "Our Father."

When the first Christian community gathered in Jerusalem after the gift of Pentecost, "they devoted themselves to the apostles' teaching and fellowship, to the breaking of bread and the prayers." (Acts: 2:42) As they lived their lives in the faith presence of the resurrected Lord and went forth to proclaim the Good News of salvation to all people they remembered the times of solitude and prayer in the life of their Lord. They taught that at his baptism by John the Baptist, Jesus was consecrated the Messiah of God in the very act of prayer. They told of his temptations and prayerful dialogue with the Father in the desert. They remembered that he prayed before he called the Twelve. They recalled with passion his prayer in Gethsemane and the agonized prayers from the Cross. Often they recalled the supreme moment of the prayer of Jesus at the moment of glory, the moment of his holy passover during which he established the new covenant of the Father's self-gift of love in the bread and wine of his body and blood. St. John remembered his words of prayer that night:

> Righteous Father, the world does not know you, but I know you and these know that you sent me. I made your name known to them and I will make it known, so that the love with which you have loved me may be in them and I in them. (17:25-26)

In remembering Jesus' life of prayer, his communion with the Father, the Christian community was surely speaking of the essence of its own very life. At the very core of the composition of the Gospel is the witness of Jesus as a man of prayer. At the very center of the faith-life of the New Testament Church we find this same prayerful Lord. Being in God, being in Christ, in prayer is essential to the life of the Church in communion with God.

In his letter to the Magnesians, Ignatius of Antioch tells of his prayer for the Churches:

> I pray that in them there may be a union based on the flesh and spirit of Jesus Christ, who is our everlasting life, a union of faith and love, to which nothing is to be preferred, but especially a union with Jesus and the Father. (1,2)

A Church that is holy, catholic, one, and apostolic is a church rooted in the life of prayer. Faithful apostles are those who are sent by God to preside at the Eucharist and provide for the sacraments, to teach the apostolic faith, and to be leaders in the Councils of the Church and a bond of unity. An essential theological element that enables this faithful ministry to be carried out with holiness and grace is the life of prayer.

The Anglican-Orthodox Dublin Agreed Statement of 1984 teaches that the fruit of prayer is holiness:

The fruit of the Spirit praying in us is holiness, and at the heart of holiness is love for God and neighbour. God's love works in us to produce holiness, restoring in us the image of God and making us and all things whole. In this life, Christians experience a tension between the call to holiness and the power of sin, the struggle between 'flesh' and Spirit (Gal. 5:17) which requires continual repentance and the assurance of God's forgiveness. God's call to holiness is also a call to work for justice, so that the Church's prayer for the coming of God's reign on earth as in heaven requires of Christians that they co-operate with God in the world. God's love for the world, embodied in Jesus Christ, works through the Holy Spirit to transfigure all things into the new creation, and we are to make manifest that love in the life of the world. (Dublin 43)

Why did God call forth the ministry of bishops? For the sake of the holy life. The bishop represents Christ to and for the people of God. His ministry is centered in the imitation of Christ.

Ignatius writes:

"The carnal cannot live a spiritual life, nor can the spiritual live a carnal life, any more than faith can act the part of infidelity, or infidelity the part of faith. But even the things you do in the flesh are spiritual, for you do all things in union with Jesus Christ." (Eph. 8,2) "Do as Christ did, for He, too, did as the Father did." (Phil. 7,2) "And thus you all are fellow pilgrims, God-bearers and temple-bearers, Christ-bearers." (Eph 9,2)

In prayer the bishop recognizes the presence of God in his ministry. Prayer, contemplative union with God, nourishes and sustains the bishop's ministry in the midst of the community of God's people and the world. Only the bishop who lives a disciplined prayer life can lead the community to encounter the gifts of God for the people of God.

The faithful life of prayer even leads to martyrdom. Ignatius sees martyrdom as the highest gift of grace in imitation of Christ.

> "May nothing seen or unseen fascinate me, so that I may happily make my way to Jesus Christ! Fire, cross, struggles with wild beasts, wrenching of bones, mangling of limbs, crushing of the whole body, and torments inflicted by the devil, let them come upon me, provided only I make my way to Jesus Christ." (Smyrn 4,2) "Permit me to be an imitator of my suffering God." (Rom 6,3)

At the heart of the bishop's ministry is his work as president of the Eucharist and provider of the sacraments. The life of prayer cannot be separated from the liturgical life of the people of God. Orthodox and Anglicans agree that:

> Prayer of the Holy Spirit in the heart of the individual Christian is inseparable from the common liturgical prayer of the Christian community. It is particularly related to the grace given in Baptism, Chrismation (Confirmation) and Eucharist and, generally, to the whole sacramental life of the Church and to common prayer and the reading of Scripture. Both common liturgical prayer and personal prayer are informed and shaped by the Church's faith in God, the Father, the Son and the Holy Spirit. (Dublin 41)

The sacramental presence of the bishop is an essential part of any sacramental action. According to Ignatius, the bishop is the high-priest of the liturgy and sacramental dispenser of the mysteries of God—Holy Eucharist, Baptism, *agape* may not be celebrated without the bishop:

> "Let no one do anything touching the Church apart from the bishop. Let that celebration of the Eucharist be considered valid which is held under the bishop or anyone to whom he has committed it." (Smyrn 8,1)

"It is not permitted without authorization from
the bishop either to baptize or to hold an agape;
but whatever he approves is also pleasing to God.
Thus everything you do will be secure and valid."
(Smyrn 8,2)

To lead, faithfully, in the sacramental life of the people of God,
the bishop needs to nurture the discipline of the prayer of the
presence of God. For only this prayerful awareness allows the
bishop to experience in these mysteries the Risen Lord.

St. Cyprian writes of the priest in the celebration of the Holy
Eucharist as one who "truly discharged the office of Christ,"
"who imitates what Christ did," "to offer...what he sees Christ
himself to have offered." It is simply impossible to carry out the
eucharistic ministry of the bishop without that constant prayer of
the heart that is presence and communion with the Holy Trinity.

St. Cyprian teaches:

For if Jesus Christ, our Lord and God, is Himself
the chief priest of God the Father, and has first
offered himself a sacrifice to the Father, and has
commanded this to be done in commemoration of
Himself, certainly that priest truly discharges the
office of Christ, who imitates that which Christ
did; and he then offers a true and full sacrifice in
the Church to God the Father, when he proceeds
to offer it according to what he sees Christ
Himself to have offered. (Epist. 63,14)

The mystical life of communion with God, in Christ, is centered in and built up in the Holy Eucharist. Gathered as one in
eucharistic worship, the people of God, again and again, meet
and are nourished by prayer, the Holy Scripture, the apostolic
tradition and teaching. In one single eucharistic life they are
sealed by the Holy Spirit with their Christian identity.

Concerning this life of communion and identity in Christ in
the Eucharist, Ignatius writes:

"Take care, then, to partake of one Eucharist; for one is the flesh of our Lord Jesus Christ, and one the cup to unite us with his blood, and one altar, just as there is one bishop assisted by the presbyters and deacons." (Phil. 4) "The eucharist is the flesh of our Savior Jesus who suffered for our sins and whom the Father in his loving compassion raised from the dead." (Smyrn 7,1)

In celebrating the Eucharistic Meal the Church, in time, becomes identified with and prefigures that communion with God the Holy Trinity that will come when the Kingdom of God is finally established. Word and sacraments signify the church's essential participation in the mystery of the life of God.

The Moscow Agreed Statement of 1976 speaks of Orthodox Anglican common faith on this essential truth.

"The Eucharist actualizes the Church. The Christian community has a basic sacramental character. The Church can be described as a synaxis or an *ecclesia*, which is, in its essence, a worshipping and eucharistic assembly. The Church is not only built up by the Eucharist, but is also a condition for it. Therefore one must be a believing member of the Church in order to receive Holy Communion.

"The Church celebrating the Eucharist becomes fully itself; that is *koinonia*, fellowship-communion. The Church celebrates the Eucharist as the central act of its existence, in which the ecclesial community, as a living reality confessing its faith, receives its realization." (Moscow 24)

The Church is called by God to be faithful to the Gospel of God and to preach this Gospel to all people at all times. The ministry of the bishop is as Eucharistic president and provider of the sacraments, apostolic teacher, leader in the Councils of the

Church, and bond of unity developed in the Church as the way to provide for fidelity to Gospel life and communion with God the Holy Trinity.

The Dublin Agreed Statement of 1984 speaks of the *esse* of the Church, and presents a vision of the Church as one, holy, catholic and apostolic:

> "The Church is one, because there is a 'one Lord, one faith, one baptism, one God and Father of us all' (Eph. 4:5) and it participates in the life of the Holy Trinity, one God in three persons. The unity of the Church is expressed in common faith and in the fellowship of the Holy Spirit; it takes concrete and visible form as the Church gathered round the bishop in the common celebration of the Holy Eucharist, proclaims Christ's death until he comes. (1 Cor. 11:26) (8)

> "The Church is holy (1 Cor. 3:17) because its members are in Christ, the head, who is holy and who lives in them (Eph. 3:17)...The Church's holiness springs from the action of God's Holy Spirit whom Christ sends to purify his people, to draw them into the reality of his risen life, and to conform them to his compassion and love for the world. (10)

> "The Church is catholic because by word and life it maintains and bears witness to the fullness of the faith, and because people of all nations and conditions are called to participate in it. (12)

> "At each local Eucharist, celebrated within the catholic Church, Christ is present in his wholeness, and so each local celebration actualizes and gives visible expression to the Church's catholicity. (13)

"The Church is apostolic because it is built on the foundation of the apostles (Eph. 2:20; Rev. 21:14) who are primary and authorative witnesses to the crucified and risen Lord. Their authority lies in the fact that they were sent by Jesus Christ, who was himself sent by the Father. (Matt. 28:19-20; John 20:21) (14)

"The apostolicity of the Church is manifested in a particular way through the succession of bishops. This succession is a sign of the unbroken continuity of apostolic tradition and life." (17)

The center of the Christian Church is the reality of *koinonia*, sharing the life of God the Holy Trinity. This mystery manifests itself in history in a Church that is one, holy, catholic, and apostolic.

The Church in the world is that community of people open to receiving the love of God and to being enfolded into the orbit of God's own life. The bishop is called by God to be transfigured by this mystery of God, the Blessed Trinity, and to serve and preserve this mystery for the people of God. The truth is that the bishop can carry out his ministry with unconditional fidelity only if his life is rooted in the discipline of contemplative prayer. The gifts of God—*koinonia*-unity, holiness, catholicity, apostolicity— are conceived and born anew each day in the faithful life of prayer.[3]

---

[3] For more on this theme, see: "The Communion of the Trinity and the Life of the Church" in *Episcopal Ministry: The Report of the Archbishops' Group on the Episcopate*, Church House Publishing, London, 1990, p. 5.

4

First Supplement
"The Communion of the Trinity and the Life of the Church"*

i. Communion Unfolded in Scripture

The Bible unfolds the story of the relationship of God to the world he has created. In the beginning God made men and women to live in a relationship of communion, with him and with one another. That is the message of the creation story in Genesis and of the history of the covenant people of the Old Testament. God established a covenant with the people: 'I will be your God, and you shall be my people' (Leviticus 26.12).

Sin and its effects are the cause of the breakdown of communion: a breakdown between God and his people and between human beings; and of disintegration within the human personality. Adam and Eve hide from God; they put the blame on each other. Cain kills Abel because he believes that Abel has stolen God's favour. The Tower of Babel leads to dispersion and mutual incomprehension. And the long history of the Old Testament recounts the narrative of the people of Israel's infidelity to their side of the covenant promises, the subsequent breakdown of their relationship with God and the consequent disintegration of the life of the people of God.

The New Testament tells the story of how God in Christ provides the means of restoring that which was, and is, lost by sin.

*From *Episcopal Ministry: The Report of the Archbishops' Group on the Episcopate* (London, Church House Publishing, 1990, pp. 5-10). This supplement is intended to accompany the preceding paper by Bishop Mark Dyer.

The purpose of the work of Jesus Christ is the restoration of communion between humanity and God and between human beings; and of the individual's wholeness. Christ is lifted up from the earth to draw all to himself. He dies to gather into one the scattered children of God (John 12.32, 11.52). The restored relationship is offered to the Old Israel and to all people and nations. This restored creation is not only a return to the beginning but a new creation in Christ.

The Church, the new Israel, is given by God in Christ as the place where the life of this new communion is offered, shared and lived out. The communion between Christians is brought into being in the sacrament of Baptism, and is maintained in the sharing of a common message and a common eucharistic life; and that life is itself a communion with the Father and the Son in the fellowship of the Holy Spirit. 'That which we have seen and heard we proclaim also to you, so that you may have communion (*koinonia*) with us; and our communion (*koinonia*) is with the Father and with his Son Jesus Christ' (I John 1.3). It is God himself who calls men and women into communion with his Son Jesus Christ; and through our communion with Christ in the Spirit we enjoy communion both with the Father and with one another. 'God is faithful, by whom you were called into the communion (*koinonia*) of his Son, Jesus Christ our Lord (I Corinthians 1.9).

The New Testament uses many images to describe the Church—it is the body of Christ, the temple, the vine, the bride, the new Israel. Underlying all these images is the idea of communion (*koinonia*).[1] *Koinonia* is more than simply human fellowship: it refers to the fact that we are drawn into the life of God the Holy Trinity and together experience something of that divine relationship. The Church, then, is that part of the world which has accepted the Gospel addressed to all people, which tries to live by it, and whose members are already drawn into communion with God the Holy Trinity and with one another in him.

---

[1] cf. *The Final Report* of ARCIC, Introduction, 4.

The New Testament shows the infant Church built up of those baptized into the life of the Holy Trinity, nurtured by Word and Sacrament, and living a common life. St. Paul sees Christians as a community, members of one body, who serve one another. It is within this community that the special ministry of service still nurtures the community and leads it in mission to the world.

There is an intimate relation between the Church and the Kingdom. The Church is already the foretaste on earth of the Kingdom portrayed in the last two chapters of the Apocalypse (Revelation 21 and 22). The end of all things, according to St. John, is a community in which there will be no more temple, sacraments or ministry, for God himself will be immediate to his people. 'Behold, the dwelling place of God is with men. He will dwell with them, and they shall be his people; and God himself will be their God.' The Church is foretaste of that kingdom, first fruits of the kingdom and sign of the kingdom.

All this points to the fact that the church is more than an institution; it is a way of 'being.' Its being is its grounding in the communion of God: Father, Son and Holy Spirit. The life of the Church partakes in the life of God the Holy Trinity. Our experience of life in the Church is confused, ragged, distorted, but there are moments of glory. That life is an incarnate foretaste of the eschatological life of the Kingdom and so it points ahead to the future consummation of the Kingdom. An understanding of communion and eschatology are thus necessary for understanding the nature of the Church and its ministry. The exercise of oversight in the Church must, equally necessarily, be related to the nurturing and maintenance of the communion of the Church and point to the vision of the Kingdom.

ii. The Communion of the Trinity

If we are to understand this character of the being of the Church and the place and role of the ordained ministry within it, we shall be helped by reflecting first on the vision of the Holy Trinity:

> We cannot have an ecclesiology until we have a

proper Trinitarian doctrine, for we cannot expect of the Church anything less than a sign and a reflection of God's way of being in creation...The Church must be conceived as the place where man can get a taste of his eternal eschatological destiny which is communion in God's very life.[2]

The key to our human understanding of the divine order lies in the Person of Christ, in the incarnation of the eternal, only-begotten son of God. Through him we know something of the life of the Trinity and the ordering of the relationships of the Persons within it. A right trinitarian theology must balance both the equality of the Persons of the Trinity and the distinction of the Persons. The Father is the Source, creating by his Word and in the power of the Holy Spirit; the Son, who is the eternal Word, became human by the power of the Holy Spirit and offered the sacrifice of his life to the Father; the Spirit nurtures God's people with life-giving power, enabling them to pray to the Father, in, with and through the Son. At the same time, the Persons are one in being and equal in their Godhead. If we are to keep before us an authentic vision of God, we must not lose sight of this balance.

In this classic Christian perception of the Triune God, we are given some insight into God's way of being as that of Persons in a relation so profoundly reciprocal that they are one in being, so perfect in its mutuality that they will one will. The interaction in love of Father, Son and Holy Spirit is a depth of participation in one another which makes the Trinity a unity.[3] From the life of

---

[2] Metropolitan John Zizioulas, unpublished essay.

[3] This unique relational character of the Persons of the Trinity is sometimes referred to as the 'social' Trinity, in which each person of the Trinity is perfectly open to the other and interdependent as in a relationship of mutual giving and receiving. This has led some recent theologians, most notably Jurgen Moltmann, to perceive God the Father through his intimate relationship with the Son, as mysteriously and paradoxically possible yet unchanging, sovereign yet vulnerable. The 1987 Report of the Doctrine Commission, *We Believe in God*, took up this theme: '...the three Persons are as inseparable in their nature as

mutuality and fellowship of the Godhead love overflows into creation, sustaining the world in being and bringing it to its appointed end in glory. The gift of God to the Church is the privilege of sharing here and now in the Divine life, and of extending the love of God in the world. The Church's vocation is to live and witness as a fellowship, a communion which seeks to be one in its ecclesial being, and one in its will to serve its Lord; and in a mutual love which gives individuals, and local communities, and diverse Christian traditions, scope to be fully themselves and to participate equally in the common life. To stress that the Church is communal is to emphasize relationships; the personal is thus prior to the institutional; the institutional exists to nurture and sustain the relations of human persons joined, as far as is possible for us as creatures, in a resemblance to that Trinitarian life. This view of the Holy Trinity has profound implications for the Church and for the exercise of all forms of authority in the Church.

In the differentiation of the Persons in the Trinity we glimpse the fundamental principle of order. The Father begets the Son and the Holy Spirit proceeds, and that is a matter of eternal order in the Being of God, and it is an eternal distinction in relation.[4]

No human society can mirror the mystery of the divine life

---

3 (continued) they are in their creative and redemptive activity. If one suffers, then all suffer, or better, if God is in Christ suffering for our redemption, then this is the sign and guarantee of the Triune God's eternal involvement in human suffering and human destiny. For authentically Christian speech about God is always speech about the Holy Trinity' (pp. 158-9).
Such reflection has been of immense importance in the thinking and spirituality of many Christians today. However, some fear that it posits a challenge to the sovereignty and impassibility of God; a view expressed in the debate in General Synod in July 1987.

4 Some would see in the Sonship of the second Person of the Trinity an exemplification of dependence on, and derivation from the Father, without any implication of inferiority, but as a proper relation of hierarchial order within the unity of the Holy Trinity.

perfectly. But we may see in the diversity in which the Father is Creator, the Son Redeemer and the Holy Spirit Comforter and Sanctifier, ground for believing that, at our creaturely level, distinction of function and differentiation of relationship are proper and necessary in the ministerial order of the Church. Creation, Redemption and Sanctification belong to God, and are his gift to his people. The co-operative ministry of the Persons in the Godhead is to be reflected in the co-operative character of Christian ministry in the Church; and God's one will for the world's good is reflected in the ways in which the community is able to act as one through the representing and focusing function of the ordained ministry, and particularly through the episcopal ministry of oversight through the ages. The bishop is focus of unity in Christ and at the same time in the sparkling diversity offered by the gifts of the Spirit. The bishop is the *polupletheia* (the multitude) in his person, the many in the one.[5]

iii. The Life of the Church

If the principles of relation and order in the life of the Trinity not only provide patterns for the life of the Church and its ministry, but are the very ground and being of the Church's life, we may take it as fundamental that the Church receives its identity from the God in whom it lives and has its being. Incorporation into the Divine life at Baptism is experienced in the life of prayer. The prayer and thanksgiving of the Church is a sharing in the priesthood of Christ, as his people offer themselves in, with and through Christ, in the power of the Holy Spirit, to the Father. We are counted worthy to stand in the presence of God, through Christ, by the Holy Spirit: we are prayed in by the Holy Spirit. In the Eucharist the Church experiences most fully that communion, in Christ the Father through the Spirit, in which the Kingdom is experienced here and now in the eschatological feast.

---

[5] See V. Lossky, *Mystical Theology in the Eastern Church* (tr. London, 1957), and Appendix I on 'the corporate person'.

Its institutional framework is an incarnational expression of that communion, and in this way too the Church is called to be an image of the Trinitarian God.

As the Church participates more deeply in the life of the Holy Trinity, as it is drawn more deeply into the eternal divine fellowship, so the human face of the Church will be conformed to the Triune God and bear God's image in the world. The Church will be an authentic sign only insofar as in and by the power of the Holy Spirit, it takes its identity from Christ, who is head of his body, the Church.

The Church must be prepared to know in its incarnate life that pain and glory which were inseparable in the incarnation of the Son; to follow his example of unconditional, vulnerable, sacrificial love; it must be prepared to walk the way of the Cross, expecting and accepting pain as it accepts responsibilities others evade; and take risks for the sake of the Gospel it proclaims. The Church has to be open to follow Christ's example of *kenosis* and poverty, ready itself to become poor for the sake of the world, ready to bear in its body the marks of crucifixion. The Church cannot escape pain, both within its own life, and in its life in relation to the world. The Church will find its identity, not on the other side of pain and suffering, but in the very midst of it, where God meets us to heal and to restore and to give new life in the power of God's resurrection. The example of the sacrificial life and death of Jesus Christ is the pattern for the obedience of the Church, and for its ministry of service. Indeed it is Christ's ministry that is entrusted to the Church: his shepherding is our shepherding. All ministry is held from Christ in the Church.

We have set out our understanding of the Church's *koinonia*, as a communion grounded in, and modelled upon, the relational and ordered and self-giving life of God the Holy Trinity and the sacrificial life of God the Son. We believe that it is within this broad understanding of the doctrinal context that the Church's ministry of oversight is best explored. That ministry is to be tested by the way it reflects the nature of God's Trinitarian life and love: by the way it images the divine life of perfect sharing, giving and receiving, receiving and giving; and by how far it is prepared to incarnate in its life the pattern of self-emptying in the incarnation of the second person of the Trinity. For guidance on the ways in which these broad principles are to be worked out in the life of the Church, we must turn to Scripture.

5

Third Paper

Bishops, Succession, and the Apostolicity of The Church

by The Rev. Canon Professor Richard A. Norris, Jr.

Professor of Church History

Union Theological Seminary, New York City

1 In each of its primary roles—viz., those of teaching, of liturgical presidency, and of leadership, governance, or administration ("shepherding")—the episcopate, embodied in the persons of individual bishops, serves the unity of each local church in the latter's identity and calling as a community of the New Covenant. Precisely in virtue of this function at the local level, the episcopate, now embodied as a college of bishops, also serves the unity of the church at regional levels and, at least in principle, at the ecumenical level. The bishop, then, is certainly, as the *Baptism, Eucharist, Ministry* document from the Faith and Order Commission of the World Council of Churches insists, a primary "sign" of unity in the church.

1.1 It is necessary to insist, however, that this unity which the episcopate serves is not just any kind of unity. It is a unity, as I have phrased it, in the church's "identity and calling" as the "community of the New Covenant." From a theological point of view, this identity and calling must be defined by reference to Christ. The church is the assembly of persons who by baptism belong to the New Covenant that God has established with humanity in Christ and who, therefore, through the gift of the Spirit, are so united with Christ in his death and new life as to be adopted children of God, sharing with Christ and with each other the new life that belongs to the flesh of God's eternal Word. With this baptismal *identity* there comes a baptismal *calling* as well—a calling to be and to make disciples whose lives and actions, individual and common, will attest, as Christ's did, the "grace and truth," the justice and mercy, of the *basileia tou theou*.

1.2 This is a theological definition of the identity and calling in which the unity of the church consists and which the ministry of bishops is meant to serve. Such a definition makes, however, a tacit appeal beyond itself. It is couched perforce in the language of the Scriptures and the creeds; and if it persuades, it does so because it offers a summary synthesis of themes and teachings that are arguably central to the witness of these sources. The church's self-understanding, therefore, and by consequence its sense of identity and calling, are rooted in what we have been taught to call "the apostolic witness." The unity of the church *in Christ* is apprehended in and through the *original Gospel*, the kerygma that is on the one hand incorporated in the Scriptures and, on the other, reiterated as faith's confessional response in the baptismal symbol. In being a "sign of unity," then, the bishop, as teacher, pastor, and liturgical president, is a servant of the original "apostolic faith" and a minister of that relation to God in Christ which "the apostolic witness" proclaims as Gospel.

1.3 Hence one must conclude that there is yet another special note which characterizes the unity of the church and hence the episcopal office that serves it. It is a unity that obtains, or is sought, not just in any and every given present, but also across generations. It binds not merely the church in one place to the church in another, but also the church of one time to the church of another: and in particular the church of *this* time (whatever that may be) to the church as originally gathered around the faith and the message of its founders. To use contemporary jargon, the church's unity is diachronic as well as synchronic. Hence the episcopate, whether taken individually or collectively, serves the unity of the church precisely to the degree that it binds past and present—precisely to the degree that it represents, in any given present, the shape of the original Gospel as that addresses the confusions, the needs, and the problems of *this* generation in *this* place. Any bishop, then, whose ministry is to serve the unity of the churches in Christ must be, above all, an *apostolic* bishop. The question, though, is what makes a bishop "apostolic" and that is the question this paper wants, though briefly and inadequately, to address.

2 The first and most obvious answer to this question is that supplied by the traditional doctrine of "apostolic succession." In this view, bishops are "successors of the apostles" in at least three senses. First, they succeed the apostles in the sense that their office or function embodies and continues at least one essential element in the office of an apostle: that, namely, of oversight or *episkope*. Second, they succeed the apostles in the sense that their office is of apostolic institution: i.e., that the apostles themselves established bishops to succeed them in the superintendence of local churches. Finally, they succeed the apostles in the sense that there is a "chain" of legitimate episcopal succession that reaches back to the original founders of the churches. Let us, then, examine these contentions by looking first at the notion of succession, and then at that of the "apostolic."

2.1 The idea of succession (*diadoche*) was thematized in the ancient world in the course of the struggles that ensued over the "inheritance" of Alexander the Great, whose death without an acknowledged or competent heir meant, in the end, that he had not one but many successors (*diadochoi*). Needless to say, the question at issue was one of legitimacy: i.e., of who could *rightly* claim to succeed to Alexander's conquests. Not surprisingly, then, the problem of succession, when, in the late second century, it was raised for the first time in Christian circles, concerned a question of legitimate inheritance. The claim that bishops "succeeded" the apostles was, in the first instance, a claim that they, and they alone, were the legitimate recipients of the "property" of the apostles, and, therefore, the legitimate successors to the apostolic office.

2.1.1 In the debates and disputes of the second-century church, this claim won the day—as against Gnostic claims to a special and esoteric apostolic inheritance. The fact that it won the day must be attributed largely to the churches' good sense: i.e., to their ability to detect whose "inheritance" was more likely to represent the lineaments of the original kerygma. By contrast, the argument that alleged an unbroken chain of succession from apostolic founders to contemporary bishops was secondary and merely supportive. It was also fragile, for the good enough reason that it was difficult to trace the links in the chain with any degree of certainty. Only Hegesippus, Irenaeus, and Eusebius of Caesarea tried; and they, as we know, did not succeed. Nevertheless, this argument was influential in two ways. In the first place, it lent additional emphasis to the theme of apostolicity by insisting that true oversight in the church must be exercised in accord with apostolic example and mandate. And in the second place, it suggested that one mark of the diachronic unity of the church is that continuity in leadership which is guaranteed by legitimate succession in the episcopal office.

2.1.2 It is difficult, then, to speak of "apostolic succession" or of "succession from the apostles," if by these expressions one intends to assert either that "the apostles" instituted the episcopal office as we know it (or even as Christians of the late second century knew it), or that one can trace a clear "chain" of succession from any given bishop at any given time in history back to one or more "apostles." The very notion of succession as an element in the continuity, unity, and identity of the church is a creation of the second century. All one can honestly say is that the pattern of leadership and of governance which on the whole prevailed in Christian communities of the second and third generations, and which, therefore, had its roots planted in the time of the churches' original founders and nurturers, was one that eventually and quite naturally evolved into a system according to which Christians in each place had a single chief pastor who was styled *episkopos*. This episcopal ministry was then perpetuated, by observance of customs having to do with election and ordination, in such a way that the identity of the community from generation to generation was safeguarded, if not guaranteed, by the regular and legitimate succession of its leaders. A bishop was understood to "succeed" his predecessor if, and only if, he was both duly elected by the clergy and people of his church and duly ordained by bishops representing the larger church.

2.1.3 This system produced a genuine succession: not, in any literal sense, a succession "from the apostles," but a succession of chief pastors whose dual "belonging"—to the local church which chose them and to the larger church which acknowledged and ordained them through other bishops—undergirded and strengthened the continuity of the churches, their diachronic as well as synchronic unity. It is, I take it, this succession to which some Anglicans have referred under the label "historic episcopate," a phrase which on the one hand renounces any claim to a clear succession of bishops "from the apostles," but on the other hand affirms the regular succession of bishops as a normal constituent of the apostolicity of the church.

2.2 This discussion of succession indicates, however, and indicates fairly clearly, that "apostolicity" and "apostolic" are terms that need no little clarification. What is more, it suggests why this is so. These words, like the word "apostle" itself, appear to refer directly or indirectly to a particular and definable group of people: namely, to the Twelve. A close reading of the New Testament, however, makes it plain that there was doubt about the names of some of the Twelve, that little was known of their activities, and that the term "apostle" was originally used to denote the much larger category of travelling missionaries (as it still does, for example, in the *Didache*)—people like Paul and Barnabas, who were certainly not members of the Twelve. Certain later writings in the New Testament (e.g., Ephesians) clearly count Paul among "the apostles," but this, as we know, was (a) denied in certain quarters in the early church, and (b) affirmed in other quarters in such wise as to deny the title "apostle" to anyone other than Paul. The fact seems to be, then, that the meaning of "apostle" and "apostolic" was not only unclear but a matter of dispute in the opening years of the second century.

2.2.1 If one attends, however, to the issues involved in this dispute, the meaning of "apostle" and "apostolic" suddenly becomes perfectly clear. "Apostle," as Ephesians straightforwardly testifies, means, roughly speaking, "one of the people on whom the church is founded"; and the debate centered around the claim of certain bodies of teaching and tradition—Pauline, Johannine, Petrine—to represent the witness of such persons. Evidently the name of James, "the Lord's brother," also figured in this debate (since he too is one of the "pillars" mentioned at Galatians 2:9). Paul, at any rate, regarded James as an apostle (Galatians 1:19), even though he was neither one of the Twelve nor a travelling missionary, no doubt because of the tradition recorded at 1 Corinthians 15:7. "Apostolic," then, is a term whose operative meaning was determined retrospectively; and it was used to qualify teaching or practice belonging to a tradition that could arguably be taken to have originated with one (or more) of the church's "pillars." What is "apostolic" is whatever of their immediate inheritance the churches of the second century took to derive from the period of the church's origins—a period with regard to which they had little precise information. And among these was the institution of episcopacy. Their concern, in other words, was to establish the churches of their own time in the witness and practice that *grounded* the Christian movement; but what they could know of that witness and practice was mediated through institutions, traditions, and writings that in most cases stood at one or more removes from the "apostolic" era and thus embodied the fruit of later reflection and experience.

3 From an historian's point of view, therefore, the epithet "apostolic," if employed naively to mean "of or pertaining to the Twelve," is something of a misnomer. What it properly means is *the heritage of the first-century churches as that was known and appropriated towards the end of the second century*, in the era of the great debate with Gnosticism (not to mention the Marcionites). What was remarkable, however, about this process of appropriation was the catholicity of its embrace.

If one attends to nothing more than the emerging New Testament canon, it is striking how frequently raging disputes were settled in effect by ignoring them. The churches accepted *four* gospels (even though they understood the Gospel to be one), and gospels that any fool could see presented variant testimonies about Jesus. More than that, they accepted, among these four, the favorite gospel of the Valentinians (John) and the gospel in which Marcion had delighted (Luke); and they set the writings of Paul and his school alongside the gospel most favored by the critics of Paul (Matthew). Whether consciously or not, the New Testament canon came to include writings that exhibited the early roots of all the conflicting tendencies of the second century. What it omitted were writings that, on the face of it, represented not the roots but the flowers of those tendencies.

The same catholicity of taste is manifest, moreover, in the fact that it was not the New Testament canon alone that was erected as apostolic. The orally transmitted pattern of baptismal catechesis and confession which later evolved into the creed(s) was also accepted as attesting the shape of apostolic teaching. Bishops in proper succession were accepted as inheritors of the apostolic teaching-office. And undergirding all of this were the sacramental liturgies of baptism and eucharist which were not only envisaged as part of the apostolic inheritance but also functioned as the framework within which canon, creed, and ministry "worked."

If we return, then, to our original question—what makes a bishop "apostolic"?—the answer has to be given in a complex form. The second century's definition-in-principle of what constitutes "apostolicity" as the criterion of the church's identity and unity *included* the episcopate; but it also included a great deal more.What Anglicans have called "the historic ministry" indeed pertained, perhaps even belonged, to the essential identity of the church. It was not a dispensable item. But neither was it, in the order of things human and creaturely, "the church's one foundation" (to quote an old hymn). Rather was it conceived as one of the concatenated set of institutions which, even though they were, in each case, contingent products of the historical evolution of the Christian movement, nevertheless functioned, in their totality, as the regular bearers and guarantors of the church's continuing identity as church of Christ. In the end, what is "apostolic" is not the episcopate, but precisely this "concatenated set of institutions," within which the episcopate—and, one might add, the presbyterate and diaconate—operates.

4 Now it is important for our purposes here, that is, for a consideration of the role of bishops *vis-a-vis* the unity and apostolicity of the church, to look more closely at this picture of the episcopate as one in a *correlative* set of "institutions" (as I have called them), which the churches of the second century identified as continuing and safeguarding their apostolic inheritance. It is this picture, I take it, that, for Anglicans, is sketched out by the so-called *Lambeth Quadrilateral*, which specified the canonical Scriptures, the two Gospel sacraments, the ecumenical creeds, and the historic episcopate as essential elements in the reunited church—and therefore, presumably, as marks of the church's *apostolicity.*

4.1 The first thing to note here is the fact, to which I have already alluded, that each of these institutions or sets of institutions is envisaged as emerging or growing up within, and out of, the life of the family of Christian assemblies. Tradition, to be sure, has, in different ways, assigned to each of them a certain priority to the life of the church. The Scriptures have been described as the inspired Word of God which addresses the church from beyond itself.The sacraments, in an Augustinian view, are not human works but visible signs of God's active presence in Christ. The ministry of the church has been described, in one ecumenical document, as "a gift of God to his Church and, therefore, an office of divine institution." The confession of faith embodied in the ecumenical creeds is, as employed in Baptism, a precondition of the existence of the church. Each of these institutions, then, is somehow *constitutive* of the church.

Nevertheless it remains true that they are institutions whose human and historical origins we can, within limits, trace; and therefore, the priority they are assigned is not a given, but a reflection of the function they perform and have performed in the life of the church. If in their different ways they signify or mediate, within the church, the transcendent source of the church's life and calling, they do so precisely because they are immanent and historically contingent products of that life.

4.2 Just because this is the case, however, none of these institutions in the forms in which we know them can be described as absolutely necessary to the life and identity of the church. It is not merely that we can imagine—not captiously but seriously and reasonably—a course of historical development that would have produced, for example, a different canon of the Scriptures or different forms of ministry; we can observe that as a matter of fact the church's history has produced such variations. Furthermore, we can observe congregations of believing Christians in which the Scriptures are not publicly read or officially accorded any normative status; congregations in which the sacraments are either neglected or deprecated; congregations in which the creeds are officially repudiated. One is free, of course, to wonder whether such groups do not so limit their experience and cripple their understanding of the life of faith as, in the end, to risk departing from what is central to it; but one cannot maintain that any one of these institutions is *absolutely* necessary, in a given time and place, to the stimulation and sustenance of living Christian faith. Indeed there is no one here, I venture, who could not, by casting about in his mind for a moment, think of a time and place when each of these institutions has been so corrupted in its use and functions, or so systematically disused, that reasonable and faithful persons might well be willing to dispense with it.

4.3 Here, then, we find ourselves in a paradoxical position. On the one hand, we see the continuing identity of the church as the community of apostolic faith to rest upon the continuity of certain distinctive and typical institutions—each of which, traditionally, has been valued for its role in opening us to the Gospel, to the self-communication of God in Christ. On the other hand, these institutions are very human affairs, to which we can ascribe no abstract necessity. What necessity they have rests upon the fact that they "happened" in the way they did to function as, on the whole, they function. We do not deduce them, we observe them as enduringly focal or nodal points in the life of the churches.

4.4 It may be, though, that part of the solution of this paradox lies in the fact that these institutions are closely interrelated: that what we have in such a formula as the *Lambeth Quadrilateral* is not so much a list of items as it is a description of a system of communication whose several parts presuppose and depend on each other. If these institutions are, in fact, constitutive for the life of the church, and can thus lay claim at any rate to a diminished and hypothetical sort of necessity, that is because of the way they function together. The Gospel set forth in the Scriptures is responsively repeated in the confession of faith represented by the creeds, sealed and enacted in the sacraments, and ministered and safeguarded by persons officially set apart for just that purpose—that is, for the purpose of keeping this system of communication, of *koinonia* between God and humanity in Christ, alive. That the system can become diseased or dysfunctional, through the failure or neglect of one of its constituent elements, we know; but we also know that, no doubt within limits, it can compensate for and correct its own weaknesses, because each of the constituent elements symbolizes and carries, in its own special way, the same Gospel. The Scriptures can reiterate what the ministry forgets; the creeds assert what disuse or overly ingenious interpretation loses in the Scriptures; the ministry proclaims what the sacraments are no longer seen or experienced as enacting.

4.5 Here, then, one can discern the logic of the outlook I have described by calling the church a "system of communication," and by referring to the episcopate as "one of a concatenated set of institutions." Such an outlook does in a sense relativize "the historic ministry;" but it does so by envisaging that ministry as real and essential only *in and through* its relation to certain other institutions from which it is inseparable; and second, by acknowledging that this whole system of institutions is relative to, because dependent upon, the historical community or communities that are its matrix. It commends none of them in and for itself, but all of them in their interrelation. If it is true, as surely it is, that continuity in episcopal succession cannot of itself guarantee the identity or faithfulness of the church, neither is it true that one can accomplish this end merely by having copies of the Bible lying about for consultation, or by repeating the words of the eucharistic liturgy. What defines and constitutes the church for practical purposes is an historically emergent system of communication "in which," as the Anglican *Articles of Religion* insist, "the pure Word of God is preached, and the sacraments be duly ministered...," by a ministry that legitimately "succeeds" to this inheritance and openly accepts this responsibility.

5 The episcopate, then, serves the unity of the church in its identity and calling not by simply being around, but by being answerable: answerable, that is, to the self-communication of God in Christ by way of Scripture, confession of faith, and sacrament. Within this system of communication, and only within it, legitimate succession of bishops is a symbol—something more than a mere sign—of the diachronic unity of the church with the Gospel that was and is its foundation, and thus of the fact that the church perdures in its given identity as the community originally gathered by "the apostles"—all of them, of whatever sort. God can, of course, dispense with bishops, and perhaps does so more frequently than we know; but the human church, in its character as an historical symbol or sacrament of the City of God, figures its continuity as the apostolic community of the New Covenant precisely through the "succession" of its legitimate officers. What is more, this is true even of Christian bodies that allege themselves to dispense with *episkopoi*. The problem of the churches' unity in their apostolic calling is not whether they shall or shall not have successions of bishops, but how their several successions shall become one.

6

Fourth Paper

Introducing "The Ministry of Bishops: A Study Document Authorized by the House Of Bishops of the Episcopal Church"

by The Rt. Rev. Richard F. Grein
Bishop of New York

Episcopalians and the Russian Orthodox Church have had cordial contacts, exchanges, and discussions for well over a century. And if one were minded to include still earlier Anglican contacts from England, such as those tentative initiatives of the Anglican Nonjurors (those Anglican bishops refusing to take the oath of allegiance to William III) we could extend those contacts back over 270 years. Ours is a history of friendship, albeit a friendship with major differences of theological perspective. But then friends do not always agree on everything.[1]

During this long history of affectionate contact the Russian Orthodox Church underwent a dark period of persecution and suffering—a suffering that we in the West can only partially appreciate. Yet at the same time we Anglicans do know the devastation that ruthless dictatorships can bring to the Church—we have had our Idi Amins in Uganda and apartheid in South Africa. For us there has also been the stress of trying to understand the meaning of faithfulness in an increasingly secularized culture.

---

[1] Herbert Waddams, ed., *Anglo-Russian Theological Conference* (London: Faith Press, 1957).

But now we enter a new era. The Russian Orthodox Church has emerged victorious, and now continues with renewed vigor its mission to the people of Russia. For this task, "there is a great need for new apostles," to quote Archbishop Clement.

In this 100-year history of our relationship, the Church of England and its daughter churches discovered themselves as a worldwide "Anglican Communion." Congregations which were established around the world as chapels of ease for English-speaking people had become indigenous churches—largely third world. The Anglican Communion is now largely made up of non-European peoples. In the Diocese of New York we now celebrate the liturgy in nine languages representing 25 nations and cultures. We are also in need of "new apostles."

We come then to this dialogue with the Russian Church in a partnership, seeking the guidance of the Holy Spirit as we both enter a new time in the Church's life. We have differing problems, but gifts to exchange as our concerns become mutual concerns. And at the heart of these mutual concerns is the role of episcopacy.

In this brief paper I would like to share with you the background of our new pastoral letter on the ministry of bishops—how it came into existence and how it will be used throughout the Episcopal Church.

I would like to begin by describing for you the way in which that document, *The Ministry of Bishops: A Study Document*, came into being. But first I need to share with you a little of the background regarding the structure of governance in the Episcopal Church.

Although the Episcopal Church is named after the ministry of bishops, it is not governed solely by bishops. The experience of the American Revolution had a profound influence on the shape of the Episcopal Church. Many of those who helped frame the Constitution of the United States of America were also involved in organizing the Episcopal Church, by framing canons, adopting a new Prayer Book and hymnal, organizing the church to be directed by a General Convention, and importantly, directing that the church be led by a Presiding Bishop, thus reflecting the civil structure of the new country, and not by an Archbishop. It was to be a church independent of all foreign authority, as was the new country, with full powers to regulate its own affairs, thereby mirroring the young nation. Thus it was given a democratic structure; and because of an acquired suspicion of the English concerning the relationship between crown and bishops, it had clear canonical limitations placed on the authority of the episcopal office.

This is not to suggest that the bishops of the Episcopal Church in the United States of America are without influence—the office is greatly honored and respected. But as I mentioned, the canonical authority is limited, so much so that American bishops probably have the fewest strictly canonical prerogatives of any Anglican bishops anywhere in the world. One must admit that at times many of our bishops experience great stress because the responsibility and expectations placed on the office are not matched by a requisite canonical authority. However, given the general goodwill and respect bestowed on our bishops by the people of the church, we are able to lead, and do have great influence on the lives of our people and in our parish communities.

The highest human authority in the Episcopal Church is the General Convention, which meets every three years. The General Convention is made up of two houses: The House of Deputies, consisting of four lay persons and four priests from each diocese; and the House of Bishops. Decisions on budgets, policy making, and resolutions on programs and mission are mandated only after gaining a majority vote in each house.

Between General Conventions, an Executive Council of bishops, priests, and lay persons elected by the Convention meets regularly to carry out the mission set forth by the Convention. The President of the Executive Council is the Presiding Bishop. Along with the Executive Council, there are twenty other "interim bodies" of General Convention which are involved in preparing legislation on policy in such areas as world mission, human affairs, ecumenism, liturgy, stewardship, and peace with justice.

Also meeting on a regular basis between General Conventions, at least annually, is the House of Bishops, with the Presiding Bishop as President. The House of Bishops gives pastoral oversight, sets forth pastoral letters, takes up theological issues, and exercises leadership in the church's mission.

At the House of Bishops meeting in 1989, the chairman of the Council for the Development of the Ministry requested that the Committee on the Pastoral Letter produce a "teaching pastoral" on episcopacy. There were two motivating reasons for this request: first, the Council for Development of Ministry was about to engage in some extensive rewriting of the canons that related to the office of bishop and wanted to draw from the theology of episcopacy to suggest the direction for their work; and second, their work in the development of ministry in the various areas of the Church's life, such as among the laity, in rural communities, the renewal of a permanent diaconate, etc., would, of course, also benefit from such a document about bishops. This request came in the form of a resolution which was voted and approved by the House of Bishops. It directed the Pastoral Letter Committee to produce a pastoral teaching on episcopacy by the next General Convention, which was to be convened in August of 1991.

It should be noted here that although the immediate impetus for the pastoral came from the theological needs of the Council for Development of Ministry, there were other underlying causes which prompted the call for the document. At the 1988 Lambeth Conference questions about authority and Anglican identity dominated. The working document on "Dogmatic and Pastoral Concerns" put the issue this way:

> The structures through which the Anglican Communion works are at present being tested and developed by the way in which decisions are being made in two important areas. One is the procedure by which, as a worldwide communion, Anglicans make their *response to the Final Report of ARCIC and to the Lima text*. The other is the way by which the matter of the *ordination of women* is

handled. Not only are these issues testing the existing structures of authority in the Anglican Communion, they are also providing a creative opportunity to realize hitherto unrecognized possibilities of communion.[2]

Put very simply: How is it possible for a communion of autonomous provincial Churches to come to a common evaluation of an ecumenical agreement, or to hold itself together in the face of potentially dividing issues such as the ordination of women? Clearly such questions foster more fundamental discussions on ecclesiology, and consequently the role of bishops. Underlying all of this is the unity we see in the doctrine of God as we have experienced it in the life of the Holy Trinity.

In the Episcopal Church there is the additional problem focused by the tension between the naming of bishops as "chief priest and pastor" and the reality that bishops function more as "corporate chief executive officers" in secular western societies. The duties of administration dominate our bishops' agendas, while pastoral contacts and activities appear to be fewer and carried out from a distance.

All of this made it clear that some serious reflection on the ministry of bishops was needed. And because of the size and great importance of the subject, I, as chairman of the Pastoral Letter Committee, decided to limit the scope of the pastoral, and proposed that it be used as a means of starting a dialogue between bishops and the Church. In beginning such a limited theological conversation I fully expected it to expand into other areas, with requests for more theological studies on the subject of episcopacy. Such a dialogical approach is very different from the work done in the Church of England; their approach has been much more systematic, and on a grander scale. Appropriately they began with

---

[2] *The Truth Shall Make You Free* (The Lambeth Conference 1988: The Reports, Resolutions & Pastoral Letters from the Bishops), London 1988, p. 113, Section 132.

doctrine of God, moving into ecclesiology and ministry, and finally dealing with practical questions unique to their situation.

It was my decision, after consulting with the Pastoral Letter Committee, to focus the discussion in our document on our Prayer Book rite for the Ordination of a Bishop, and in particular on the exhortation which precedes the examination:

> My *brother*, the people have chosen you and have affirmed their trust in you by acclaiming your election. A bishop in God's holy Church is called to be one with the apostles in proclaiming Christ's resurrection and interpreting the Gospel, and to testify to Christ's sovereignty as Lord of lords and King of kings.
>
> You are called to guard the faith, unity, and discipline of the Church; to celebrate and to provide for the administration of the sacraments of the New Covenant; to ordain priests and deacons and to join in ordaining bishops; and to be in all things a faithful pastor and wholesome example for the entire flock of Christ.
>
> With your fellow bishops you will share in the leadership of the Church throughout the world. Your heritage is the faith of patriarchs, prophets, apostles, and martyrs, and those of every generation who have looked to God in hope. Your joy will be to follow him who came, not to be served, but to serve, and to give his life a ransom for many.[3]

This exhortation sets forth a clear statement regarding the ministry of bishops, and is carefully rooted in the early church Fathers—in particular Ss. Ignatius, Hippolytus, Irenaeus, and Cyprian. This had the double benefit of making it clear that our

---

[3] The Book of Common Prayer, p. 517.

relatively new Ordinal is based in the Church's earliest tradition; and also it set the context for the pastoral in a time when the theology of episcopacy was developing.

Here a word needs to be said about the 1979 Book of Common Prayer of the Episcopal Church in the U.S.A. and its relationship to previous Prayer Books. The first American Book of Common Prayer was adopted in 1789. It followed from the English books of 1549, 1552, and 1662; the latter was in use in the American colonies before the Revolution. The 1789 Book of Common Prayer was revised in 1892 and again in 1928.

The framers of the 1979 book broke with the tendencies of making only modest revisions in succeeding Prayer Books; instead they went back to the Church's earliest liturgical texts to find the basis for their work. This was a bold move. Such an approach meant that the American Book of Common Prayer would have a very different style and tone from other Anglican Prayer Books, which in general were similar, using the English Book as a basis. Subsequently many other Anglican churches have followed the American lead, with the result that one of the key factors which united Anglican churches around the world, the commonality of Prayer Books on an English model, is gradually being lost. For although there are still similarities because of a common theology, the differences are now more remarkable because of cultural influences.

But this radical change in our liturgical texts is also notable because of our Anglican propensity to express our theology through liturgy. *Lex orandi, lex credendi*—the law of prayer is the law of faith—characterizes our Anglican way of making faith statements. What we believe is best understood through our liturgy—our worship is not only an action expressing our theology but is an act of believing. Therefore, the return to patristic texts in the shaping of our Prayer Book will ultimately have an enormous influence on the shaping of the people of God in the Episcopal Church, as over time their way of worship becomes their way of believing.

One need only compare the texts of the initiatory rites and

ordinals of the 1928 and 1979 Books of Common Prayer, focusing on the implied ecclesiology which lay behind the texts, to get a sense of the change. The relationship between the baptized and the ordained is very different in the two books. In the old 1928 Prayer Book we might characterize the clerical charge with regard to the laity as: a treasure to protect, to be removed from the world, a flock to be led to salvation.

Conversely, in the new 1979 Prayer Book the clergy are part of a total ministry of the people of God; they are to prepare the baptized for mission, to send them into the world. Thus while both ecclesial understandings are true, and remain part of a total view of the Church's mission, there is a shift in emphasis from a church preoccupied with saving its own to a church sensing the need to express its mission to the world. In our present book the candidates for baptism promise to be evangelists, to "proclaim by word and example the Good News of God in Christ"; to be servants, to "seek and serve Christ in all persons"; and to be prophets, to "strive for justice and peace among all people, and respect the dignity of every human being."[4]

It is clear in this that the baptized are the chief ministers of the Church's mission. It is also clear that the ministry of the ordained is defined in relationship to the baptized. For example, in the examination at the ordination of a bishop the candidate promises as a chief priest and pastor to "encourage and support all baptized people in their gifts and ministries," to "nourish them from the riches of God's grace, pray for them without ceasing, and celebrate with them the sacraments of our redemption."[5]

And in the exhortation preceding the examination of the candidates for priesthood we find this statement: "All baptized people are called to make Christ known as Savior and Lord, and to share in the renewing of his world... As a priest, it will be your task to proclaim by word and deed the Gospel of Jesus Christ, and to fashion your life in accordance with its precepts. You are to love

---

[4] Ibid., p. 305.
[5] Ibid., p. 518.

and serve the people among whom you work, caring alike for young and old, strong and weak, rich and poor."6

In all of this it is clear that the ordained render a service to the people of God, a service which is characterized both by their nurture and their preparation for ministry. Such an orientation of leadership offered as service is understood in fulfillment of our Lord's command to the Apostles when he contrasted the exercise of authority among the Gentiles, who lord it over others, with that of the church: "But it shall not be so among you; but whoever would be great among you must be your servant [*diakonos*], and whoever would be first among you must be slave [*doulos*] of all. For the son of man also came not to be served but to serve, and to give his life as a ransom for many." (Mk. 10:43ff.)

The servant image of the Church has had notable popularity among many in the Episcopal Church in recent years. This in itself may be due in part to the fact that it is easily deduced from the Prayer Book rites already mentioned. Clergy are called to service on behalf of the baptized, and the people of God are called to ministries of service in the world.

Presently in the Episcopal Church servant ministries abound. I am constantly impressed with the number of volunteers from our parishes in the Diocese of New York offering their ministries to people in desperate situations. They work among the hungry and homeless, in special programs for people with AIDS, in training programs for young people and those without jobs. They organize people to gain their rights with regard to housing, schools, and hospital care. Presently in our national Church's overseas program, "Volunteers for Mission," we have two priests working among the poor in Panama, a pediatric nurse setting up an AIDS program in Liberia, another nurse training medical assistants in Zimbabwe, and recently we have had a priest in Moscow working with the problems of alcoholism.

One would not want to claim that all of this mission activity was a result of a change in our liturgy. But certainly such min-

6 Ibid., p. 531.

istries of service are sustained and supported by the presentation in our liturgical rites of an ecclesiology which promotes the image of a servant church. And also important, because such good work can take on a life of its own and thus become an end in itself, is the solid theological foundation which helps maintain proper balance and perspective. The liturgy of the Book of Common Prayer maintains this foundation.

Now, let me briefly recap the causal forces and conditions which made the production of the study document *The Ministry of Bishops* seem propitious. The immediate cause was the request of the Council for the Development of Ministry for a theological standard for their work. In the background, but no less important, was the Anglican Communion's concern with structures of authority; and the developing tensions between the bishop as chief priest and pastor and the bishop as administrator and manager. And finally, there was the clear shift in the implied ecclesiology of the Prayer Book which apparently redefines the relationship between the ordained and unordained.

After the House of Bishops voted to have the pastoral letter written, as chairman of the Pastoral Letter committee I consulted with the Committee to select the theologians who would write the document on behalf of the bishops. Three theologians were selected who had expertise in the three areas to be considered— the bishop as preacher/teacher, as celebrant of the Church's sacraments, and as conciliar leader. Two of those theologians are part of this conference—the Rev. Canon J. Robert Wright and the Rev. Canon Richard A. Norris. By the way, both are Canon Theologians to me as Bishop of New York.

The first draft was written and edited, then sent to all the bishops of the Episcopal Church and a select list of theologians for comment. Over a period of about three months we received comments from about 30 bishops and theologians. Some of the bishops wanted the document expanded to include more of the pastoral dimension, particularly with regard to clergy and difficult pastoral situations; in other words, the practical side of episcopacy.

Still others thought we needed something on the bishop as missionary, or a discussion on suffragan and assisting bishops. One theologian felt we needed to clarify the distinction between proclamation [*kerygma*] and teaching [*didache*].

The comments were collected by the editor, and after discussion with the Pastoral Letter Committee, it was decided to stay with the previous exclusive focus on only three areas, promising the bishops that a future paper would address their other concerns. The editor then gave the pertinent comments to each of the three authors to produce a second draft, which also added an introduction and conclusion to the pastoral letter. This second draft was again sent out to the bishops in time to be read before the General Convention.

At the General Convention the Pastoral Letter Committee met to take up still other comments we had received from the bishops. A few minor adjustments were made and the document was presented to the House of Bishops for vote (Pastoral Letters do not go to the House of Deputies—priests and laity—for their approval since it is generally agreed that the teaching role belongs to the bishops). The bishops gave their approval to the Pastoral Letter, which meant that they accepted it as their own and that it would now be distributed throughout the Episcopal Church for study and discussion.

It might be pointed out here that the Pastoral Letter on episcopacy is itself an example of how we understand that bishops teach the Church. For even though it was not written by bishops, they were part of the process from the beginning, they had input to its contents, and in the end made it their own by vote.

Now to the document itself. In the precis of the Pastoral Letter it is claimed that the document "examines the role of a bishop in light of the promises made in the Ordination of a Bishop in the 1979 Book of Common Prayer." The Examination in the Ordinal most clearly sets forth our understanding of the role of the bishop in a diocese. And although the precis speaks of "redefining" and "renewal" with reference to the contemporary church and episcopacy, it does not intend to imply that something new is being set forth. Rather it is a matter of reclaiming the patristic understanding of episcopacy as a way of reclaiming and refocusing the essentials of the ministry of bishops for our time.

Again, the precis tells us that the authors, the three theologians, "were asked to focus on three pastoral roles or functions which are vital to the office of bishop..." These three pastoral roles were not simply selected from a list of possibilities but were given to us from the past by a young church—the early patristic church before the time of Constantine—in the process of formation. For me this means that they are of vital importance to any age when the Church is in a transitional process and trying to reclaim its foundational theology.

The three roles can be understood as three functions—preacher/teacher, celebrant of the sacraments, and conciliar leader—but, of course, they are more than that. In fact, all that a bishop does finds its locus in each of these three central activities. This is in part because the emergence of each is tied to a particular moment in early church history when the Christian community faced a crisis. In this way the Church under the guidance of the Holy Spirit was able to find in the office of bishop a functional role to face the challenge. Thus it was that St. Ignatius would claim for the bishop that essential role as the personal symbol of unity in the eucharistic community when his church faced persecution and incipient heresies which threatened to divide. Or some 80 years later, St. Irenaeus, faced with a full-blown gnosticism claiming a secret tradition, began to define the bishops as "successors of the apostles"... as the personal guarantors in the process of transmission of the apostolic witness. Or still later, as the church faced division and even schism over differences in local practice, St. Cyprian would describe the episcopate as "a single whole, in which each individual bishop has a right to and a responsibility for the whole."[7] Cyprian makes clear that each bishop exercises his episcopal ministry in union with all the other bishops—espe-

---

[7] *On Unity*, 5.

cially as they meet in council. "The Church, which is Catholic and One, is not separated nor divided, but is in truth connected and joined together by the cement of bishops mutually cleaving to each other."[8]

Here then, through the challenges of history, the Church has defined episcopacy in three fundamental roles which shape and determine all else that a bishop might do. So fundamental are these three roles that it is possible to see them as different expressions of the unity of the Church in time. For Cyprian, the bishop in council with other bishops is the focus of unity for the Church in the present; for Irenaeus the bishop connects the Church to its past history in the tradition of the apostles; and for Ignatius the bishop as the center around which the eucharistic community gathers connects the Church to the future—the eschatological dimension.

So then we are dealing with more than three important functions; rather we have in them the essence of episcopacy. They were shaped by history, each receiving a special emphasis at a particular time. The questions for us now are: How shall we understand these three roles in this new era? What needs to be emphasized at this time in this or that particular situation to assure the unity of the Church, and the carrying out of its mission? What more needs to be said?

When the Pastoral Letter was published there was added to it a foreword by our Presiding Bishop and Primate explaining the process used to produce the document, and to encourage response. There was also added a precis outlining the basic principles about the episcopate found in the Pastoral, and a study guide to foster its use.

The Pastoral Letter has at this time been sent to all dioceses of the Episcopal Church, and to all our seminaries. We have asked the faculties of our seminaries to study the document, to comment on its contents and suggest areas where further work needs to be done, both theologically and in its practical application.

---

[8] Epistle 66, to Florentius.

This will begin the dialogue with our academic community, and, as I mentioned before, such a dialogical approach should bring about an expansion of our initial theological work. We would also expect the pastoral to serve as a very important part of our ecumenical dialogues which, as this one, often involve questions about the episcopacy.

Apart from its use as a study document, the Pastoral Letter on episcopacy will also serve several other very practical purposes. The most important of these is as a guide for dioceses which are in the process of electing bishops. Most dioceses follow a similar pattern when an election is called for. A committee is selected to nominate several candidates who are then introduced to the diocese through written material, and sometimes in person with sessions for verbal presentations and questions and answers. This helps introduce the nominees to the people of a diocese, and especially to those who will be part of an electing convention. Our bishops are elected by a special convention of a diocese, sitting in two orders—clerical and lay. To have an election, a candidate must receive a majority of votes cast in each order on the same ballot. In other words, the clergy and laity of a diocese must agree on who will be elected as a bishop. (After the election a majority of consents must also be received from the bishops and from the Standing Committees of the other dioceses in the Episcopal Church before the consecration can take place.) It is our hope that those responsible for electing a bishop will carefully read the Pastoral Letter so that they will be well informed about the office of bishop before voting.

But it is the nominating committees that will make the greatest use of this Pastoral. They are charged with the task of making a profile of the diocese, describing geographical, social, and economic factors, and also detailing such things as the number and kinds of congregations, the number of clergy, and budget information. If the diocese has a mission strategy plan, that will also become part of the profile.

This profile will then be used to describe the kind of episcopal leadership the diocese will need. It is at this point that the

Pastoral on bishops will have a key role to play. The study guide in the back of *The Ministry of Bishops* document suggests a process for discernment of key roles and functions needed to lead the diocese. Even though the three episcopal roles described in the Pastoral are considered essential, because each diocese is different the emphasis in setting priorities will vary. For example, a rural diocese without many educational resources might want a bishop who is personally a very good teacher, while a metropolitan diocese that has plenty of such resources might want a bishop who is not necessarily a good teacher but who can organize those resources for the benefit of the diocese. In this way the document will help to focus for the nominating committee the chief strengths and gifts needed in episcopal leadership.

One other way the Pastoral Letter can be used by a diocese is in the process of evaluating leadership. Most dioceses in the Episcopal Church have some sort of mission statement containing the primary goals of the diocese. These goals call for a particular kind of leadership. From time to time a diocese will evaluate the progress made in its mission goal, and as part of that process, evaluate its leadership in carrying out those goals. Here again it is hoped that the document will help dioceses in this evaluation process by keeping the essentials in perspective, while at the same time helping it change an emphasis in leadership style.

Finally, the pastoral will help individual bishops discuss their ministry with the people of their dioceses. Such an intentional, organized discussion can only prove to be fruitful in helping the Church better understand the episcopate, and what bishops have been called to do since patristic times.

As you can see, we have high hopes for the many ways in which *The Ministry of Bishops: A Study Document* may positively affect the Episcopal Church. We want the people of the Church to become better acquainted with the theology of episcopacy as it is presented in our Ordinal, but we also want that theology applied in practical ways. We believe that in this way our House of Bishops can be involved both as teachers of the Church, and as leaders of the Church in this critical time.

7

Second Supplement

"The Ministry of Bishops: A Study Document Authorized by The House of Bishops of the Episcopal Church"*

[At General Convention, Phoenix, Arizona, July 10-19, 1991]

Foreword
by the Presiding Bishop

It gives me great pleasure to commend to you this study document on "The Ministry of Bishops" which has grown out of dialogue in the House of Bishops on the role of the episcopate in the contemporary Church. The demands of the Episcopal ministry are extraordinary. As this document suggests, it is time for the Episcopal Church to take "a close look at what it wants its bishops to be and to do."

At the House of Bishops meeting in Philadelphia in September, 1989, Bishop John Ashby, Chairman of the Committee on Ministry, called for a theological statement on the episcopate. Responding to that request, the Committee on the Pastoral Letter, under the leadership of Bishop Richard Grein, decided to underwrite a commentary on the Ordinal for a Bishop found in the 1979 Book of Common Prayer. With funds provided by Trinity Institute, the Committee on the Pastoral Letter commissioned three scholars to co-author the study. Those chosen were Robert Wright of General Theological Seminary (General Editor), Richard Norris of Union Theological Seminary in New

---

* Published by Trinity Institute, Parish of Trinity Church, New York, 1991.

York, and Louis Weil of Church Divinity School of the Pacific. Drafts of the document were circulated to all bishops for comment twice before this version was adopted by the House of Bishops at the General Convention in July 1991 for study throughout the Church.

The paper before you examines the role of the episcopate in the life of the church historically and singles out several pastoral functions set forth in the ordinal which the authors believe could be helpful in considering the renewal and reform of the episcopate. I invite you to consider this document as the first step in a church-wide conversation on the role of the bishop in the Episcopal Church. I encourage you to study it carefully, both individually and corporately, in parishes and dioceses, as laity and clergy. Then I urge you to send your comments to Trinity Institute at the address provided on the back of this title page. The Institute will receive and correlate your responses on behalf of the Committee on the Pastoral Letter which will report its findings to the House of Bishops.

Faithfully yours,
Edmond L. Browning
Presiding Bishop

Precis

This document examines the role of a bishop in light of the promises made in the Ordination of a Bishop in the 1979 Book of Common Prayer. Prior to reading this text, it may be helpful to read through the ordination service focusing in particular upon the examination of the bishop-elect on pages 517-518.

The authors of "The Ministry of Bishops" were asked to focus on three pastoral roles or functions which are vital to the office of bishop but are sometimes misunderstood or neglected today. As you read, you will discover that these three central activities also subsume virtually all of the other promises the bishop-elect makes. The three pastoral functions discussed are:

1. The Bishop as Proclaimer of the Gospel and Teacher of the Christian Faith.

2. The Bishop as Provider of and Presider over the Sacraments. (Baptism and Eucharist)
3. The Bishop as leader in the Councils of the Church, local, national and supra-national.

In each of these cases the function of the bishop is examined historically, but the uniqueness of our present circumstances is fully acknowledged. In fact, several basic historical lessons concerning the communal nature of the church and the bishop's relationship to that community are used to redefine the contemporary church and the role of the bishop in a most instructive way. These basic principles, taken from the document, could be the starting points for the rethinking and renewal of episcopal ministry.

1. This document is about the place of the Bishop in the life of a Christian community.
2. The church, the people of God, is a community not a corporation.
3. The bishop is a member of that community.
4. The bishop's role grows out of, not apart from, the community.
5. The bishop presides over the sacraments as a member of the assembly of the baptized rather than as someone apart from it.
6. The church, as an evolving community, is a body of lifelong learners, constantly striving to live more fully in "the Christian way."
7. The bishop is an apostolic link between the tradition and the contemporary community of learners.
8. The bishop, therefore, is the "anchor" person in the church's entire ministry of proclamation and instruction.
9. In the early church there were two regular occasions for the ministry of proclamation and teaching: i)the process of Christian initiation culminating in baptism (catechesis), and ii) the Sunday liturgy. As the 'first citizen' and chief teacher, the bishop presided at both the baptismal and

eucharistic liturgies, the two public actions in which the church most definitively enacted its identity.

10. Though it is impossible today for the bishop to preside at every baptism or Sunday liturgy, the symbolic significance of these pastoral roles and their roots in the worshiping community are a good place to start rethinking the vocation of a bishop and the bishop's essential connection with the local congregation.

11. Finally, the bishop's role as a leader and an administrator grows out of and is dependent upon the bishop's pastoral roles associated with teaching and presiding at the sacraments, which are theologically prior.

12. The form of church government symbolized in the bishop's presidency of the eucharist is collegial and conciliar in character. This model should apply to all the bishop's leadership functions.

13. The collegial character of the bishop's relationship with the clergy of the diocese is established symbolically in the ordination of a priest, when the other presbyters present at the ordination join the bishop in laying hands on the ordinand. That same collegiality is also implied in the bishop-elect's promise to sustain and take counsel with fellow presbyters in the diocese.

In conclusion, the document proposes the recovery of a specifically pastoral/liturgical model of the bishop's role in the parishes and missions of a diocese. "When this model is followed," the authors maintain, "the assembly is offered an opportunity which, in spite even of infrequency of personal contact, will reveal the place of the bishop in the community, not as a visiting dignitary, but as one who fulfills a specific and crucial role of symbolic presence and unity for all the congregation of the diocese. The bishop will be seen as one who leads the people in the great common signs of Christian identity and as a bridge between the local community and all other parishes and missions of the diocese, and of the diocese with the church throughout the world."

THE MINISTRY OF BISHOPS
Introduction

1. It is not easy to find out what we Episcopalians, or Anglicans generally, make of the office of bishop. On the whole, we have tended simply to take bishops for granted. In ecumenical dialogues, we have regularly insisted upon "the historic episcopate" as an institution that directly serves the unity of the churches and, therefore, has an essential place in any scheme for the reconciliation of different Christian traditions. On the other hand, we have, with equal regularity, been hesitant to insist either upon a particular theological understanding of the office of bishop or upon a particular constitutional form of it. Bishops, as we see them in practice, are simply the heads or presidents of what might best be called extended local churches[1]: Local churches articulated into a number of parishes, congregations, communities, and other institutions, but united in communion with their single pastor, the bishop.

2. Generally speaking, this model of episcopal ministry has worked well with us. Its economy and modesty are from many points of view commendable. In different historical and local circumstances, the office of bishop has varied in its shape and functions, and no one wants to foreclose flexibility for the future by insisting dogmatically upon a particular style of episcopacy. On the other hand, too easy a satisfaction with

---

[1] "Local church" is best defined as that assembly (*ekklesia*) of believers in which all the interlocked orders of ministry—i.e., the *whole* ministry of Word and Sacrament—are represented: laity, deacons, bishop, and presbyters. Hence in an episcopally ordered body, "local church" means what we normally call the "diocese." Thus the diocese is not, as it is sometimes called, a "middle judicatory," since in the Episcopal Church there are no judicatories in the ordinary sense of that term below the level of the diocese; and a parish is not "the local church."

this very general characterization of the office can blind us to the need for critical attention to the way in which episcopacy actually functions in our own time and place.

3. The Episcopal Church is always, more often in informal than in formal and considered ways, making decisions that affect the manner in which the pastoral office of the bishop is *seen* and *exercised*. Thus the very procedures followed in the election of a bishop project an image of the office itself and of the sort of person who might normally seek or be nominated for it; yet few inquire what this image is or how well it corresponds to the requirements of pastoral leadership in the church. To take another example, canon law makes provision for the election of suffragan bishops, while at the same time the extra-canonical practice of employing assisting bishops seems to be growing. Each of these devices meets an obvious need, but at the same time each of them raises, and indeed creates, problems about the pastoral role and responsibility of the bishop—problems that the Episcopal Church has never seriously addressed. There are, moreover, practical pressures upon bishops to concern themselves more and more exclusively with administrative concerns, institutional policy-making, and crisis-management; and these pressures too generate questions about what Episcopalians think bishops are for, questions which are often, and rightly, echoed by our partners in ecumenical dialogue.

4. For these reasons, and others that might be cited as well, it is time that the Episcopal Church took a close look at what it wants its bishops to be and to do—and in particular, perhaps, at what it says about them in its new Book of Common Prayer.[2] To be sure there is not, and probably cannot be, a prescription for a style of episcopacy that will fit the circumstances of every local church. Nevertheless, there are deep and weighty traditions about the meaning of the office of bishop which

---

[2] The Church of England has recently published a fine study of 354 pages, *Episcopal Ministry: The Report of the Archbishops' Group on the Episcopate* (Church House, London, 1990).

need to be taken into serious account in any consideration of this matter—and none more seriously than the characterization of episcopacy that appears in The Book of Common Prayer's rite for the ordination of a bishop.

5. There the pastoral role of the bishop incorporates at least three central activities: that of proclaiming and teaching, that of providing the sacraments and especially presiding in the church's eucharistic service of God, and that of exercising supervisory or administrative leadership in the councils of the Church, local, national, and supra-national. In what follows, we have tried to explicate these roles and their significance in the life of the Church *historically*, with two particular aims: first, that of calling attention to elements in the pastoral office of the bishop which, in our present situation, run the risk of being forgotten or neglected; and second, that of raising the question how these elements can be incorporated in a reformed and renewed episcopate. We are here engaged, then, not in prescription but in exploration.

1. The Bishop As Proclaimer And Teacher

6. The Preface to the Ordinal in the 1979 Book of Common Prayer describes bishops as persons "who carry on the apostolic work of leading, supervising, and uniting the Church" (p.510). In later statements and expressions which expand and develop this brief and summary description, it becomes plain that one essential dimension of the "apostolic work" consists in proclaiming and teaching. The address of the Presiding Bishop which opens the ordinand's Examination (p. 517) reminds the bishop-elect that to be "one with the apostles" entails engagement in the activity of "proclaiming Christ's resurrection and interpreting the Gospel"; and this injunction is later rephrased in the form of a question: "Will you boldly proclaim and interpret the Gospel of Christ, enlightening the minds and stirring up the conscience of your people?" (p. 518). The bishop, in fact, is to "feed the flock of Christ," and to do so by guarding and defending them "in [Christ's] truth"

and by being "a faithful steward of his holy Word" (p.521). For just this reason, the bishop promises to "be faithful," not only in prayer, but also "in the study of Holy Scripture," that he or she "may have the mind of Christ" (p.518).

7. This emphasis on the role of the bishop as teacher of the Church is nothing new either in Anglican tradition or in Christian tradition generally. It was the conviction of such Anglican reformers as John Jewel that "the key, whereby the way and entry to the Kingdom of God is opened unto us, is the word of the Gospel and the expounding of the law and Scriptures";[3] and they were, therefore, convinced that the ordained ministry as a whole had as its most prominent function "to instruct the people."[4] When, indeed, they spoke of the administration or governance of the Church, it was for the most part the Church's guidance by and under the Gospel that they had in mind: a "spiritual" and interpretative function that belonged in a pre-eminent way, as they saw it, to the Church's official overseers and leaders, the bishops. No doubt the Reformers, when they sounded this theme, did so in an idiom that reflected the problems and prepossessions of their own time and place; but they were nevertheless right in claiming that in this matter they had merely "returned to the apostles and old Catholic fathers."[5] They no doubt remembered how Gregory of Nazianzus had characterized the work of the priestly and episcopal ministry as "education" and "healing," which consisted in "giving in due season to each his portion of the Word," and which required above all "wisdom, which is chief of all things, and holds in her embrace everything which is good, so that even God himself prefers this title to all the names by which he is called."[6]

---

[3] John Jewel, *An Apologie of the Church of England* II (in T.H.L. Parker, ed., *English Reformers* [Library of Christian Classics 26, Philadelphia, 1966], p. 24.

[4] *Ibid.* (LCC 26, p. 21).

[5] *Ibid.* I (LCC 26, p. 17).

[6] See the sermon "In Defense of His Flight," esp. 22, 35, 50 (*Post-Nicene Fathers* VII:209ff.).

8. This image of the bishop as teacher, interpreter of the Scriptures, and bearer of the Word of redemption has concrete historical and institutional roots. The gospels picture Jesus as, among other things, the teacher of a band of disciples. Acts portrays the Apostle Paul as "teaching...in public and from house to house," and "declaring...the whole counsel of God" (Acts 20: 20,27) and Paul himself speaks of a tradition which he bears and hands on (see 1 Cor. 15:1-5) and of the "treasure" of the gospel conveyed, by him and others, "in earthen vessels" (2 Cor. 4:7). Early Christian communities— the churches that produced the gospels and collected the letters of Paul—were, therefore, acutely conscious of their responsibility to transmit and inculcate the authentic message of redemption in Christ as the core and basis of a particular "truth," that is, a particular way of seeing, and living in, the world.

9. From early times, therefore, there were special "places" in the life of the Church that were marked out and reserved for a ministry of proclamation and teaching. One of these, of course, was the Sunday liturgy, which, as it developed, in effect institutionalized the reading and exposition of the Scriptures as an essential element in the business of the assembled Church. A second—more prominent in the early church than it is today—was the whole process of Christian initiation, culminating in baptism. Elaborated over the centuries, this initiatory process involved lengthy and systematic catechesis, whose aim was the intellectual and moral formation of new disciples of "the way." The centrality of the catechumenate in the life of early Christian churches is attested by the fact that some of the texts we have inherited under the name of "creeds" are, in fact, products of this initiatory process. They originally evolved as syllabi of doctrinal instruction that at the same time, because they took the form of professions of faith, signified believers' acceptance of the New Covenant with God in Christ—a covenant sealed by the gift of the Spirit.

10. The ministry of proclamation and teaching, then, was quickly institutionalized—in homiletic exposition of the Scriptures and in the instruction of neophytes—in connection with the eucharistic and baptismal liturgies, the two public actions in which the churches most definitively enacted their identity under God. For just this reason, however, the bishop early became the focal representative of the Church's ministry of teaching. As "first citizen" and shepherd of the community, the bishop presided in both the eucharistic and the baptismal liturgies. Thus bishops were the normal expositors of Scripture in the Sunday liturgy, and there also devolved upon them the responsibility of expounding the "faith" (i.e., the creed in one or another of its various local forms) and the "mysteries" (i.e., the liturgical enactment of believers' union with Christ: baptism and eucharist) in the course of the catechumenate.

11. This did not mean—and the point needs to be emphasized—that the bishop enjoyed a monopoly of the Church's teaching ministry. Presbyters might be delegated to preach (though one ordinarily hears of their preaching on week-days); and lay-persons[7] as well as deacons and presbyters played prominent roles in the instruction of neophytes. The bishop, however, was understood to sit at the center of all this activity: to be, as it were, the "anchor" person of the Church's entire ministry of proclamation, instruction, and formation.

12. This image of the teacher-bishop first surfaces as an explicit theme in Irenaeus of Lyons' five books *Against Heresies*, probably written around 180-185, especially in his lengthy polemic against the gnostics of the school of Valentinus. In Irenaeus' eyes, these particular Christian gnostics, and indeed the whole movement of thought to which they belonged, were guilty of offering an explication of the Church's

---

[7] By modern standards. The reference is, of course, to catechists, who in the ancient church often figured in lists of "clergy," though they were not ordained. It is this role that Origen filled—no doubt in an extraordinary way—during his years in Alexandria as head of the "catechetical school."

Gospel—its *kerygma* or "tradition"—which, in fact, over-turned and contradicted that gospel. They spoke the Church's language, he insisted, but when they set out to explain it—and especially in their interpretation of the Scriptures—they turned out to say something entirely different from what it was intended to convey. He argued, therefore, that the true key to the Scriptures was the ordinary instruction given to converts when they sought baptism—instruction whose con-tent he summarized, in varying forms of words, as "the rule of faith" or "the rule of truth." In his eyes, this "rule"—a near ancestor of our creeds—was, as near as might be, a setting out of the "plot" of the Scriptures; and for just that reason it could both be used to interpret them and at the same time be established by their testimony. It represented, in fact, a sum-mary expression of the very same apostolic teaching, the same *kerygma*, that could be found in the four Gospels, the Acts of the Apostles, and the Letters of Paul; it differed from them only in its form and in the fact that it is handed down orally in the churches.

13. "Orally," however, did not imply, for Irenaeus, some vague, hidden process that no one could detect or point to. It meant, as we have seen, public transmission by way of the increasing-ly institutionalized practice of baptismal catechesis. It was entirely natural, therefore, that Irenaeus should find the ulti-mate guarantors of this process of transmission in the bish-ops, who at once administered, presided over, and participat-ed in the regular, rhythmical process of instructing neophytes. That is why he could say that the bishops had received the apostles' own "place of teaching" (*Against Heresies* 3.3.1): The apostolic mission of conveying, in and for the Church, the authentic message of redemption and liberation in Christ. Indeed it is this fact that constitutes the heart of Irenaeus' notion of "apostolic succession." In the first instance, bishops are "successors of the apostles" in the very precise sense that they have inherited both the apostolic message as that was publicly transmitted in the Church's teaching ministry, and

also the apostolic responsibility and authority as "stewards of the mysteries of God" (1 Cor. 4.1).

14. Any present-day appropriation of this image of the bishop as teacher must, therefore, in the first place, stress the responsibility that belongs to the episcopal office. The bishop is, to begin with, a person under authority: one committed in virtue of office to sustaining the Church's identity and mission by "proclaiming Christ's resurrection and interpreting the Gospel" (BCP, p. 517). The stress here is on what is to be proclaimed and interpreted: the bishop's teaching must answer to the apostolic proclamation of Christ's resurrection and to "the Gospel"—what Irenaeus would also have called "the *kerygma*"—as those are given to the Church both in the written books of the old and new covenants and in the catechetical tradition that is distilled in the "rule of faith" or "creeds." Hence the Book of Common Prayer expects, and indeed requires, of the bishop that he or she be a serious student of the Scriptures; not merely one who is knowledgeable about the fruits of academic study of the Bible, but also one whose personal experience and understanding of the world are informed by meditative appropriation of the wisdom of the Scriptures in all their variety. As a teacher of the Church, the bishop must be a seeker after "the mind of Christ," who himself is "our wisdom, our righteousness and sanctification and redemption" (1 Cor. 1.30).

15. In the second place, though only as a person under authority, the bishop in teaching speaks with authority. The word "authority" here does not of itself connote coercive power, nor does it connote any sort of incorrigibility. It means that bishops, as their communities' "first citizens," speak weightily; that their official word of teaching grows out of, and points people back to, the truth on which the community is founded. A bishop may or may not be a professional student of theology; for the bishop's primary concern is not with theologies as such, but with people's knowledge of God, their ability to understand themselves and their world, and to

direct their lives and actions, in accord with the realities attested in the Scriptures and in the Church's language of teaching, praise, and prayer. Furthermore, this authority is of the very specific sort that belongs properly to a teacher; its aim is to bring people to that point of maturity in Christian faith and life where they can function, in their own spheres, as teachers and so as "authorities" themselves.

16. In the third place, the Book of Common Prayer must be taken with the utmost seriousness when it insists that the teaching office of the bishop involves a work of interpretation. To appropriate the sense of the Church's *kerygma* as that is conveyed in the Bible and the catechetical tradition is always a matter of "rendering" it—both in the light of the interpreter's particular circumstances, cultural setting, and problems, and in the light of earlier interpretations. To transmit the tradition, then, is to interpret it: to grasp new dimensions of its meaning, to envisage it in fresh perspectives. To be sure, no interpretation ever captures the full range or depth of the Gospel's significance; and for that reason the wise teacher never allows a particular reading of the tradition, however engaging or fruitful it may be, to displace or to replace its gnarled and knotty sources. Nevertheless, every honest reading of that tradition opens a new way into its depths. The bishop, then, as the Church's principal teacher, will play the interpreter unashamedly—and weigh with critical sympathy the interpretations of others, ancients and moderns alike; but no more than a loving expositor of Shakespeare's plays will he or she suppose that people are better off in making do with such interpretations than they are in coming to terms with the original. Good teachers delight more in what they interpret than they do in their own renderings of it.

17. Finally, it needs to be said that the image of the bishop as teacher, writ large as it is in the Book of Common Prayer, corresponds to a picture of the Church as a body of learners or apprentices—disciples of the Lord, or of "the Way" (see

Acts 9:1-2, 19:9,23). The church whose bishop is a student-teacher of the tradition is a body of people who are in the business of appropriating a certain way of life as their own—of learning and "trying on," both theoretically and in practice, the dispositions, attitudes, and values that belong properly to persons who share the destiny and the calling of God's Christ. To recover a sense of the Church's teaching function, and especially as that takes shape in the office of bishop, therefore entails an ongoing reconsideration of the very life of the Church itself.

2. The Bishop As Provider Of The Sacraments

18. From a contemporary perspective, the relation of a bishop to the sacraments as indicated in much early Christian literature runs the risk of being a merely theoretical link drawn from a model of pastoral oversight which is now remote from the situation of the Church in modern society. When in the Prayer Book at the Examination of a bishop-elect the Presiding Bishop (or a bishop appointed by the Presiding Bishop) says that the new bishop is "to celebrate and to provide for the administration of the sacraments of the New Covenant" (p. 517), the gathered assembly take for granted that in the experience of the majority of the baptized members of the diocese, that specified relation of the bishop to the ordinary sacramental life of the diocese will be expressed most frequently in "providing for the administration of the sacraments" through the ordination of presbyters as the usual celebrants of the sacraments in the various parishes and missions of the diocese. Actual contact with the bishop as celebrant will for most be limited to the canonical visitation and perhaps some major diocesan event.

19. It is important to recognize that the modern Church is thus heir to a dislocation of model which originates in the radically transformed social situation of the Church in the fourth century. From that time, as a consequence of the great expansion of the Church which followed its liberation under the

Emperor Constantine, the bishop's relation to the eucharist became less that of a sign of direct pastoral relation to the local community and more that of a remote overseer of all the baptized in a given geographical area. The response of the Catechism concerning the ministry of a bishop reflects this altered model: the bishop is "pastor of a diocese," not of a local assembly which can gather on Sunday with the bishop to participate as a body in the fundamental sign of their baptismal unity. The primary expression of the bishop's relation to the baptized in the regular celebration of the eucharist has thus shifted from a direct relation as pastor to that of provider for the sacramental life of the diocese as a whole.

20. This shift, although it occurred in early Christian history, is significant for us today as we work to recover a fuller sense of the relation of sacramental responsibility to pastoral oversight. In the early Church, bishops presided at the eucharist because they presided over the common life of the Christian community. Sacramental responsibility was the articulation of a pastoral relation to a specific body of people. We have tended to work from an inversion of that model. As soon as a person is ordained to the presbyterate, they are understood by the Church to have the authority to preside at the eucharist. A former vocabulary, somewhat alien to us today, makes the point clear: the newly ordained priest had the "power to confect the sacraments." This vocabulary reflects an understanding of the sacraments in which the act has become narrowly the action of the priest rather than a sign of faith within the general context of pastoral ministry. For many centuries the Church resisted this concept of what was called "absolute ordination." Ordination was conferred until the late twelfth century with reference to specific pastoral responsibility; presiding at the eucharist was an expression not of sacerdotal power but of pastoral care. The change in attitude which permitted absolute ordinations from the end of the twelfth century is indicative of a dissociation of the ordained from the ordinary lives of Christian laity.

21. This historical development is important in our consideration of episcopal ministry since the break between presbyteral ordination and pastoral care is a kind of delayed reverberation of an earlier break between the bishop and the local congregation. In fact, one can interpret the historical evolution of delegation of pastoral/sacramental ministry to presbyters as the result of an underlying theological energy from within the nature of the Church to preserve this personal link. At an earlier time, the bishop had been able, within a less complex geographical situation, to preserve this link personally. The eventual separation of the priest's sacramental ministry from a specific context of pastoral responsibility, however, is indicative of a gradual alienation of all the ordained ministries from an ecclesial context as the basis of their meaning. At the same time there was a consequent clericalization of the sacramental rites of the Church in which they became sacred actions which only the ordained could perform rather than common actions of the whole people of God in union with their pastoral leaders.

22. This ecclesial perspective is an imperative for the Church today, and it is one for which enormous insight can be gained from the understanding of pastoral oversight during the first centuries of Christianity. We find in the early evidence an affirmation of the role of pastoral and sacramental leadership, but also a firm sense that it is the entire assembly of the baptized that celebrates the eucharist. Although the New Testament does not specify who presided at the earlier eucharistic assemblies, there is no evidence to suggest that this presidency was exercised in an arbitrary fashion. Even if we assume that when one of the apostles was present he would appropriately have offered the eucharistic blessing, the itinerant nature of their ministry meant that others would fulfil that role when the apostles moved on. This presider was perhaps often the host in whose home the community gathered. There is evidence from the immediate post-apostolic period that it was thought a prophet should (when present)

pronounce the blessing (*Didache*, ch. 10). At this same time, i.e., the end of the first century, the *Letter of Clement to the Corinthians* speaks of bishops-presbyters as "those who have presented the gifts," which most commentators understand as a reference to the eucharistic elements. In this document, those presiding at the eucharist are the leaders of the local community "with the consent of the whole church" (44,3).

23. It is in the writings of Ignatius of Antioch that we find most clearly the bishop as the sign of the unity in the Church in his role as presider at the eucharist. In his *Letter to the Smyrnaeans*, Ignatius writes: "Only that eucharist is to be considered legitimate which is celebrated under the presidency of the bishop or under that of the one he appoints. There where the bishop appears let the community be, just as where Jesus Christ is, there is the whole Church" (8:1-2). In the model of leadership reflected in the writings of Ignatius, the local church is presided over by a bishop who is assisted in his ministry by presbyters and deacons. For Ignatius, the role of the bishop is that of a personal symbol of the unity of all those who gather with him in the celebration of the eucharist. The unifying ministry of the bishop is so reflected in the bishop's presidency over the eucharistic assembly that it can be said for Ignatius that in this common action the unity of the Church is created (*Trallians 1.1, Ephesians* 1.3).

24. It is important to remember, however, that in the time of Ignatius the local church was not a diocese, to employ a later canonical term, but a single body or a single eucharistic assembly of all the Christians in a given area. The image of the bishop's role in the eucharist as the unifying symbol of the local church was thus supported in the regular experience of Christians of each Sunday's assembly. From the fourth century onward, the Church's situation in society led to a gradual shift away from that model toward an administrative model in which the bishop was increasingly experienced as the overseer of clergy to whom the immediate pastoral/sacramental relation to the local communities had been delegated.

25. One other witness from pre-Constantinian Christianity is especially relevant to our subject. About a century after Ignatius, Hippolytus of Rome wrote *Apostolic Tradition* as a conservative summary of the tradition in which the author had been formed. *Apostolic Tradition* is thus generally held to reflect usages dating back to the youth of Hippolytus, that is, about 180 A.D. The ordination of the one "chosen by all the people" to be their bishop takes place in the context of the eucharist, and the first act of the new bishop is to proclaim the eucharistic prayer over the gifts which are the oblation of the entire Church. Hippolytus thus witnesses to the continuity of the tradition which we observed in Ignatius: The one who presides over the Church is the one who presides at the eucharist. The emphasis does not seem to be one of a narrowly conceived sacerdotal power, but rather that of a fundamental relation of pastoral oversight for which the presiding role in the eucharist is seen as its primary public expression. If one wants to use the language of "power" in this context, the power to preside at the eucharist must be ascribed to the responsibility of pastoral oversight. This assertion rests upon the decisive testimony of *Apostolic Tradition*: The liturgical actions of the new bishop are not manifestations of an isolated power but rather are the liturgical expression of his presidency over the community of the baptized in an act of corporate worship. The episcopate does not appear so much as a ritual function but rather as a charism whose purpose is to build up the common life of the Church. Nor can the charism be seen as a purely individual gift to the ordinand; the gifts pertain to the collegial order into which a person is ordained. The newly ordained comes to participate in the gifts of the Holy Spirit to that order for the upbuilding of the community of the baptized.

26. What emerges from this approach to the ministry of the bishop is that it is the entire Christian assembly which is the subject of a liturgical action, and that all the various participants, whether lay or ordained, constitute a single celebrating

assembly. The laity are not merely observers of what the clergy perform. The ancient liturgical texts clearly support this view. Not a single prayer in the early sacramentaries of both the eastern and western rites has the bishop or priest speak in the first person singular, but rather always to proclaim the prayers using the "we" of the entire Christian assembly. This suggests that, even acting in that role as head of the assembly, the presider at the eucharist acts as a member of the assembly rather than in distinction from it.

27. The recovery of such a sense of the presiding role for the bishop or the bishop's ordained delegate has important implications for the renewal of our self-understanding as the Church, and for the way that self-understanding is imaged in the ordinary liturgical models of our parishes and missions. Our recovery of a more adequate theological understanding of our baptismal identity as the people of God must find its appropriate connection with our understanding of the eucharistic action: the only qualification for participating in the offering of the sacrifice of praise and thanksgiving is the baptism which has made each of us an active participant in the eucharistic assembly. The eucharist is not the action of clerical suppliers to essentially passive lay consumers. The recovery of a baptismal framework as the context of the eucharistic action permits us to get beyond the debates of the sixteenth century with their opposing views of, on the one hand, the priest offering Christ, or, in the reaction to that, of the Christian people offering only themselves. The action in the eucharist is that of the whole body of Christ, head and members, offering the whole body of Christ to God. In *The City of God*, Augustine states the theological basis for this view: "This is the sacrifice of Christians; we being many are one body in Christ. And this also the Church continually celebrates in the sacrament of the altar,...that it may be plain to her that in that which she offers she herself is offered" (10,6).

28. This corporate understanding of liturgical celebration is echoed in one of the questions put to the bishop-elect in the

Examination: "As a chief priest and pastor, will you encourage and support all baptized people in their gifts and ministries,...and celebrate with them the sacraments of our redemption?" (BCP, p. 518). The bishop's liturgical role is at the center of the pastoral office accepted in ordination. Given present geographical realities as to the size of most dioceses, it is evident that, at the level of ordinary experience, most of the people of a diocese will share only rarely with their bishop in the realization of this promise. Unless the Church is sensitive to the dislocation between the image behind this promise and the occasions in which it is realized, it is an invitation to the parishes and missions of a diocese to operate within a narrowly congregational experience of the Christian life. The 1979 Book of Common Prayer marks a potentially significant recovery of the pastoral/liturgical role of a bishop in the parishes and missions of a diocese by its rubrical norms for the bishop's role in what may be, in practical reality, only a canonical visitation every twelve or eighteen months. In the specifications, for example, of the bishop's role at the rite of Holy Baptism, the directions (p. 298) indicate that the bishop should preside at the celebration of the rite. When this model is followed, the assembly is offered an opportunity which, in spite even of infrequency of personal contact, will reveal the place of the bishop in the community, not as a visiting dignitary, but as one who fulfills a specific and crucial role of symbolic presence and unity for all the congregations of the diocese. The bishop will be seen as one who leads the people in the great common signs of Christian identity and as a bridge between the local community and all the other parishes and missions of the diocese, and of the diocese with the Church throughout the world.

3. The Bishop As Leader In The Church

29. The bishop is to give leadership to the diocese and to "share in the leadership of the Church throughout the world," as the third paragraph of the Examination in the Ordinal (p. 510)

puts it. The bishop's particular ministry is described "as apostle, chief priest, and pastor of a diocese" in the Catechism, where this episcopal ministry is contrasted with the priest's ministry of "sharing" with the bishop in oversight (*episcope*) and the deacon's ministry of "assisting" bishops and priests (pp. 855-856). Thus we may say that, whereas the ministry of all Christians ("the laity") from the viewpoint of the Catechism is to "represent Christ," each of the three orders within the Body does this in a particular way, whether by leadership, sharing, or assistance. Already in the *Apostolic Tradition* of Hippolytus from the early third century, these three roles are foreshadowed, and in the Prayer Book's ordination rites these relationships are expressed in the different ways that hands are laid on: bishops together in the ordination of a bishop, both bishop and fellow presbyters in the ordination of a priest, and the bishop alone in the ordination of a deacon (pp. 521, 533, 545). At the same time it remains true, of course, that the bishop's primary relationship to the community of faith is through baptism.

30. The particular role of a bishop in leadership was vividly described as early as the year 240 by the eminent African theologian, Origen: "Those who faithfully discharge the office of a bishop in the Church may appropriately be called the rafters, by which the whole building is sustained and protected, both from the rain and from the heat of the sun" (*Commentary on the Song of Songs*, 3.3). This concept of *episcope*, or oversight, the bishop serving as conciliar leader and president in synod, is set forth in the Prayer Book where the bishop is asked to "share with fellow bishops in the government of the whole Church, to sustain and take counsel with fellow presbyters, and to guide and strengthen the deacons and others" (p. 518), but this episcopal ministry or function of administrative leadership is not compartmentalized by the Prayer Book or divorced in any narrow way from the bishop's other two ministries as president of eucharistic worship and as apostolic witness to Christian teaching. Thus, in

order for the bishop "to guard the faith, unity, and discipline of the whole church" (pp. 518, 855), drawing upon "the faith of patriarchs, prophets, apostles, and martyrs and those of every generation who have looked to God in hope" (p. 517), it is also necessary that affirmative answers be given to all other questions posed to the bishop-elect on page 518. As administrator both within and beyond the bounds of the diocese, and yet operating within established constitutional and canonical limits, the bishop is also expected to be the chief priest or leader of worship, as well as the principal teacher and preacher, within the diocese.

31. Because the bishop exercises this sort of leadership in the whole Church, he or she also pledges fidelity to the Holy Scriptures and to the Church's doctrine, discipline, and worship (pp. 513, 518). It is for this same reason that the bishop always presides at Confirmations, Receptions, Reaffirmations (pp. 412-419), Ordinations (pp. 510-555, 855) and Consecrations of Churches (pp. 566-579), as well as being the normal presider and preacher at baptism (p. 298), the eucharist (pp. 13, 322, 354), and celebrations of new ministry (p. 558). Thus the bishop's role in "leading, supervising, and uniting the Church" (preface to the ordination rites, p. 510), in "building up the Church" (prayer of episcopal consecration, p. 521), is directly related to everything else that the bishop does. Sacramentally and iconographically, the bishop's wider role in the leadership of the diocese and of the whole Church is thus given visual expression at a new bishop's Ordination by the presidency of the Presiding Bishop or the Presiding Bishop's episcopal delegate as chief consecrator (p. 511), by the joining of other bishops in the laying-on-of-hands in the prayer of consecration (p. 521, a practice tracing back to the earliest surviving ordination rites in the history of the Christian church, the *Apostolic Tradition* of Hippolytus in the early third century), and by the recommended presence of other bishops and representative presbyters standing together "with the new bishop at the Altar as fellow ministers of the Sacrament" (p. 553).

32. Classically, the pattern for this role of the bishop as administrative and conciliar leader is derived from the early church in the model of St. Cyprian, bishop of Carthage who died in 258, who portrays the bishop as the bond of unity between each local church or diocese and all the others. It is especially to his writings that we must turn in order to find the patristic foundations for the doctrines of episcopal collegiality and conciliar leadership that are today developed and expounded in the third paragraph of the Examination of a bishop-elect in the Ordinal of the Book of Common Prayer (p. 517). Cyprian emphasized that bishops have inherited both the apostolic message and also the apostolic responsibility and authority (Letter 3.3). Stressing the need for unity with one's bishop, a point already made in the letters of Ignatius of Antioch in the early second century, Cyprian continues, "The Church is the people united to the bishop, the flock clinging to its shepherd. From this you should know that the bishop is in the Church, and the Church in the bishop" (Letter 66.8). Even more, to be "in communion" with one's bishop is to be "in communion with the Catholic Church" (Letter 55.1). In Cyprian as well as in the North African church of at least a generation before his day, we find an emphasis on the need for bishops to meet together and to reach a "common mind" under the Spirit's guidance. "The episcopate is a single whole, in which each individual bishop has a right to and a responsibility for the whole," writes Cyprian (*On Unity*, 5), by which he seems to mean that each bishop shares in the one episcopate, not as having a part of the whole but as being an expression of the whole. Thus for Cyprian, writes Bishop Kallistos Ware, "The universal Church is not a monolithic, totalitarian collectivity, in which the individual is swallowed up by the greater whole. It is, on the contrary, a family of local churches."[8] In Cyprian's own words, "there is one Church

---

[8] Kallistos Ware, "Patterns of Episcopacy in the Early Church and Today: An Orthodox View," 25, in *Bishops, But What Kind?*, ed. Peter Moore, London, 1982, p. 18.

throughout the whole world divided by Christ into many members, also one episcopate diffused in a harmonious multitude of many bishops" (Letter 55.24). For Cyprian, therefore, as for the Episcopal Church today, there is a collegiality that the bishop shares with the priests of a given diocese, as well as a different sort of collegiality that the bishop shares with other bishops in the wider church at large.

33. As for those bishops who deny this by insisting on their own teachings or actions even to the point of schism, Cyprian declares, perhaps idealistically by the standards of our own day: "He, therefore, who observes neither the unity of the Spirit nor the bond of peace, and separates himself from the bond of the Church and from the college of the bishops, can have neither the power nor the honor of a bishop since he has not wished either the unity or the peace of the episcopate" (Letter 55.24). Finally, in a way that could not anticipate the questions raised in our time by the existence of suffragan bishops and of overlapping jurisdictions in full communion, Cyprian expounds the Lord's words in John 10:16, "There shall be one flock and one shepherd" by stating his own maxim: "A number of shepherds or of flocks in one place is unthinkable" (*On Unity*, 8). Providing an ecclesiological foundation for his doctrine of episcopal collegiality, Cyprian summarizes, in the earliest surviving treatise on the nature of the Church: "It is particularly incumbent upon those of us who preside over the Church as bishops to uphold this unity firmly and to be its champions, so that we may prove the episcopate also to be itself one and undivided" (*On Unity*, 5).

34. The bishop's bonds with the diocese and with the wider church, of which Cyprian writes so eloquently and which are epitomized by the Prayer Book in the words of the Examination that is addressed to the bishop-elect (p. 517), are actualized in every proper area of episcopal ministry in the Church today. Ideally speaking, therefore, the bishop's role as administrative leader is an all-but-literal replication of the advice given as early as Ignatius of Antioch to the Church at

the beginning of the second century: "Do nothing without the bishop" (*Trallians*, 2.2). Yet, precisely because this advice cannot be obeyed literally, the bishop from very early on, as still today, follows this advice by leading, presiding, and overseeing, rather than by direct participation alongside every baptized person in every area of the Church's work and ministry. The bishop does not need to do everything personally, but to see that every necessary thing does happen. The bishop must hold up the vision, articulate the basic theology, and help provide the institutional structures by which it can occur.

35. The comprehensive role that the Prayer Book sets out for the bishop as sign of unity in Christ and the one through whom each member of the diocese is in communion with the whole Church and its mission has still further dimensions beyond those that are expressed in the office of teaching and proclaiming as well as in the liturgy. There is also the service of leadership that the bishop performs when appointing committees, when presiding at the diocesan convention, when making visitations of parishes, when proposing names to fill vacant cures, and when serving as pastor to, and co-worker with, the clergy of the diocese, as well as when speaking in the House of Bishops, attending Lambeth Conference, and taking part in the wider councils of the Church. These are not just disparate and humdrum tasks that need to be completed but, rather, essential elements continuous with the episcopal work of Ignatius and Hippolytus and Irenaeus and Cyprian in the nurture and formation and inspiration of the Church for its own proper ministries today. In each of these ways the bishop is exercising *episcope*, oversight and leadership and governance that is the proper ministry of the episcopal office, and so also when preaching the Gospel, when teaching the Catholic Faith, and when calling for initiatives in evangelism, ecumenism, and mission. The bishop defines the diocese; it is the jurisdictional region over which he or she is the ordinary. As its sign of unity, as the one charged to "boldly proclaim and interpret the Gospel of Christ, enlightening the

minds and stirring up the conscience of the people" (p. 518), the bishop unites the diocese within itself and to the whole Church, both articulating the vision and making sure that it happens, gathering the people of God and then dispatching them. As Cyprian might say, the bishop is not only the one who is sent but the one who sends, or, as the Prayer Book puts it, the bishop is "chief priest and pastor," charged to "encourage and support all baptized people in their gifts and ministries" (p. 518).

36. The episcopate is a unique, distinct and different, but not "superior," order in the Church, functioning both individually and collegially, calling each parish or congregation beyond itself to those wider obligations and responsibilities that transcend what could otherwise become a parochialism or congregationalism that might be inward-looking and narrowly based. A proper doctrine of the Church, or ecclesiology, thus depends upon a proper ministry of the episcopate. It is the bishop's distinct vocation to translate into personal reality within the Church's life that which is already, liturgically and theologically, in the Prayer Book itself.

Conclusion

37. We have ended this exploration with a consideration of that pastoral role of the bishop which is easiest for Christians who are members of a "corporate society" to understand: that of leadership connected with administration and supervision. For us, it is neither difficult nor inconvenient to envisage the bishop as a kind of "chief executive officer," overseeing varied functions in the complex organizational life of a modern diocese. The corporate world itself today is engaged in an ongoing search for patterns of leadership which adequately describe the relationships between leaders and followers, between corporate goals and the common good. There is a striking congruence between much of that effort and the search outlined in this paper. What does it say to the church when secular institutions seriously use such words as "vision-

ary," "servant," and "responsibility" to characterize effective leadership?

38. Nonetheless, it is important to recognize that a bishop is not simply a corporate executive. He or she presides not over a corporation but over a "people" to which he or she *belongs*; and from this point of view the bishop is more like a "first citizen" than an imported manager. It is this circumstance above all that is conveyed and symbolized by the bishop's presidency at the Eucharist (and, in that setting, at the rites of Christian initiation): that role sets the bishop *within* the community, standing *with* the laity, the presbyters, and the deacons in the action by which the whole assembly enacts its common identity in Christ—its new relation to God in the Spirit. Thus the bishop's presidency at the Eucharist intimates and symbolizes the proper *form* of episcopal government: its essentially collegial and conciliar character, whether within or beyond the local church.

39. Then too, this people in whose midst the bishop stands and works, is—or at any rate ought to be—itself a body of disciples of "the way." Hence a significant part of the bishop's leadership role is summed up in a responsibility for *proclaiming and teaching*—for reaching out and for bringing the community along in the understanding and practice of its calling to follow Christ.

40. This picture presents neither an impossible role nor a farfetched ideal. To actualize it in some significant degree in our society would, however, require much practical thought and effort; for the very style of authority classically associated with pastoral office is in many respects foreign to contemporary habits of mind. It would, in fact, require deliberate institutional changes calculated to change people's perception of the nature of leadership and authority in the Church and hence the way in which that leadership and authority function in practice. On the other hand, it is also true that to rethink episcopacy in this manner would indeed be to re-form the life of the church—and hopefully to bring it closer to its calling

under God. The question which these explorations raise in our minds is whether—and how—the Episcopal Church could undertake such a rethinking for the sake of its own faithfulness in mission and life.

Study Guide

The following suggestions for studying "The Ministry of Bishops" are offered for the use of diocesan committees and other church groups that are engaged, either in the search for a bishop, or in the review and renewal of the office of the episcopate.

First, read through the liturgy for the Ordination of a Bishop in the Book of Common Prayer, focusing, in particular, on the examination of the bishop-elect on pages 517-518.

Second, make a list of all the roles and functions mentioned in the course of the examination and in the promises, the charges, and the prayers.

Third, add to that list any additional roles or responsibilities which you think are appropriate to the office of bishop.

Fourth, prioritize your list.

Fifth, read the study document contained herein, identifying all the roles and functions in particular categories and subcategories as you proceed.

Sixth, compare your prioritized list with the list derived from the study document. Are your priorities similar to those of the document?

Seventh, ask yourselves how, in light of the study document, you would revise your list.

Finally, knowing that no bishop could possibly fulfill all our expectations, carefully revise and limit your list and your priorities to accord with reality.

For an ecumenical perspective, follow again these same steps together with a representative group of Roman Catholics and/or of Lutherans.

Possible Diocesan Study-Program On The Ministry Of Bishops

Six possible sessions, which can, however, be reduced to two, depending upon the intensity desired and the time available. There can be two speakers, the first, a theologian, to lead the sessions in part one, and the second, a bishop, to lead the sessions in part two.

Part I: Bishops In The Past
1. Bishops in the New Testament
2. Bishops in the Early Church
3. Bishops in the Anglican Tradition

Part II: Bishops In The Present
1. The Bishop as Proclaimer and Teacher
2. The Bishop as Provider of the Sacraments
3. The Bishop as Leader in the Church

Two Alternative Schemas For Part III:
1. The Bishop in the Diocese
2. The Bishop in the National Church
3. The Bishop in the Anglican Communion

1. The Bishop relating to laity, deacons, and priests
2. The Bishop relating to other bishops
3. The Bishop relating to non-Episcopalians and to non-Christians

8

Fifth Paper

Teachers and Evangelists for the Equipment of the Saints: Prayer Book Doctrine Concerning the Bishop as Teacher, Evangelizer and Focus of Unity

by The Rev. Charles P. Price
Professor Emeritus of Systematic Theology
Virginia Theological Seminary

I. The Task

When one consults the Book of Common Prayer of the Episcopal Church in the United States in order to learn what it has to say about the Bishop as teacher, evangelizer and focus of unity, one may be surprised at first, as the writer of this essay confesses that he himself was, to discover how little is stated directly and explicitly on these matters. In the service for the Ordination of a Bishop, for example, the word *teacher* (or *teaching*) does not appear. Neither does the word *evangelizer* (or *evangelist*). Moreover, the Bishop is called upon, both in the words which the ordaining Bishop addresses to him, and in one question of the subsequent examination, to "guard the faith, unity, and discipline of the Church" (BCP, pp. 517, 518), but nothing at all is said in the service or elsewhere in the Prayer Book about the Bishop's being a "focus of unity" in so many words. The Prayer Book apparently considers unity to be inseparable from faith and discipline.

The title of this paper, on the other hand, expresses an understanding of the ministry of Bishops which would be commonly accepted throughout the Anglican Communion. Bishops are expected to teach and to evangelize. In the current "Decade of Evangelism" on which the Anglican Communion is embarked, Anglicans look to their Bishops for leadership. And in the controversial questions which have put considerable strain on the unity of our Church, matters like the ending of racial segregation in the 1960's and the ordination of women as Priests in the 1970's and now Bishops in the 1980's, the role of our Bishops is providing steadying balance and healing care, and in preventing more fragmentation of the Church than has, in fact, occurred, has been notable. Our Bishops have served as foci of unity in these particular instances, and they do so in general.

It is the task of this essay to present Prayer Book teaching about the office of Bishop in such a way that these three functions—teaching, evangelizing, and being a focus of unity—will be manifest.

II. Some Preliminary Observations

Several introductory remarks will be helpful in setting the Ordination Rites of the American Book of Common Prayer in the proper perspective.

1. The first is that the three traditional orders of ordained ministry are deemed essential in the Episcopal Church. The Preface to the Prayer Book Ordination Rites (BCP, p. 510) begins by asserting the continuity of our Church in this respect with the apostolic community.

> "The Holy Scriptures and ancient Christian writers make it clear that from the apostles' time, there have been different ministries within the Church. In particular, since the time of the New Testament, three distinct orders of ordained ministers have been characteristic of Christ's holy catholic Church" (BCP, p. 510).

The Preface continues by naming and describing the three sacred orders: bishops, presbyters, "generally known as priests" (ibid), and deacons. This Preface is a modernized version of the Preface which first appeared in the English Ordinal of 1550 and has been prefixed to every subsequent set of English and American Ordination Rites.

This remark is important for present purposes because it establishes for our Church that these three orders belong together and are interdependent. In the American Episcopal Church, as in the Roman Catholic and Eastern Orthodox Churches, a candidate for Bishop must already have received ordination as a Priest and a Deacon. The gifts conferred at each ordination are "cumulative." A Bishop remains both Priest and Deacon. (Cf., Marion Hatchett, *Commentary on the American Prayer Book*, Seabury, 1980; p. 505.) "Once a Deacon always a Deacon," is a sentiment frequently expressed among us.

Hence the full Prayer Book understanding of the Bishop's role as teacher and evangelizer depends in part on what is said about the teaching and evangelizing roles of Priests and Deacons. The Examination of the Bishop in the 1979 Ordination Rite focuses and particularizes these functions, as we shall see in later sections of this paper; but the Ordination Rites assume for Bishops what has already been established for Priests and Deacons, although Bishops are expected to exercise these functions in a way characteristic of their particular office.

2. It also follows from the Preface to the Ordination Rites that the Office of Bishop in the American Episcopal Church in the late twentieth century is essentially the same as it has been down through the ages. "The order of bishops...carry(s) on the apostolic work of leading, supervising, and uniting the Church" (BCP, p. 510). Although the *way* in which bishops perform their roles may vary from age to age, the substance of their ministry is unchanged. (See below, Section VI) This observation gives us the liberty to examine the teaching office of Bishops as it has been expressed in earlier Ordinals, both English and western medieval. Different epochs in the life of the Church have presented different challenges to its existence and, therefore, have generated differently nuanced expressions of the meaning of Holy Orders. At

certain times it was considered necessary to stress certain aspects of Order more than others. Neither in the Church of England nor in the American Episcopal Church has there ever been an intention to deny any essential element of Holy Orders. From the very beginning of the life of the Church, the gift of the Spirit has insured that there would be teachers and evangelists. (Cf. Rom 12.7, I Cor 12.28, Eph 4.11) As far as unity is concerned, the Spirit Himself *is* the unity of the Church, and the ordination of our Bishops by the Spirit to be leaders in the Church makes them by that very act to be symbols of our unity in Christ.

3. The final point to be made regarding the continuity between Holy Orders in the American Episcopal Church and the Church Universal is indicated by a statement in the Preface to the American Prayer Book. This same Preface has appeared in every American Prayer Book since the first one was adopted in 1789.

> "...it will also appear that this Church is far from intending to depart from the Church of England in any essential point of doctrine, discipline, or worship; or further than local circumstances require" (BCP, p. 11).

The intention of each revision of American and English Books of Common Prayer has always explicitly been to retain the essential features of ancient apostolic ministry. This intention is made clear both by the continued use of the Preface to the English Ordinal of 1550 and of the Preface to the first American Prayer Book. This element of considered continuity allows us to say that according to the American Book of Common Prayer of 1979, Bishops function as teachers, evangelizers and foci of unity as they always have, though "local circumstances may require" some variation in the details of implementing these roles.

III. The Bishop as Teacher

1. *A word of definition.* We must begin this section with a word of explanation. This paper is written with the assumption that teaching is to be understood in its broadest reference—the communication of ideas from one person to another. Teaching in

Christian context involves not only instruction in doctrine and morals but also the communication of basic Christian attitudes.

2. *Notes on tradition.*

(a). Teaching was a fundamental aspect of Jesus' own ministry. In his earthly life, he functioned most notably and obviously as a teacher. He was often addressed as Teacher, or Good Teacher. He was a teacher of the Law and of the new Law. By his teaching Jesus prepared his disciples to accept his messiahship, although they did not comprehend his teaching until after the resurrection when the Spirit reminded them of all that he had said (Jn 14.26).

(b). In an only slightly different sense, the apostolic ministry was a teaching ministry. The apostles, after Jesus' resurrection, were concerned to teach about Jesus' place in the coming kingdom of God and, therefore, to proclaim the future resurrection of all. On the list of ministries of charismatic, Spirit-filled persons in the earliest Church, teachers are mentioned immediately after apostles and prophets; and when the ministries of apostles and prophets ceased, teaching and evangelizing were the most significant roles. To be successors of apostles, Bishops necessarily have to teach and evangelize.

(c). The teaching of early Bishops is well known and crucial in the life of the Church. One has to think only of Ignatius, Irenaeus, Athanasius, Basil, Chrysostom, Ambrose, Augustine. It would be foolish and unnecessary to try to give a longer list. Many, if not most, of the great teachers of the patristic Church were Bishops; so were many teachers in later times. As is well known, Bishops anciently sat on a chair when they preached. It was the posture of teachers. The Church of England has continued this tradition of teaching Bishops: Cranmer, Jewel, Butler, Temple, Ramsey. The Episcopal Church in America too has an honored succession of Bishops who have been teachers: William White, our first Presiding Bishop; John Henry Hobart; Charles Henry Brent, an early leader in the ecumenical movement; Edward Lamb Parsons, liturgiologist and social reformer; Angus Dun—to name a few.

(d). Medieval western Pontificals and the several editions of the English Ordinal make the teaching role of the Bishop unmistakably clear. In medieval western ordination rites, only new Bishops were publicly examined. Priests and Deacons were not interrogated. Therefore, the teaching office comes to its expression in this examination. Here the new Bishops promised "to teach by word and example those things which [they] learn from Holy Scripture," "to teach purity of living and sobriety of life by the help of God," "to teach others [the] humility and patience" [which they are to observe themselves], and "to teach the traditions of the orthodox fathers..." In the *Pontifical of Magdalen College* (consulted for this essay), the Postcommunion prayer runs, "O Lord Jesus Christ,...you have deemed this bishop worthy to teach the doctrine of the apostles..." (*The Pontifical of Magdalen College*, ed. by H.A. Wilson, Henry Bradshaw Society, 1910; pp. 70, 71, 78; translation mine.) Those phrases suggest a major emphasis on the teaching role of the Bishop.

(e). In earlier English and American Ordination Rites, on the other hand, an examination is provided for each of the three Orders. In the Examination of the Bishop-elect, there are two questions somewhat related to the one quoted from the Pontifical regarding teaching the people doctrine learned from Holy Scripture; a third question requires the Bishop-elect "to show yourself in all things an example of good works." (Cf. BCP 1928, pp. 554, 555.) In this Ordinal, Priests are also entrusted with instructing the people "out of said Scripture" and ministering Doctrine as well as Sacraments. (BCP 1928, p. 542.) Deacons too are expected "to instruct the youth out of the Catechism." (BCP 1928, p. 533.) Here, as in the medieval Pontifical, these themes recur in the Postcommunion Prayer. If anything, there is greater emphasis on the teaching role of the ordained ministry in the sixteenth century Ordinal and its English and American successors than in the medieval Pontifical, and it is distributed among all three Orders. This emphasis is almost certainly a reflection of the Reformation emphasis on sound doctrine.

3. *American Prayer Book 1979.* In the trajectory provided by these texts, we can approach the doctrine of the 1979 American Book of Common Prayer regarding the teaching office of the Bishop.

In the first paragraph of the address which the Presiding Bishop makes to the Bishop-elect, the Presiding Bishop charges the new bishop "to be one with the apostles in proclaiming Christ's resurrection and interpreting the Gospel, and to testify to Christ's sovereignty as Lord of lords and King of kings" (BCP p. 517). Proclaiming, interpreting and testifying are the three actions which in this liturgy focus the teaching ministry of the Bishop. This statement at the beginning of the Examination is reinforced by two of the questions subsequently addressed to the Bishop-elect:

> *Bishop:* Will you be faithful in prayer, and *in the study of the Holy Scripture*, that you may have the mind of Christ?
>
> *Answer:* I will, for he is my help.
>
> *Bishop:* Will you boldly *proclaim and interpret* the Gospel of Christ, enlightening the minds and stirring up the conscience of your people?
>
> *Answer:* I will in the power of the Spirit.
>
> (BCP, p. 518, italics added.)

First we notice the focus on resurrection. As we shall see presently, Presbyters are also charged to teach in these Ordination Rites, but in the Examination of Priests no explicit mention is made of the resurrection. In the New Testament, of course, *apostles* were eyewitnesses to the resurrection. Matthias was chosen as a successor to Judas because he too had been with Jesus "from the baptism of John until the day when he was taken up from us" (Acts 1.22). Matthias was chosen to be a witness to the resurrection. Bishops are to be "one with the apostles" first and foremost in their proclamation of the resurrection of Christ.

The calling of Bishops to proclaim the whole Gospel is, to be sure, not removed by this primary emphasis on the resurrection.

The more encompassing task is assumed here from the presbyterial teaching office. (Cf. BCP, p. 531.) But the teaching role of the Bishop is not only initially focused on the resurrection; it is also broadened by the insistence that Bishops are "to interpret the Gospel of Christ." A comparison with the Examination of Priests in these Ordination Rites (BCP, pp. 531-532) will reveal that the element of interpretation does not come to expression there. Needless to say, one must not make too much of an argument from silence. Teaching can scarcely go on at all without some kind of interpretation. Yet it is at least worth pointing out that it is to Bishops that the delicate and sensitive task of interpretation (*hermeneia*) is openly entrusted. They are to be the authoritative interpreters. Interpretation always involves the translation of the Gospel not only from one language to another but also from one culture to another. Our Church undertakes to translate the Gospel from its bearing on the lives of people in first-century Palestine to its bearing on people in the twentieth-century United States. Any such translation runs the risk of distortion. *Traduttore traditore* runs an Italian proverb. To translate is to betray. Official decisions about interpreting the Gospel are laid on the shoulders of our Bishops in the hope that they will, both because of their experience and in the expectation of their trustworthiness, keep interpretation as faithful as possible to the original sense of the text.

The phrase used in connection with the Bishop's study of the Holy Scripture is also striking. "...that you may have the mind of Christ," it concludes. Such language does not appear in the ordination services for either Priests or Deacons. Deacons are asked simply, "Will you be faithful in prayer, and in the reading and study of the Holy Scriptures?" (BCP, p. 544). Presbyters undertake a more solemn obligation: "Will you be diligent in the reading and study of the Holy Scriptures, and in seeking the knowledge of such things as may make you a stronger and more able minister of Christ?" (BCP, p. 532). In neither case is that lovely and searching qualification about "having the mind of Christ" added.

It is profoundly desirable that all baptized Christians should have the mind of Christ. Yet to set forth the expectation that Bishops above all others should have the mind of Christ expresses in a liturgical and ritual way the central role of our Bishops in teaching the truth of the Scriptures. They must be shaped by the mind of Christ so that as they teach, enlightening minds and stirring up wills of others, they will help the others to be shaped by the mind of Christ.

4. After the Examination in this Ordination Service, the Bishop-elect is asked by the Presiding Bishop to lead the congregation in confessing its faith by reciting the Nicene Creed. That act is an eloquent liturgical expression of the Bishop's role as guardian of the faith and as teacher of the whole community. This element of the 1979 American Ordination Rites has been borrowed from Eastern Orthodox practice. (Cf. Hatchett, op. cit., p. 523.)

5. After the consecration the new Bishop is handed a Bible. In the earlier English and American Ordinals, the sentence which accompanied the delivery began, "Give heed unto reading, exhortation, and doctrine...," a clear reference to Bishop as teacher. In 1979, the formula runs, "Receive the Holy Scriptures. Feed the flock of Christ..." This reference to Jesus' resurrection charge to Peter beside the Sea of Galilee combines both the teaching and sacramental aspects of the episcopal office under the figure of feeding. The Petrine reference makes it especially apt for Bishops.

6. How do bishops in the American Episcopal Church fulfil their teaching roles? The answer to this question lies in two directions: (1) in the opportunities provided for the Bishop to teach within the liturgy; (2) in extra-liturgical occasions for instruction. Only the first set of considerations properly falls within the scope of this paper. In the final section of the paper there will be found a brief discussion of the extra-liturgical opportunities for Bishops to teach, evangelize, and guard and focus the unity of the Church.

How then does the American Prayer Book provide for our Bishops to be teachers within the liturgy? When Bishops make their official visits to a parish, they are "expected to preach the

Word and preside at Baptism and the Eucharist" (BCP, p. 298). The Prayer Book, in other words, envisions the Bishop as fulfilling the ancient role of liturgical President of the congregation—baptizing, confirming, receiving new members from other Christian denominations, hearing parishioners reaffirm their baptismal vows, and also teaching. The Bishop teaches as one aspect of proclaiming the Word. We recall the examples of great teaching bishops in the patristic Church. Bishops are given an opportunity by the Prayer Book to teach every time they visit a parish. In fact, the Prayer Book expects them to teach. Bishops usually make an official visitation, and sometimes two visitations, on nearly every Sunday of the year. Thus this Prayer Book provision alone offers our Bishops many occasions to teach in the way that the Ordination Rite expects them to do. Extra-liturgical occasions, however, may be even more significant, since they probably put the Bishop in touch more frequently with a larger proportion of the members of the diocese. We shall turn to them later.

IV. The Bishop as Evangelizer

1. *A word of definition.* As in the case of teaching, our consideration of evangelizing must be prefaced with some words of explanation.

The word *evangelizer* does not appear in the Prayer Book. The Prayer Book does use the word *evangelist*, but designates by that term only the four Gospel writers, Matthew, Mark, Luke and John. Of course, the passages from Ephesians (4.11) and II Timothy (4.4) which mention the ministry of evangelists are read from time to time in course. Also, Ephesians is cited directly in the Prayer of Consecration for Priests (BCP, p. 533). The trouble is that no one is exactly sure what New Testament evangelists did.

It is tempting to think that they were charismatic figures who proclaimed the Evangel, the Good News of Jesus Christ, by telling the story of Jesus. The four Evangelists whose names we know may then have committed to writing the orally transmitted work of nameless predecessors. Perhaps in a similar way John committed to writing on Patmos an Apocalypse of the kind which might have been uttered by New Testament prophets (I Cor

14.29-32), and the *Didache* may be a written form of the instruction of teachers, which at the beginning would have been orally transmitted. Some such theory would have the advantage of accounting for the appearance of prophets, teachers and evangelists in Romans, I Corinthians and Ephesians. In a certain sense they are all aspects of apostolic ministry.

But here we are interested in a different word, *evangelizer*. It stands for a different ministry, though we hope it is closely related to the work of the evangelists.

As is well known, Anglican Churches around the world are embarking on a "Decade of Evangelism" to mark the close of the second millennium of the Christian Church and the opening of the third. What the work of evangelism ought to mean for twentieth-century Western life has been discussed and pondered within Anglican circles for nearly three-quarters of a century. One definition of it has gained fairly wide acceptance. It was developed in England in 1918 by the *Archbishop's Committee of Inquiry on the Evangelistic Work of the Church*, and was republished in 1945 as the starting point of another English Commission appointed by Archbishop Temple to consider the same subject. The report of this second Commission was published only after Temple's death and the end of the Second World War. This definition runs as follows:

> To evangelize is so to present Christ Jesus in the power of the Holy Spirit, that men shall come to put their trust in God through Him as their Savior and serve Him as their King in the fellowship of the Church.
>
> (*Towards the Conversion of England*, J.M. Dent and
> Sons, Toronto, 1946; p. 1)

An only slightly modified form of this same definition was accepted in 1973 by the General Convention of the American Episcopal Church (our highest legislative authority) when it established a Program Committee on Evangelism; and another General Convention reaffirmed it in 1991, after the Decade of

Evangelism had started. (Cf. *The Decade of Evangelism in the Episcopal Church*, by Robert Harrison, 1991, unpublished; p. 3.)

The 1988 Lambeth Conference section report on Mission and Ministry gave a more succinct definition of evangelism: "the communication of the good news of Christ's Kingdom and his accompanying command to people to repent, believe, and be baptized into his body, the Church" (Para. 65, p. 43). Evangelism, we thus might say, is "the making of new Christians" (Para. 22, p. 34).

2. *A note on tradition.*

(a). As Jesus was a teacher, so also he was an evangelizer. He told the disciples of John the Baptist that "the poor have the good news brought to them" (Mt. 11.5).

(b). After Jesus' resurrection the good news of the victory of God's Kingdom spread like wildfire to the ends of the known world. The tradition of the far-flung missions of the individual Apostles is well known. After they died, the evangelization of the Roman Empire continued apace. In that world there were many evangelizers.

(c). In the Middle Ages, there was not the same concern for "making new Christians" as existed at the beginning or as has been reawakened in the contemporary Western Church thanks to the inroads of secular society. In the medieval Pontifical to which we have already referred, there is no mention of evangelism or evangelists. New Christians in that age were made mostly by baptism and formed by the teaching and sacramental life of the Church. The emphasis on the role of Bishops lay in their identity as providers of sacraments, as offerers of the sacred gifts and the source of Holy Orders. We note, however, that one prayer for the new Bishop in the Pontifical ran, "May you be an apostle" (*Magdalen Pontifical, op. cit.* p. 78).

(d). In the English Ordinal of 1550, the passage from Ephesians 4, "...some Apostles, some Prophets, some Evangelists..." is cited in the Consecration Prayer for Bishops, as it is in the subsequent revisions of that Ordinal in the English Books of

1552 and 1662, and in the American Books of 1789, 1892 and 1928. We have already noted that in the present American Book, this reference now appears in the Consecration Prayer for the Priest (BCP, p. 557). Emphasizing the evangelical nature of the episcopal office, these earlier Ordinals ended this part of the Consecration Prayer with the clause, "...that he may be evermore ready to spread abroad thy Gospel." (e.g., BCP 1928, p. 557.) It is as good a definition of being an evangelizer as one could desire. Thus one could say that in the liturgical tradition which we are tracing in this paper, the function of evangelization was never lost, although under the circumstances of life in the epochs which produced the earlier Rites, that function was not emphasized.

3. *The American Prayer Book.* What does it mean, then, in the context of BCP 1979, for Bishops to be evangelizers? To be an evangelizer is to tell the story of Jesus and to preach the Good News in such a way that people will come to a decision to commit themselves to Christ. In the contemporary world, this decision must involve a conscious reorientation of values and style of living.

The Prayer Book, as we have seen, makes ample opportunities for our Bishops to preach to the congregations of their Dioceses. We have discussed the preaching office as a vehicle for teaching. Preaching has at least as much to do with evangelism as with teaching. It accounts for no small part of the Bishops' evangelizing role. Although both teaching and evangelism involve a wider range of activities than preaching alone, the preaching part of these roles is what the Prayer Book makes obvious, because preaching is a liturgical act.

The teaching and evangelizing aspects of the episcopal office, though distinguishable, are quite inseparable. The relationship between the two functions might be stated in this way: The Bishop as teacher is concerned to communicate the substance and meaning of the Gospel. The emphasis in this case is on intellectual communication—mind to mind. One notes, though, that minds must be moved to accept teaching. Emotions must be enlisted at some level, at some point in the process, if teaching is to be effective. On the other hand, the Bishop as evangelizer is concerned to stir hearts and move wills. Evangelization requires a response from those who hear the message. The emphasis is on conversion. It is obvious in this case that if no substantive ideas are communicated during the evangelizing process, the resulting conversion will be hollow and futile. Ideally both teaching and evangelizing aspects of preaching are present together in every act of proclamation. In our secular age, we need to be more self-conscious about both.

And we must recognize that the liturgical opportunities to teach and evangelize afforded by the preaching role assigned to the Bishop in the Prayer Book are simply symbolic of a much more far-reaching evangelistic ministry. Especially in the extra-liturgical aspects of the Bishops' evangelizing program, *the interpretation of the Gospel, which the Prayer Book teaches as a primary part of the Bishops' teaching role, is crucial for the work of evangelizing also. Without interpretation, without new language sensitive to a new world, the Gospel cannot be heard in the world, and so will not be accepted.*

V. The Bishop as Focus of Unity

1. *A word of definition.* The role of Bishops in guarding the unity of the Church is mentioned unmistakably and explicitly three times in BCP 1979: (1) in the address of the Presiding Bishop to the Bishop-elect, the Presiding Bishop says, "You are called to guard the faith, unity, and discipline of the Church" (BCP, p. 517). (2) In the sixth question of the following interrogation, the Bishop-elect is asked, "Will you guard the faith, unity, and discipline of the Church?" The Bishop-elect answers, "I will, for the love of God" (BCP, p. 518). (3) In the Catechism, in response to the question, "What is the ministry of a bishop?" the following reply is given:

The ministry of a bishop is to represent Christ
and his Church, particularly as apostle, chief
priest, and pastor of a diocese; to guard the faith,
unity, and discipline of the whole Church...

(BCP, p. 855).

In addition to these clear references to unity, there is a significant description of the unity of the People of God in John 17.20-21, part of one of the Gospel passages which may be read at the ordination of a Bishop.

"I ask not only on behalf of these, but also on
behalf of those who will believe in me through
their word, that they may all be one. As you,
Father, are in me and I am in you, may they also
be in us."

What do these passages tell us about a Bishop as focus of unity?

2. *The verses from the Fourth gospel establish the nature of the unity of the Church.* It is a unity like that which exists among the *Personae* of the Trinity—a unity of love, a unity in the Holy Spirit and effected by the Holy Spirit. This unity preserves and encourages difference. The unity of the Church which the Bishop is charged to preserve is not a unity of grudging assent and suppressed argument, but a unity of mutual love and forbearance and complete openness. It "bears all things, believes all things, hopes all things, endures all things" (I Cor 13.7). This unity permits frank disagreement and free discussion, and waits patiently for newer and deeper understandings to emerge after sufficient dialogue.

Our Bishops, like all Bishops in the Church of God, are ordained by this same Spirit and in this Spirit exercise leadership in the Church. The emergent and designated leaders of any organization or institution summarize and symbolize that organization. They *focus* it, and in that sense produce its unity. In the recent experience of the West, for example, Winston Churchill during the Second World War served this function for the allied nations in a remarkable degree. He focused for us our resistance to fascism in the spirit of Western civilization and values. He inspired a whole generation with that spirit.

The spirit of Western civilization is not the Holy Spirit, needless to say. But the analogy is helpful. In a far more perfect way, Jesus was anointed with the Holy Spirit. In the power of that Spirit he was able to represent God to humanity. He also represented humanity to God. He was the "last Adam" (I Cor 15.45) and the new mankind. He was and is the focus of unity for all humanity.

In an analogous way, Bishops, ordained by the Holy Spirit, focus the life of the Church in their dioceses. They sum up and symbolize the life of the Church and inspire it with that same Spirit, with *agape*. The ordination prayer in the American Prayer Book begins,

> Therefore, Father, make *N.* a bishop in your Church. Pour out upon *him* the power of your princely Spirit, whom you bestowed upon your beloved Son Jesus Christ, with whom he endowed the apostles, and by whom your Church is built up in every place...

> (BCP, p. 521).

Because Ignatius, for example, recognized the power of that Spirit to focus the unity of the Church in the person of the Bishop, he could write to the Ephesians,

"Seeing then that I received in the name of God *your whole congregation* in the person of Onesimus, a man of inexpressible love and your bishop..." (ad Eph 1.8; cf. ad Mag 2.1, ad Trall 1.1, etc.)

Ignatius was able to see the whole congregation in its Bishop because Bishops are the representative figures of the Church of God in their diocese, by virtue of their ordination by the Spirit to be leaders in a Spirit-filled Church. The Spirit focuses the unity of the Church, and focuses that unity significantly through Bishops because Bishops are called and ordained by the Spirit as the emergent and recognized leaders.

3. *A note on tradition.* It would be tedious and unnecessary in this context to prove that the ordination of Bishops in the Church of

God has always had this character. It may have begun when Paul and Barnabas "appointed elders for them in each church" (Acts 14.23), if *cheirotonesantes* can be read to mean, as some think, "appoint by a show of hands."

In the patristic Church, Bishops were customarily acclaimed by the laity before they were ordained. Then and now, Bishops are both acknowledged by the Church and empowered by the Spirit. Hence they focus unity.

4. *Teaching of the American Prayer Book.* More needs to be said, however, on the ways in which the American Prayer Book expresses this aspect of the episcopal office.

In the first place, the Ordination Service itself is a focus for the life of the whole Church. Prior to the service, the new Bishop was elected at a session of the representative Convention of the Diocese where he (or now she) is to serve, by a majority of the Presbyters and a majority of the elected laypersons. At the ordination itself, the Presiding Bishop or someone appointed by him is the chief consecrator assisted by at least two other bishops (BCP, p. 511). The ordaining Bishops represent the wider Catholic Church on this occasion. Moreover, the consent of a majority of the Bishops and of the Standing Committees of the dioceses of the American Church (consisting of elected presbyters and laypersons) is required. Thus the very act of electing and ordaining a new Bishop in this Church makes the Bishop a symbol and focus for its unity.

In the second place, the Bishop is ordained to celebrate the sacraments. The Bishop is the liturgical President of the congregations of the diocese. As Bishops are expected to preach the Word on the occasions of their official visits, they are also expected to baptize and celebrate Eucharist, that "blest sacrament of unity," so that their role as the source of sacramental life in the diocese can be made manifest. As the one who confers Holy Orders, the Bishop is also the source of the local ministries of Deacons and Priests. *The sacramental ministry of our Bishops set forth in the American Book of Common Prayer is one powerful way in which they focus the unity of the Church.*

This aspect of the Bishop's office has been more fully expressed in BCP 1979 than in the earlier English and American Ordinal. The ordaining action of the Holy Spirit is given vigorous expression by means of the prayer adapted from the *Apostolic Tradition* of Hippolytus. ("Pour out upon *him* the power of your princely Spirit,..." (BCP, p. 521). The role of the Bishop as high priest and offerer of the holy gifts is made explicit. (*Ibid.*) The references to the sacerdotal ministry of Priests are fuller in this Book than in earlier Ordinals, and apply to Bishops by virtue of the "cumulative effect" already mentioned. (Cf. BCP, p. 534; Hatchett, *op. cit.* p. 527.) Ecumenical discussions and criticism of the earlier rites combined to produce these new emphases in the 1979 service. (See, for example, *Russian Observations upon the American Prayer Book*, Alcuin Club Tract XII, Mowbray, 1917; pp. 8-21.)

In the third place, it is significant that the Prayer Book sets the role of Bishops as guardians of unity squarely in the context of guarding also the faith and discipline of the Church. The unity of love is not an "empty" unity. It is, in fact, doubtful whether any significant unity of any human group can be empty. People are always united by *something*, by common purpose, common love, even common fear. Christians are united first and foremost by faith in the risen Christ. That is why Bishops are teachers and evangelizers first and foremost of the resurrection. Christians are also united by a common discipline, by common action. When the Catechism of the Prayer Book asks, "What is the duty of all Christians," the response is given,

> "The duty of all Christians is to follow Christ; to come together week by week for corporate worship; and to work, pray, and give for the spread of the kingdom of God."

(BCP, p. 856)

Bishops maintain the unity of the Church by maintaining the faith of its members and encouraging them in their regular worship, in doing acts of charity and generosity, and in prayer. Unity is expressed and achieved by such actions and nourished by such faith. Bishops guard the unity of the Church in no small measure through their teaching and evangelizing ministries, for the unity of the Church is necessarily unity in Christ and unity in the Spirit which binds Father and Son together. The episcopal office is a focus for that kind of unity in each diocese. If unity is conceived in a different way, which does not keep Christ at the center and acknowledge the love of the Spirit, then Bishops become symbols of disunity, as has unfortunately happened from time to time, to the shame and sorrow and division of the Church of God.

VI. The Weight of Non-Theological Factors in Shaping the Ordained Ministries of the Church

The American Prayer Book presents the office of Bishop, considered as teacher, evangelizer, and focus of unity, as continuous with the episcopal office of the Church of the ages. We have directed our attention to the doctrine of the Prayer Book in these matters and we have noted the liturgical opportunities provided within the Prayer Book for Bishops to function in these ways. At the end, however, some brief attention must be devoted to making a distinction between the essential theological and liturgical aspects of the episcopal ministry and its non-theological, sociological aspects.

When the Presiding Bishop and the co-consecrators lay their hands on the head of the Bishop-elect, the Presiding Bishop prays that

> "...*he* may feed and tend the flock of Christ, and exercise without reproach the high-priesthood to which you have called *him*, serving before you day and night in the ministry of reconciliation, declaring pardon in your Name, offering the holy gifts, and wisely overseeing the life and work of the Church."

(BCP, p. 521.)

All the items in that list except the last are liturgical and theological in character. The last item in that description of what bishops do, however, designates them as leaders of the People of God in the world, as they encounter "the cosmic powers of this present darkness" (Eph 6.12).

From the beginning, the shape of the Church *in the world* has been determined at least in part by the necessities of that encounter. The Church has taken a number of shapes in the two millennia of its history. At the beginning it was a tiny and persecuted flock, gathered for worship on the Lord's Day and scattered during the week like salt throughout the structures of Hellenistic society. In the Middle Ages, it became a hierarchical structure with ministries devised to meet the power structure of the feudal system. Patriarchs ministered to emperors, archbishops to kings, bishops dealt with nobles, priests ministered to local townsfolk or country folk. The very words *province, diocese, parish*, grew out of the refashioning of the Roman Empire under Diocletian.

To make a long story short, the *shape* of the American episcopate has been determined by many of the same historical forces which shaped the United States government at its inception. The American Episcopal Church is a constitutional body. Its highest earthly authority is vested in an elected assembly which meets once every three years. The assembly, called General Convention, consists of Bishops in one House, and four Presbyters and four Laypersons from each Diocese in a second House. Bishops, as we have seen, are elected for life by representative Diocesan Conventions, and those Conventions also elect the clerical and lay representatives to each session of the General Convention. It might be said that the constitutional structure of the American Episcopal Church is a characteristically American creation.

Our Bishops function essentially and theologically in traditional ways. This essay has attempted to exhibit that fact. But they function *in the world* through these constitutionally, sociologically and historically determined structures. Authority among us is shaped to reside in these elected assemblies, where laypersons along with presbyters and bishops take their constitutionally determined parts, where decisions are made after due deliberations by majority vote in each order. In certain important matters a majority is specified to be more than simply half the voters. Thus bishops do not have their will unless clergy and laity agree;

but they can veto any measure which they hold to be wrong or unwise. Dissent is not only tolerated but appreciated, on the view that truth is better served by thorough discussion than by fiat. Measures enacted in these assemblies are carried out by appointed committees or by individual persons who then can act in the name of the whole Church. In this political aspect of its life, the American Episcopal Church is thoroughly democratic, and has all the strengths and weaknesses of that form of government. Action is taken with the consent of the governed and dissent is, on the whole contained within the body. On the other hand, compromise is often weak and action slow. As Americans like to say about their national government, democracy is a very poor form of government except when compared to others.

It would go beyond the scope of this paper if it were to describe the many extra-liturgical opportunities and mechanisms afforded to our Bishops by this constitutional structure to function as teachers and evangelists *in the world*. But at least this much should be said. Bishops are our constitutional leaders. As such they are our chief teachers and chief evangelists, and are in a good position to encourage and enable the other orders of ministers, especially the laity, to teach and evangelize the world. By virtue of their office they usually have many resources at their disposal. There are often programs devised and developed by the National Church which Bishops can implement on diocesan levels. In addition, Bishops can launch courses in teaching and evangelizing directed specifically to their own diocesan clergy and people. Beyond that, Bishops can communicate with the people in their dioceses by means of pastoral letters and articles prepared for diocesan newsletters.

In all those ways and probably many more, Bishops can lead the clergy and people of their dioceses to equip themselves to teach and evangelize. We believe that in our world every Christian needs to be a ready teacher and evangelizer whenever she or he encounters a neighbor. The leadership role of Bishops is critical in moving the Church to a situation where Laity are ready to take up their roles as ministers of Christ, and the leadership role of Bishops is amply and eloquently taught by the Prayer Book.

> "With your fellow bishops you will share in the leadership of the Church throughout the world,"

the Presiding Bishop tells the new Bishop. Later in the Examination the new Bishop is asked,

> "Will you sustain your fellow presbyters and take counsel with them; will you guide and strengthen the deacons and *all others who minister in the Church?*"

and responds, "I will, by the grace given me" (BCP, pp. 517-518, italics added).

The 1979 Prayer Book has a liturgy in which Church members can reaffirm their baptismal vows in the presence of the Bishop, and receive from the Bishop an empowering gift of the Spirit. This act is a liturgical recognition of the Bishop's role in encouraging these lay ministries. It is a new possibility in the 1979 Book.

It is easy enough to point out then that the Prayer Book charges and enables our Bishops to equip the whole Church and to teach and evangelize in the power of the love of Christ. It is proving to be quite difficult to put into place programs for training Laity to be effective in their several ministries. Our Church has only begun during the last one or two decades to take the ministry of Laity seriously. Nevertheless, we believe that it holds for us the promise of the future in an increasingly secularized and alienated world.

9

Third Supplement
"Episcopacy in the Anglican Communion"*

The story in outline

The expansion of Anglicanism outside the British Isles began as a result of the commercial enterprises which took members of the Church of England abroad to live. In America, the Colony in Virginia, for example, had royal patronage and Anglican members. In the seventeenth century chaplaincies were set up in European ports and spread further afield with the formation of the East India Company, which had chaplains in India from 1614. These members of the Church of England abroad were regarded as being under the jurisdiction of the Bishop of London.[1] The foundation of the first Anglican missionary societies, and the expansion of their work in the eighteenth century, provided a further impetus to Anglican expansion and resulted in new conversions to Anglicanism.

Although many missions were committed to establishing an indigenous clergy (the first African priest was ordained in 1765) England retained control. An Act of Parliament was required to create a new bishopric and new bishops had to be consecrated in London under royal mandate. In 1783 Samuel Seabury was elected by the clergy of Connecticut in America to be their bishop. But this was after the Declaration of Independence; he could not

---

* From *Episcopal Ministry: The Report of the Archbishops' Group on the Episcopate* (London, Church House Publishing, 1990, pp. 119-133).
[1] See Chapter 7, para. 237.

take the Oath of Allegiance to King George III as part of the consecration service; so he could not be consecrated by English bishops. Seabury was consecrated by bishops of the Episcopal Church in Scotland in 1784. This created a precedent unwelcome in England, and led to the 1786 Act which allowed the Archbishop of Canterbury to consecrate those who were not subjects of the British Crown. In 1788 two further bishops were consecrated for America. By 1836 bishops for Nova Scotia, Quebec, Calcutta, the West Indies and Australia had also been consecrated. In 1864 the first African bishop was consecrated in Nigeria.

At an early date it became clear that both legally and practically the Churches in the colonies were to become separate and distinct self-governing entities. Prior to 1866 the Crown granted Letters Patent creating dioceses and appointing bishops with ecclesiastical jurisdiction wherever it was considered desirable to do so. However, this practice ceased after the Privy Council expressed the opinion that the Crown could not confer ecclesiastical jurisdiction upon such a new bishop, in a colony which had an independent legislature.[2] The individual Churches thereafter organized themselves on a synodical basis and it was their own national legislatures which gave many of them statutory recognition and powers.

The various Churches within the Anglican Communion are regarded in law as voluntary bodies organized on a basis of consensus. The essence of the Anglican Communion is that it is a fellowship of Churches historically associated with the British Isles. It embraces all those Churches and dioceses which are in communion with the See of Canterbury and recognize the Archbishop of Canterbury as the focus of unity.

The desire to come together for 'common counsels and united worship'[3] has led the bishops of the Anglican Communion to meet periodically at Lambeth since 1867 under the presidency of the Archbishop of Canterbury (see paras. 272-8). The Lambeth

---

[2] Re: Lord Bishop of Natal (1865), 3 Moo. P.C.C. N.S. 115.
[3] Introduction to 1867 Lambeth Conference.

Conference is, however, a voluntary gathering with no legislative powers and no basis in canon, ecclesiastical, civil or common law. Nevertheless, where Resolutions passed by the Conference have been received with general acceptance by the Churches represented they have thereby attained what may be regarded as, in strictly non-legal terms, an 'authoritative' character.

The relationship between the Church in the Colonies and the 'mother' Church in England was complicated by the fact that the relationship of Church to State in England[4] could not be extended outside the British Isles. This was by virtue of a declaration by order in Council in the time of Charles I and made necessary the beginning of local synodical government, first in New Zealand in 1844; and the eventual granting of independent constitutions, to New Zealand in 1857, South Africa in 1876, the West Indies in 1883, for example.

The development of episcopacy in this wider Anglican world was, and still continues to be, influenced by the local cultural context and local styles of leadership and structures of authority. Nevertheless, the reports of successive Lambeth Conferences from the first in 1867, show that a coherent understanding of the nature and function of episcopacy is shared by the various parts of the Anglican Church. The understanding fundamental to the different local expressions of episcopacy remains consonant with that which we have traced through the centuries.

A. The bishop in the local church

The earlier Lambeth Conferences were concerned to lay down guidelines for the maintenance of an episcopal system in a Communion which was still growing in the mission fields and in what was still conceived of as a 'colonial' framework. The Conferences emphasized repeatedly the fundamental character of the relationship between a bishop and his diocese and upheld the principle of one bishop in one diocese. In 1867 it was allowed there might be 'peculiar cases' of race or language, but 1920

---

[4] On which see Chapter 12.

maintained that difficulties should not be allowed to interfere with the principle that there can be 'but one Church and one Authority.'[5] In 1930 there was a clear statement of 'the ancient Catholic principle that the fundamental unity of Church organization is the territorial Diocese under the jurisdiction of one Bishop,' with an assertion of the ecclesial completeness and autonomy of such a local church. 'A duly organized Diocese under its Bishop has the right, subject always to its duty to the whole fellowship of the Church, to decide and act for itself in its own affairs.'

A significant test of the 'one bishop, one diocese' principle, and of the rule that a diocese is a territorial unit, has been the demand for 'ethnic' bishoprics, with what might be called 'cultural' rather than geographically defined areas of jurisdiction. These may coincide, but they need not necessarily always do so, as in the case of the Diocese of Aotearoa in New Zealand, the Order of Ethiopia in Southern Africa, the Navajoland Area Mission in the United States of America.

The principle that the territorial diocese is the fundamental unit of church organization was underlined by early Lambeth Conferences in the repeated insistence that clergy going from one diocese to another should carry Letters Testimonial from their own bishop, without which the bishop of their new diocese would not grant a license to minister among his priests. An especially difficult problem[6] was the relationship of religious communities to their diocesan. A Committee of the 1897 Conference recommended that every priest ministering to a religious community should be licensed for that purpose by the Diocesan Bishop: it stressed that care should be taken that the Community should not interfere with the canonical obedience which each clergyman owes to the Bishop of the diocese in which he ministers. It was this same principle of safeguarding the relationship between

---

[5] Committee on Development of Provinces, Lambeth Conference, 1920.

[6] As it has been from the beginning of Western monastic communities in late patristic times.

diocesan and his people that lay behind Resolution 72 of the 1988 Lambeth Conference. This Conference:

1. Re-affirms its unity in the historical position of respect for diocesan boundaries and the authority of bishops within those boundaries; and in the light of the above.

2. Affirms that it is deemed inappropriate behavior for any bishop or priest of this Communion to exercise episcopal or pastoral ministry within another diocese without first obtaining the permission and invitation of the ecclesial authority thereof.

Thus there has been a careful insistence in a time of overseas expansion on maintaining the relationship between bishop and diocese and taking a stand against parallel jurisdictions. The tasks in which the bishop exercises his oversight in his diocese have been set out in some detail by the Lambeth Conferences of 1968, 1978, and 1988, with a notable emphasis on mission.

Within the wider context of the mission and ministry of the whole Church, the diocese is often seen as basic to the life and unity of the local Church. This unity is personified and symbolized in the office of the bishop. Under God, the bishop leads the local church in its mission to the world. Among other things, the bishop is:

(a) a symbol of the Unity of the Church in its mission;

(b) a teacher and defender of the faith;

(c) a pastor of the pastors and of the laity;

(d) an enabler in the preaching of the Word, and in the administration of the Sacraments;

(e) a leader in mission and an initiator of outreach to the world surrounding the community of the faithful;

(f) a shepherd who nurtures and cares for the flock of God;

(g) a physician to whom are brought the wounds of society;

(h) a voice of conscience within the society in which the local Church is placed;

(i) a prophet who proclaims the justice of God in the context of the Gospel of loving redemption;

(j) a head of the family in its wholeness, its misery and its joy. The bishop is the family's centre of life and love.[7]

B. Linking the Churches
a. The establishment of Provinces

The function of bishops as ministers of unity was underlined by the Lambeth Conference of 1920.[8] Its Committee on Development of Provinces endorsed the view that this ministry of unity should normally be discharged collegially by the gathering together of local dioceses into Provinces. This was already the case in the British Isles: the Church in Ireland was brought into a new relationship with the State by the Irish Parliament of 1560. Struggles between Presbyterians and Episcopalians in Scotland resulted in a presbyterian organization for the Church of Scotland. An Episcopal Church in Scotland survived, however, among those who kept to episcopacy at the Revolution Settlement of 1690. Scotland is now a province in full communion with the Church of England. The Welsh Church became a separate province when it was disestablished in 1920. With the consecration of Samuel Seabury in 1784, and three years later two further American bishops, an episcopate derived from the Church of England was constituted, and the first Anglican Province outside the British Isles and independent of the Church of England was formed. The first Lambeth Conference expressed the view that 'The association or federation of Dioceses within certain territorial limits, commonly called the Ecclesiastical Provinces, is not only in accordance with the ancient laws and usages of the Christian Church, but is essential to its complete organization.'[9] It is seen as the best means by which discipline

---

[7] *The Truth Shall Make You Free*, Report of the Lambeth Conference 1988 (London, 1988), p. 61.

[8] Resolution 9, vii.

[9] Committee D, 1867.

may be maintained, the election of bishops confirmed and the Church enabled 'to adapt its laws to the circumstances of the countries in which it is planted.' The 1867 Conference also stated a belief that the relationship of diocese to province should be governed 'on the one hand by the subordination of the bishops of the Province to a Metropolitan, and on the other by the association of the Dioceses in Provincial action.'

b. The emergence of world-wide Anglican collegiality
i. The Lambeth Conference

The development of the wider episcopal fellowship in the collegial gathering of Lambeth Conferences came naturally within Anglicanism, and was consonant with the Church of England's view that it continued the ministry of the universal church at the Reformation. In the 1860's, there came from Canada a suggestion that there should be a 'National Synod of the bishops of the Anglican Church at home and abroad.'[10] This they saw as a 'means...by which the members of our Anglican Communion in all quarters of the world should have a share in the deliberations for her welfare, and be permitted to have a representation in a General Council of her members gathered from every land.'[11] The Canadians envisaged this as an essentially conciliar gathering, the next best thing to 'the assembling of a General Council of the whole Catholic Church.'

The Canadian proposal was heatedly discussed in both the Lower and the Upper House of Convocation in England. Different views were expressed on the implication of bishops coming together in such a way. Some thought that it would

---

[10] Printed in R.T. Davidson, *Origin and History of the Lambeth Conferences, 1867 and 1878* (London, 1888), p. 32. The suggestion was prompted by an incipient crisis over jurisdiction in South Africa. The 'Colenso Affair' in 1863, in which John Colenso, Bishop of Natal, appealed to the Judicial Committee of the Privy Council against a ruling of his own Metropolitan (deposing him because of his views on Scripture), led to the questioning of the existing arrangements between the Provinces and the mother Church in such matters of jurisdiction.

[11] *Ibid.*, pp. 34-5.

enable those who held authority from God in the Church to say what is 'the faith of the Church from the beginning.' The bishops in Council would 'maintain to the end that given faith.'[12] Others thought it a much simpler matter: 'to bring them to a better understanding of the common wants of the Church' and 'to give them heart and courage to undertake their several duties.'[13] The Dean of Westminster made the point that the history of Councils had not been encouraging—'the general course of their steps has been marked by crime and sin.'[14] The question of the 'bindingness' of such Councils was also at issue. Canon Seymour contributed the view that 'it was a received axiom in the Catholic Church that...articles of faith were not binding upon the whole Church until the Church had received them...laymen giving their assent in the ancient church.'[15] Some had a vision that once Anglicans met in Council, they might unite first with the Greek Church, and afterwards with other Churches. On the question of bindingness the Bishop of Oxford commented, 'that which is not a Council of the Churches cannot pretend to do that which it belongs to a Council to do—i.e., to lay down any declarations of faith,'...'such declarations are binding when laid down by a properly constituted council or Synod because such bodies have a right to claim the inspiration and overruling presence of him who guides the Church to a right decision.'[16] All this shows how uncertain members of the Church of England were about the best pattern of conciliarity to adopt for their growing Communion of Churches, and in those Churches themselves similar reservations were expressed.[17]

---

[12] The *Chronicle of Convocation*, Feb. 13, 1876, p. 724.

[13] *Ibid.*, p. 729.

[14] *Ibid.*, p. 731-2.

[15] *Ibid.*, Feb. 14, p. 778.

[16] *Ibid.*, p. 804. On the questions of 'reception' and 'bindingness,' see further Chapters 10 and 13.

[17] 'Historically, it was in England itself that the sharpest challenge to the authority of the Lambeth Conference and therefore to the wider primacy of the Archbishop of Canterbury was first expressed in 1867 and it was, in fact,

Nevertheless, the First Lambeth Conference met in 1867. The Archbishop in his opening speech said:

> It has never been contemplated[18] that we should assume the functions of a general synod of all the Churches in full communion with the Church of England, and take upon ourselves to enact canons that should be binding upon those here represented. We merely propose to discuss matters of practical interest and pronounce what we deem expedient in resolutions which may serve as safe guides to future action. We have no direct precedent to guide us.[19]

Lambeth Conferences are thus not (and cannot be) legislative bodies for the whole Anglican Communion; their Resolutions are not binding upon the Provinces and cannot be enforced. Nevertheless, because of the view of episcopacy to which Anglicans are committed, expressed in Ordinals and in the statements of the Lambeth Conferences, the Resolutions of a Lambeth Conference count for a good deal. When all those charged by their local Church, within the ministry of the Universal Church in its Anglican expression, are gathered together to seek a common mind, then that counsel of assembled bishops must be, and is, taken very seriously indeed by those on whose behalf they give guidance.

While the meeting together of all the bishops of the Anglican Communion has clearly filled a need, and made it possible to experience and express the communion that exists amongst Anglicans, the question of the authority of the Lambeth

---

[17] (continued) The particular relationship of the Established Church of England with the Crown that was largely responsible for preventing an earlier movement from independence to interdependence.' R. Greenacre, *Lost in the Fog?* (London, 1989), p.8.

[18] This does not, of course, quite accurately reflect what the Canadians had in fact, asked for at first.

[19] Davidson, p. 10.

Conference has always been a sensitive matter. Lambeth 1920 remained clearly of the opinion that its authority was a moral one:

"The Lambeth Conference...does not claim to exercise any powers of control or command. It stands for the far more spiritual and more Christian principle of loyalty to the fellowship. The Churches represented in it are indeed independent, but independent with the Christian freedom which recognizes the restraints of truth and love. They are not free to deny the truth. They are not free to ignore the fellowship...the Conference is a fellowship in the Spirit."

The question of the authority of the Lambeth Conference has been raised recently increasingly sharply owing to the need for provinces, free to act autonomously, to consider the case for restraint when they come to take decisions in matters that affect the life of the whole Communion: matters concerning an Anglican response to international bilateral and multilateral dialogues and the development of the ordained ministry, particularly the opening of the episcopate to include women.

Anglicans have consistently been aware of the anomaly of holding such a conference in a divided Christendom. And statements of Lambeth Conferences have shown the bishops aware of the incompleteness of their Communion when there is a division in the universal Church. They have continued to look forward to a greater unity and to the possibility of holding a genuinely Ecumenical Council, and have correspondingly affirmed the provisionality of Anglicanism.[20] Both the ecumenical agendas of Lambeth Conferences, and the presence of ecumenical observers (from episcopal and non-episcopal churches) testify to the felt need of Anglicans for a fully universal Church. The welcoming of all of the bishops of the United Churches of the Indian sub-con-

---

[20] On 'provisionality,' see further our discussion under that heading in Chapter 13 on *Women in the Episcopate*.

tinent into the fellowship of the 1988 Lambeth Conference was a sign of a move towards this greater wholeness.[21]

ii. The Anglican Consultative Council

From the end of the last century the need has been felt for some organ or organs of 'higher authority' for the Anglican Communion. But just as the Communion has stopped short of turning the Lambeth Conference, or any other body, into an organ with 'teeth' and with jurisdiction (and indeed that is a constitutional impossibility), so other organs of higher authority have restricted powers. In the debates surrounding the establishment of a Lambeth Conference, questions of representativeness were often raised. After a lengthy discussion of possibilities in previous Lambeth Conferences, the Lambeth Conference of 1968 recommended the establishment of the Anglican Consultative Council (ACC) with representatives from the Anglican Churches. (This discharges responsibilities previously carried out by earlier bodies—The Lambeth Consultative Body; the Advisory Council on Missionary Strategy.) Its notable feature is that it brings together bishops, clergy and laity under the presidency of the Archbishop of Canterbury. The ACC thus provides a forum for episcopal, clergy and lay participation at a Communion-wide level. It meets every three years. Its functions have been clearly set out and agreed to by the Provinces. But questions remain unresolved about the kind of body the ACC is and the nature of its authority, in what sense it is 'synodical' and what is its relationship to the form of collegial oversight which has been a part of the life of the

---

[21] 'If the 1968 Lambeth Conference was able to declare that episcopal collegiality is an apostolic heritage given to the whole body or college of bishops, the context showed clearly that this body was not thought to be limited to the bishops of the Anglican Communion. It must, nevertheless, be admitted that we find less clarity in the language of the 1978 conference where Resolution 13 could speak of the collegial responsibility of the whole episcopate in a context which apparently did not look beyond the episcopate of the Anglican Communion.' R. Greenacre, 'An Anglican Response,' The Nature and Future of Episcopal Conferences. *The Jurist*, XLVIII (1988), p. 394.

Church since early times. These points were debated at the 1988 Lambeth Conference and there was a consensus in favor of retaining the seniority of the Lambeth Conference as a forum of those who exercise episcopal oversight.

iii. The Primates' Meeting

The Meeting of Primates was established at the Lambeth Conference in 1978. The advantage of this smaller episcopal meeting is that it can gather more frequently and help the Archbishop of Canterbury make major decisions about Lambeth Conferences, or about any matter affecting the whole Communion. The minutes of the 1979 meeting comment:

"The role of a *Primates' Meeting* could not be, and was not desired as, a higher synod in that sense. Rather it was a clearing house for ideas and experience through free expression, the fruits of which Primates might convey to their Churches."[22]

The Primates' Meeting concerned itself with initiating and leading a discussion in the early eighties on authority in the Anglican Communion and in 1987 produced a background report for the Lambeth Conference on *Women and the Episcopate*. More recently it has, amongst other things, produced a report, *Communion, Women and the Episcopate*, passing it to the Provinces for debate. Resolution 18 of the 1988 Lambeth Conference wanted to see 'a developing collegial role for the Primates' Meeting under the presidency of the Archbishop of Canterbury, so that the Primates' Meeting is able to exercise an enhanced responsibility in offering guidance on doctrinal, moral and pastoral matters.'[23]

iv. The development of Primacy[24]

The break with Rome and the establishment of Royal Supremacy inevitably raised questions over the position of the

---

[22] Minutes of the Primates' Meeting, 1979, p.4.
[23] *The Truth Shall Make You Free*, Report of the 1988 Lambeth Conference, p. 216.
[24] Cf. paras. 83, 102,124-125, 127, 147, 321 ff.

Archbishop of Canterbury. In the sixteenth century there were those, like Cartwright, who believed that Archbishopric is an innovation, a 'new ministry.' Others followed Whitgift in maintaining that the Council of Nicaea 'doth not only allow of the name but also the office of Metropolitan, archbishop' and that 'mention is made of a patriarch,' so that such higher episcopal oversight has ancient precedent. His view was that, in the ancient church, Primates, 'first bishops,' Patriarchs, Metropolitans, 'Bishops of the mother city,'and Archbishops, were all one. Generally, Anglican apologists maintained that there was room for Patriarchs in the West, but not for universal primacy. That is to say, they stopped short of allowing a universal bishopric, but held that Metropolitans in their provinces had the right to make bishops and the duty to care for them. Anglicans accepted the standing of the ancient Orthodox patriarchates and in England recognized the seniority of Canterbury's position over that of York, reflected in the title of the Archbishop of Canterbury as 'Primate of All England.'[25]

In practice, medieval tradition made it plain what an archbishop ought to do. In 1571 it was possible to list the duties of an archbishop thus: all that pertains to bishops also pertains to archbishops, but over and above his ordinary episcopal duties the archbishop has a responsibility to know how things are going throughout his province, and he ought, if he can to visit the whole province at least once. If a see is vacant, he must fulfil the duties of its bishop until he is replaced. If his bishops need discipline, he must give them fatherly counsel and warning. He hears and judges appeals to his archiepiscopal Courts, and he convokes provincial synods, this last at Royal command. It is his responsibility to install the bishops of his province once they have been chosen and elected. Hence the Archbishop of Canterbury was never simply a symbol of unity of

---

[25] It should be noted that some Anglicans from at least the seventeenth century were open to the idea of a universal primacy located in Rome. See 'Primacy and Collegiality: an Anglican View,' *Lambeth Essays on Unity* (SPCK, London, 1969), p. 16 *et al.*

the Church of England with moral authority and no jurisdiction. There was, through the Church courts, always a legal and jurisdictional component to his primacy.

With the growth of the Communion and the establishment of fresh Provinces, new 'metropolitans' have come into being as Primates or Presiding Bishops in the Anglican Communion. Not all of these primacies are attached to 'fixed' sees,[26] and it is not everywhere the case that the Primate has a see of his own. In the Episcopal Church in the United States (ECUSA) and now in Canada the Presiding Bishop or Primate has been 'freed' from diocesan responsibilities to be a 'chief executive.' Both these variants raise certain questions about the relationship of *episcope* and pastoral ministry.

The Lambeth Conferences have been cautious about the concept of a single primacy of the Anglican Communion, and have not gone far towards defining its authority. The 1908 Lambeth Conference said that 'no supremacy of the See of Canterbury over Primatial or Metropolitan Sees outside England is either practical or desirable.'[27] Nevertheless, the 1908 Conference wished to bear witness to the universal recognition in the Anglican Communion of the ancient precedence of the See of Canterbury. The 1930 Conference contrasted as two 'types of ecclesiastical organization' a 'centralized government' and a 'regional' authority 'within one fellowship.'[28] The 1948 conference commented that 'former Lambeth Conferences have wisely rejected proposals for a formal primacy of Canterbury.'[29] Lambeth 1968 described the role of the Archbishop of Canterbury in greater detail:

> Within the college of bishops it is evident that there must be a president. In the Anglican Communion this position is at present held by the occupant of the historic See of Canterbury, who

---

[26] E.g. Wales and Scotland.
[27] Lambeth, 1980, p. 418.
[28] Lambeth, 1930, Committee Report on the Anglican Communion.
[29] Without defining fully what such 'formality' would entail (Lambeth, 1948, p. 84).

enjoys a primacy of honor, not of jurisdiction. This primacy is found to involve, in a particular way, that care of all the churches which is shared by all the bishops.[30]

There has thus been a strong sense of the reality of a Canterbury primacy. Lambeth 1978 added that the fellowship of the Anglican Communion is grounded in loyalty to the Archbishop of Canterbury as 'the focus of unity,' and that loyalty was warmly evident at the 1988 Conference. Underlying the Anglican understanding of the role of the primate is the theology of the ministry of oversight which makes the bishop representative and focus of the life of the community. This is thoroughly in line with the development of ministry in the early Church in which primacy, exercised in collegiality and conciliarity, was regarded and experienced as a symbolic primacy, caring for the unity and well-being of the Church, rather than a 'primacy of jurisdiction.' This was the character of the universal primacy envisaged by the Archbishop of Canterbury when he spoke of the future in a united Church during his visit to Rome in 1989.

It is, however, clear that in spite of the desire that the primacy of the Archbishop of Canterbury should be supremely one of focusing unity, and a primacy of honor rather than jurisdiction, certain functions have accrued to the office. The Archbishop of Canterbury has always invited bishops to the Lambeth Conference. He is president of the Lambeth Conference and the Anglican Consultative Council, a 'permanent link' between the two bodies; as president of both he exercises metropolitan authority over isolated dioceses, which are not yet within provinces; in 1988 it was the Archbishop of Canterbury and not the Primates' Meeting that was asked in the first Resolution of the Conference to convene a Commission to consider the implications of a woman being consecrated a bishop.[31]

---

[30] Lambeth, 1968, p. 137.
[31] The Eames Commission. See Chapter 13.

We ought not to leave the subject of primacy without noting that there remains a tension, and an increasing one, between the responsibilities of the Archbishop of Canterbury within the Church of England, and his primatial functions in relation to the Anglican Communion as a whole. This is partly a matter of division of time and energy; and partly of loyalty, where (as in principle may be the case) Provinces make independent legislative decisions which test the bonds of common faith and order.

C. Continuity through time

The Lambeth Conferences have upheld the view that the episcopate is the ministry of continuity. Lambeth 1958 describes its role here:

> In ordination...the individual must affirm that he believes himself to be called of God to the ministry, and the Church must be satisfied of...his call and his fitness for the work. Then the Church also calls and the body of the faithful assents to the ordination. Ordination must be performed by those who have received and are acknowledged to have received, authority to exercise *episcope* in the Body, and to admit others to share in that ministry. This acknowledgement by the Body of the ministry of *episcope* must be recognized and accepted. From this arises the principle of continuity by succession, which appears to be indispensable, at least from the human point of view.[32]

It is of importance ecumenically that the same Conference notes: 'This is not to say that God cannot dispense with the succession if he wishes, as indeed he did when the Aaronic priesthood was superseded by the appointment of the High Priest of our Confession' (Hebrews 7:11-28).[33] The 1958 Conference

---

[32] Lambeth, 1958, pp. 2,88 and 137.

[33] (1958, 2.88) There are points here of relevance to the search for mutual recognition of ministry between episcopal and non-episcopal Churches.

sums up the Anglican position economically: 'The Anglican tradition has always regarded episcopacy as an extension of the apostolic office and function both in time and space, and, moreover, we regard the transmission of apostolic power and responsibility as an activity of the college of bishops and never as a result of isolated action by an individual bishop.'

Something needs to be said here about 'the historic episcopate locally adapted in the methods of its administration to the varying needs of the nations and peoples called of God into the unity of this Church' (Lambeth Quadrilateral, 1888).[34] This is the fourth article of the Chicago-Lambeth Quadrilateral, in the form of words adopted by the Lambeth Conference of 1888. Dr. Vincent, Assistant Bishop of Southern Ohio, was anxious in the debates of the 1880's to make it clear that the phrase 'the historic episcopate' 'was deliberately chosen as declaring not a doctrine but a fact, and as being general enough to include all variants.'[35] The intention was to make the Anglican doctrine of episcopacy as capacious as possible within the limits set by the realities of what episcopacy had been in the history of the Church; and at the same time to emphasize the importance of a history which contains tradition. As the Report of the Joint Commission on Approaches to Unity to the American General Convention of 1949 put it, episcopacy is 'a fact accompanied by its historical meaning.'[36] It is what might be described as a fact of revelation, and thus a fact carrying doctrinal implications.

Those doctrinal implications we have sought to draw out from the history in our earlier chapters. But one or two further points ought to be made here. In 1920, the Lambeth Conference addressed the difficulty that the episcopate has not seemed the natural instrument of unity to those Churches which have, since the sixteenth century, rejected episcopacy. The Conference

---

[34] See, too, para. 187.
[35] *Quadrilateral at One Hundred*, ed. J. Robert Wright (Ohio, London and Oxford, 1988), pp. 118-9.
[36] *Ibid.*

stressed that there was no question of denying 'the spiritual reality of the ministries of those communions which do not possess the episcopate.' But it held that the episcopate is, nevertheless, 'the best instrument for maintaining the unity and continuity of the Church.' With the same proviso, the 1958 Conference spoke more strongly of the belief 'that a ministry acknowledged by every part of the Church can only be attained through the historic episcopate.' The role, not only of episcopacy as a particular form of *episcope*, but of the 'historic episcopate,' that is, the actual episcopate as it has existed in the Church and exists today, remains of crucial importance.

It is also of importance for unity that we should see our way clearly on the subject of what does and does not constitute an admissible 'local adaption' to different cultural contexts.[37] A test here must be whether the 'local adaption' allows the episcopate to continue to act collegially with full interchangeability of ministries and a shared sacramental life under a single episcopate. For example, in African dioceses the leadership role of the bishop may have about it something of the tribal chief, head of an extended family, settling squabbles in the congregation in a fatherly way.[38] In the developed world the bishop can seem chiefly administrator and public figure. In Brazil he may be doing a secular job as well as being a bishop. The spiritual role of the bishop may seem in African, Asian or Latin American cultures to make him a 'holy man' in all the different ways that idea has been understood in these different parts of the world. In Asia and parts of Africa the missionary role of the bishop may predominate. None of these 'local adaptations' is divisive; on the contrary, they enrich the corporate pastorate of the episcopate of the whole Communion. And none is incompatible with the profound continuity of the Church through the ages as the one Body of Christ.

---

[37] A striking case in point is the consecration of women bishops in some parts of the Communion. See Chapter 10.
[38] *Bishops: But What Kind?* pp. 140-1.

By way of brief summary, we may perhaps underline again the consistent adherence of Anglican theology and practice, in this world-wide arena of a growing and diversifying Communion, to a view of episcopacy derived from Scripture and earliest Christian tradition; and in which the intersection of the three planes of the Church's life in the person of the bishop makes him the focus and minister of unity.

10

Fourth Supplement

"The Episcopal Church and the Ministry of the Historic Episcopate"*

A. The Legacy of the Church Of England

It is well-known that during the reformations of the sixteenth century the Church of England maintained the threefold order of the ordained ministry with the episcopate at its heart. Under Henry VIII the royal supremacy replaced papal supremacy and separated England from the jurisdiction of the bishop of Rome. An Act Restraining the Payment of Annates (1534) took for granted the threefold order focused in the episcopate and ordered that from henceforth the king, in his role as Supreme Head of the Church in England, should nominate to the proper electing body the person to be elected archbishop or bishop.[1] In the reign of King Edward VI an ordinal was devised and published in 1550 with the title, "The forme and maner of makynge and consecratyng of Archebishoppes, Bishoppes, Priestes and Deacons." It was revised and bound up with the 1552 Book of Common Prayer and is to be found in subsequent prayer books. The preface to the Ordinal stated "that from the Apostles' time there hath been these

---

*From *"Toward Full Communion"* and *"Concordat of Agreement"* (the Report of Lutheran Episcopal Dialogue, Series III), ed. William A. Norgren and William G. Rusch (Minneapolis, Augsburg and Cincinnati, Forward Movement Publications. 1991. pp.59-71.

[1] G.R. Elton, *The Tudor Constitution* (Cambridge University Press, 1960), p. 350.

orders of Ministers in Christ's Church,"[2] and this was seen as sufficient reason for the continuance of the threefold order.

After the brief and troublesome reign of the Roman Catholic Queen Mary, during which doctrinal reforms were reversed and papal jurisdiction reintroduced for a short time, Queen Elizabeth came to the throne, Parliament restored royal supremacy, and the historic episcopate was again set free from the jurisdiction of the bishop of Rome. Elizabeth did not seek the restoration of the Edwardian legislation (repealed under Mary) that had directed the crown to appoint bishops by letters patent rather than following the traditional canonical procedures. She did clarify the supremacy, claiming rather less than did her father, Henry VIII, preferring to be known as "Governor" rather than "Head" of the church, firmly stating that she did not take to herself any authority other than that provided by law, would not tamper with inherited doctrine or ceremony, and would not claim any "function belonging to any ecclesiastical person being a minister of the Word and Sacraments of the Church."[3] She would, so she signified, maintain the historic order of the Church's ministry and its essential integrity. And yet, although the ancient threefold pattern of the ordained ministry was thus retained under reformation, one significant change from the years of Edward VI may be noted as surviving the tumultuous events of that century: bishops, priests, and deacons were permitted to marry.[4]

Anglican attitudes toward the episcopate and understandings of its meaning and functions developed during the sixteenth and seventeenth centuries. At the outset there were those who continued to regard bishops as primarily servants of the state. On the other hand there were bishops such as John Hooper who labored

---

[2] Cf. Paul F. Bradshaw, *op. cit.*, Chapter 2.

[3] "A Declaration of the Queen's Proceedings Since Her Reign," in W.E. Collins, *Queen Elizabeth's Defence of Her Proceedings in Church and State* (London: SPCK, 1958), p. 45.

[4] Cf. Richard Spielmann, "The Beginning of Clerical Marriage in the English Reformation: the Reigns of Edward and Mary," *Anglican and Episcopal History*, Vol. 56, No. 3 (September 1987), pp. 251-263.

diligently in his diocese to provide a learned clergy and to correct the faults of those perceived to be in error, chiefly through the ecclesiastical courts.[5] The expectation of bishops' attendance at court, necessitating long absences from their dioceses, declined markedly under Elizabeth. John Jewel, Queen Elizabeth's first bishop of Salisbury, reflected the Reformation point of view, stating: 'Those oily, shaven, portly hypocrites, we have sent back to Rome from whence we first appointed them: for we require our bishops to be pastors, laborers, and watchmen."[6] Although in the early years of Queen Elizabeth's reign there were those who did not take a high view of episcopacy, the dominant attitude of that time was probably expressed by the final Elizabethan archbishop of Canterbury, John Whitgift, who believed that episcopacy best suited monarchial government which, incidentally, he regarded as the best form of government. But where the civil government was oligarchical, he considered, the ecclesiastical government might appropriately be presbyteral,[7] and thus foreigners ordained abroad only by presbyters were allowed to minister in England. But none were to be ordained in England save by bishops. The evidence thus suggests that in the sixteenth and early seventeenth centuries the prevalent theological opinion in the Church of England was that where episcopal ordination was available, it should be retained; but in cases of necessity where this was not possible, such as on the continent, then presbyteral ordination might suffice. Richard Hooker expressed the Anglican understanding this way:

> When the exigence of necessity doth constrain to
> leave the usual ways of the church, which other-
> wise we would willingly keep, where the church
> must needs have some ordained and neither hath

---

[5] F.D. Price, "Gloucester Diocese under Bishop Hooper," *Transactions of the Bristol and Gloucester Archeological Society* 60:51-151.

[6] Cited in J. Booty, *John Jewel as Apologist of the Church of England* (London: SPCK, 1963), p. 23.

[7] Cf. P.M. Dawley, *John Whitgift and the English Reformation* (New York: Charles Scribner's Sons, 1954), pp. 140ff.

nor can have possibly a bishop to ordain, in case of such necessity, the ordinary institution of God hath given oftentimes, and may give, place. And, therefore, we are not simply without exception to urge a lineal descent of power from the Apostles by continued succession of bishops in every effectual ordination. These cases of inevitable necessity excepted, none may ordain but only bishops: by the imposition of their hands it is, that the church giveth power of order, both unto presbyters and deacons.[8]

Nonetheless, there was pressure of invective from Rome and from Puritans and Separatists in England. Some of the more militant Puritans sought to replace episcopal government with presbyterian government, such as that of Calvin's Geneva, regarding bishops not as "pastors, laborers, and watchmen," but as "that swinishe rabble," as "pettie Antichrists, proud prelates, intolerable withstanders of reformation, enemies of the gospel, and most covetous wretched priests."[9] Indeed, episcopacy was altogether suppressed in the Church of England following the Civil War during the Commonwealth period (1649-1660), but it was restored after the Interregnum. The result of all this controversy, however, was that, rather than merely accepting the threefold order as an historic given, there were now those who began to argue that the historic episcopate was of divine origin and necessary, somewhat in imitation of the Puritans who argued that presbyterian government was of divine origin and necessary. Richard Hooker had argued that the first "institution of bishops could be traced back to Christ himself, through the Apostles," but he was

---

[8] Richard Hooker, *Ecclesiastical Polity*, Book VII Chapter xiv, 11: *The Works of that Learned and Judicious Divine, Mr. Richard Hooker*, ed. John Keble, sixth edition, Vol. III, pp. 231-232; punctuation modernized.

[9] Cited in Leland H. Carlson, *Martin Marprelate, Gentleman: Master Job Throckmorton Laid Open in His Colors* (San Marino: Huntington Library, 1981), p. 9.

careful to qualify this argument by insisting that episcopacy was a matter of "positive law." Bishops thus owed "their continued existence in the church since the death of the Apostles to the authority of the church that had chosen to retain them, rather than to any immutable command of divine law."[10] There would be those in the future who would hearken back to Hooker's judicious understanding, but there would also be those who took a simpler view: Christ instituted bishops, so there must be bishops. The bishops after the Interregnum of the seventeenth century insisted on ordaining (or re-ordaining) all ministers previously not episcopally ordained during the Commonwealth period, and the Ordinal of the 1662 Book of Common Prayer as well as the Act of Uniformity in the same year now insisted that episcopal ordination was necessary for the holding of ecclesiastical benefice or admission to the pastoral ministry of the Church of England. Henceforth, no one would "be accounted or taken to be a lawful Bishop, Priest, or Deacon" unless he were admitted "according to the form hereafter following, or hath had formerly Episcopal Consecration or Ordination." This requirement applied to ministers from all non-episcopal churches, whether in England or elsewhere. The traditional attitude of the Church of England was, nevertheless, maintained toward reformed churches elsewhere: they were true churches, whose ministries, though irregular and anomalous, were real and effective.[11] But a clear boundary had been set for the limits of Anglican comprehensiveness that has survived even in the latest (1979) Book of Common Prayer of the Episcopal Church in the United States:

> No persons are allowed to exercise the offices of
> bishop, priest, or deacon in this Church unless
> they are so ordained [by "the laying on of episco-

---

[10] W.D.J. Cargill Thompson, "The Philosopher of the 'Politic Society': Richard Hooker as a Political Thinker," in *Studies in Richard Hooker*, ed. W. Speed Hill (Cleveland and London: Case Western Reserve University, 1972), p. 57.

[11] Cf. especially LED II, *op. cit.*, p. 42, note 1; also Norman Sykes, *op. cit.*, and Richard Norris, "Episcopacy," *op. cit.*, pp. 304-305

pal hands"], or have already received such ordination with the laying on of hands by bishops who
are themselves duly qualified to confer Holy
Orders (preface to the Ordinal, page 510).

During the latter half of the seventeenth century there was
thus a shift of theological emphasis in Anglican understandings of
episcopacy. Partly this shift was due to the exigencies of polemics,
as noted above. It was also stimulated, however, by the rediscovery and authentication of certain patristic texts, especially the first
epistle of Clement and the letters of Ignatius. The texts dealt
with matters of church order and seemed to indicate a separate
and distinct episcopal order from early times.[12] Hence the episcopal ordering of the church began to be envisaged, in some
quarters, not only as historically normative or of divine approba-
tion and apostolic origin (though certainly not as necessary to salvation), but as a divine gift that defines the sphere of covenanted
grace and as an apostolic office which is the basis for the Church's
authority and identity independent of civil society. One example
of this tendency is the bishop of Chester, John Pearson (1673-
1686), active in the process of authenticating the genuine letters
of Ignatius of Antioch, who became "sure that there can be no
power of absolution or authority to consecrate the elements in
the Lord's Supper on the part of one who has not been episcopally ordained."[13]

After this shift in theological emphasis, three ways of understanding episcopacy come to the fore in the following centuries.
First were those for whom episcopacy was still a secondary matter. Among many latitudinarians, episcopacy remained a conve-
nient and traditional manner of ordering the ministry. Emerging
eighteenth-century Anglican evangelicals largely shared this view

---

[12] Manuscripts of these patristic texts, which had been lost to the medieval
Western church, were rediscovered in the seventeenth century and led to
authoritative editions in England: *The First Epistle of Clement* (1633), and the
Letters of Ignatius of Antioch (1644, 1672).

[13] Norris, "Episcopacy," *op. cit.*, p. 305.

with their latitudinarian adversaries. The other two ways of understanding episcopacy, however, accorded it greater theological significance.

The second of these understandings made episcopacy primary. When confronted with latitudinarian theological understandings combined with whig political views of ecclesiastical reformation, the shift of emphasis resulted in the assertion of the Tractarian Movement (1833-1845) that not only was episcopacy of apostolic foundation, but it was necessary to authentic ecclesial life. Appealing to the example and teaching of the early church fathers, such as Cyprian of Carthage, emphasis was placed on the church's self-governance through the episcopate. In Tract 74, for example, it was asserted that non-episcopal forms of ministry, "men thus sending themselves, or sent by we know not whom," have no authority to administer the Sacraments. John Henry Newman (1801-1890) considered bishops to be of the *esse* of the church and urged "the clergy to remember 'the real ground' on which their authority was built, their 'apostolical descent.'" He called upon them "to join with the bishops, and support them in their battle to defend the Church."[14]

A third way of understanding episcopacy, broader but not entirely dissimilar, represents a more comprehensive view resulting from the revolutionary challenges to Christianity coming with the nineteenth century, yet stemming from the shift in emphasis noted above, and was encouraged by the thought of F.D. Maurice (1805-1872). He commended the institution of the episcopate as "one of the appointed and indispensable signs of a spiritual and universal society,"[15] and he also held that "the main constituent of the Church's polity is the episcopate. Bishops have

---

[14] Desmond Bowen, *The Idea of the Victorian Church: A Study of the Church of England, 1830-1889* (Montreal: McGill University Press, 1868), p. 51 and see p. 87 (citing Tract 1). Also E.R. Fairweather, *The Oxford Movement* (New York: Oxford University Press, 1964), pp. 55-59.

[15] Frederick Denison Maurice, *The Kingdom of Christ* (1838; reprinted London: S.C.M. Press, 1958, ed. A.R. Vidler), Vol. II, p. 106.

the direct commission of Christ, as much as did the original holders of the apostolic office."[16] In the case of the Tractarian and Maurician ways of understanding episcopacy, though, the shift of attitude corresponds to a shift in the position of the church in state and society and, as such, informs contemporary discussions of the episcopate that have been stimulated in part also by the ecumenical movement.

B. Anglicanism in the American Cultural Context

It is remarkable that after the American Revolution colonial Anglicanism survived in the newly founded Protestant Episcopal Church, the first autonomous Anglican Church outside the British Isles but now independent of the civil society. Anglicanism was associated with the tyranny of the British crown, and it might have perished in the United States with the end of British rule. It is also remarkable that the episcopate survived in the new world. There were no resident bishops in colonial Anglicanism and the colonists on the whole had opposed any suggestion of episcopacy, regarding bishops as "proud prelates." The 1789 founding convention of the Episcopal Church met in Philadelphia facing the necessity of resolving widespread differences, principally between those who believed that there could be no discussion of church government without bishops being present and in charge and those who had been prepared to go forward without bishops if for a time the proper consecrations could not be procured, insisting that in this new land it was the faithful people who mattered most. The result was that the historic threefold order of the ordained ministry was continued, though the bishops were elected by both clergy and laity, who were to share in the government of the church in diocesan conventions and in the General Convention.

Although Samuel Seabury, the first bishop of the Episcopal Church in America, and some others like him, maintained a high-

---

16 Maurice's view as summarized in B.M.G. Reardon, *From Coleridge to Gore: A Century of Religious Thought in Britain* (London: Longman, 1971), pp. 180-181.

church estimation of the vital necessity of episcopacy not only to the church but also to Christian life and salvation, and would have preferred for bishops a greater degree of authority,[17] it was, nonetheless, determined at the insistence of William White, first bishop of Pennsylvania, that laity were also to participate in every level of church government and even in the selection of those to be ordained. Though reminiscent of conciliar patterns in the early church, such changes in the structure, practice, and understanding of the episcopate were influenced by American colonial experience as well as by the history of the English convocations of Canterbury and York and by a positive theological evaluation of American governmental philosophy and practice, the Articles of Confederation being of particular influence. Collectively, these arrangements in the Episcopal Church have come to be known as "the constitutional episcopate." The bishop continued to be understood to fulfill a particular and historic ministry within the community of the faithful, but not apart from it.

As a result of their new situation, Anglicans in the United States were given further opportunity to explicate their understanding of the historic episcopate. A case in point is the famous Memorial presented to the 1853 General Convention by, among others, William Augustus Muhlenberg, an Episcopal priest whose great-grandfather was the famous Lutheran "patriarch," Henry Melchior Muhlenberg. It petitioned other House of Bishops to take an initiative by ordaining ministers of the traditions (especially on the frontier) without binding them to the Thirty Nine Articles of Religion and the rubrics of the Book of Common Prayer. While the Memorial met with some enthusiasm, no practical action resulted.[18]

---

[17] Cf. Frederick V. Mills, Sr., *Bishops by Ballot: An Eighteenth Century Ecclesiastical Revolution* (New York: Oxford University Press, 1978).

[18] Robert Goeser and William H. Petersen, *Traditions Transplanted: The Story of Anglican and Lutheran Churches in America* (Cincinnati: Forward Movement Publications, 1981), p. 36.

C. New Understandings from the Ecumenical Movement

Yet as the nineteenth century progressed, the existence of many competing communions in the U.S.A. caused leaders such as William Reed Huntington to address the issue of church unity. In 1886 the Bishops of the Episcopal Church, meeting in Chicago, appealed to "principles of unity exemplified by the undivided Catholic Church during the first ages of its existence," which they understood to be "essential to the restoration of unity among the divided branches of Christendom." This Chicago-Lambeth Quadrilateral, as it came to be known after it had been affirmed by the 1888 Lambeth Conference (in a slightly amended form), identified four principles "as a basis for an approach to reunion":

> **a)** The Holy Scriptures of the Old and New Testament, as "containing all things necessary to salvation," and as being the rule and ultimate standard of faith.
>
> **b)** The Apostles' Creed, as the Baptismal Symbol; and the Nicene Creed, as the sufficient statement of the Christian faith.
>
> **c)** The two Sacraments ordained by Christ Himself—Baptism and the Supper of the Lord—ministered with unfailing use of Christ's words of Institution, and of the elements ordained by Him.
>
> **d)** The Historic Episcopate, locally adapted in the methods of its administration to the varying needs of the nations and peoples called of God into the Unity of His Church.[19]

It remained for the twentieth century ecumenical movement to multiply conferences and dialogues on matters standing in the

---

[19] Book of Common Prayer (U.S.A., 1979), p. 877.

way of visible unity. At times the very instruments of unity have appeared to some as barriers, not least the historic episcopate. The bishops of the 1920 Lambeth Conference sought to break the impasse with "An Appeal to All Christian People":

> The vision which rises before us is that of a Church, genuinely Catholic, loyal to all truth, and gathering into its fellowship all "who profess and call themselves Christians," within whose visible unity all the treasures of faith and order, bequeathed as a heritage by the past to the present, shall be possessed in common, and made serviceable to the whole Body of Christ. Within this unity Christian Communions now separated from one another would retain much that has long been distinctive in their methods of worship and service. It is through a rich diversity of life and devotion that the unity of the whole fellowship will be fulfilled.[20]

The Appeal was to "an adventure of goodwill and still more of faith, for nothing less is required than a new discovery of the creative resources of God." The four principles of unity in the Chicago-Lambeth Quadrilateral were reworded as follows:

> The Holy Scriptures, as the record of God's revelation of Himself to man, and as being the rule and ultimate standard of faith; and the Creed commonly called Nicene, as the sufficient statement of the Christian faith, and either it or the Apostles' Creed as the Baptismal confession of belief;

> The divinely instituted sacraments of Baptism and the Holy Communion, as expressing for all the corporate life of the whole fellowship in and with Christ;

---

[20] *Conference of Bishops of the Anglican Communion holden at Lambeth Palace, July 5 to August 7, 1920* (London: SPCK, 1920), PP. 27-28.

A ministry acknowledged by every part of the Church as possessing not only the inward call of the Spirit, but also the commission of Christ and the authority of the whole body.[21]

The Appeal addressed the reality of the ordained ministries of communions without the historic episcopate:

May we not reasonably claim that the Episcopate is the one means of providing such a ministry? It is not that we call in question for a moment the spiritual reality of the ministries of those Communions which do not possess the Episcopate. On the contrary we thankfully acknowledge that these ministries have been manifestly blessed and owned by the Holy Spirit as effective means of grace. But we submit that considerations alike of history and of present experience justify the claim which we make on behalf of the Episcopate. Moreover, we would urge that it is now and will prove to be in the future the best instrument for maintaining the unity and continuity of the Church. But we greatly desire that the office of a Bishop should be everywhere exercised in a representative and constitutional manner....

We believe that for all, the truly equitable approach to union is by way of mutual deference to one another's consciences. To this end, we who send forth this appeal would say that if the authorities of other Communions should so desire, we are persuaded that, terms of union having been otherwise satisfactorily adjusted, Bishops and clergy of our Communion would willingly accept from these authorities a form of commission or recognition which would commend our ministry

---

[21] *Ibid.*, p. 28.

to their congregations as having its place in the one family life....

It is our hope that the same motive would lead ministers who have not received it to accept a commission through episcopal ordination, as obtaining for them a ministry throughout the whole fellowship.

In so acting no one of us could possibly be taken to repudiate his past ministry. God forbid that any man should repudiate a past experience rich in spiritual blessings for himself and others. Nor would any of us be dishonoring the Holy Spirit of God, Whose call led us all to our several ministries, and Whose power enabled us to perform them. We shall be publicly and formally seeking additional recognition of a new call to wider service in a reunited church, and imploring for ourselves God's grace and strength to fulfill the same.[22]

Thus we have a moving admission of the impoverishment of all ordained ministries by the fact that they are not in communion with each other.

Responses to this Appeal and to like messages from other communions have been deliberate but steady. Notable examples are the unions of Anglican dioceses with Christians of other traditions in the Churches of South India, North India, Pakistan, and Bangladesh. Discussions have continued in the World Council of Churches Commission on Faith and Order and between communions in many parts of the world, including the Anglican-Lutheran dialogues. Reflection on the experience of steadily widening dialogue, as well as on that of full-communion concordats with the Old Catholic Churches of Europe, the Philippine Independent Church, and the Mar Thoma Church, has led the

---

[22] *Ibid.*, p. 28-9.

Episcopal Church to an understanding of the goal of visible unity as "one eucharistic fellowship...a communion of Communions."[23] The work of the Consultation on Church Union in the U.S.A. with churches of the Reformed and Methodist traditions has produced a proposal in light of this goal statement which seeks to incorporate the historic episcopate.[24]

The Anglican-Reformed International Commission has produced the report *God's Reign and Our Unity*, which is rich in material concerning the reconciliation of ordained ministries. On the issue of continuity of succession, it declares:

> We have been led to acknowledge...the reality of one another's churchly life. But this gives us no ground for concluding that the historic continuity of ordinations is an irrelevance. On the contrary it is an element in the proper visible form of the Church's unity in space and time, to the end of the age and the ends of the earth. We, therefore, affirm that the ways by which our separated churches are brought into unity must be such as to ensure (a) that the reality of God's gift of ministry to the churches in their separation is unambiguously acknowledged; and (b) that the continuity of succession in ordination with the undivided Church is—so far as lies in our power—visibly restored and maintained.[25]

---

[23] *Journal of the General Convention, 1979*, p. C-46. Cf. J. Robert Wright, editor, *A Communion of Communions: One Eucharistic Fellowship* (New York: Seabury Press, 1979), pp. 3-29, and especially pp. 23-24 for application to Lutheran-Episcopal dialogue, and pp. 185-211 for the essay on "The Concordat Relationships."

[24] *The COCU Consensus: In Quest of a Church of Christ Uniting*, edited by Gerald F. Moede (1984), pp. 48-50.

[25] *God's Reign & Our Unity:* The Report of the Anglican-Reformed International Commission 1984 (London: SPCK, 1984), p. 57, Par. 90.

The Standing Commission on Ecumenical Relations of the Episcopal Church reassessed the relation of the historic episcopate to apostolic succession in light of the ecumenical dialogues, and in 1976 produced what it called a "working statement" which acknowledged that "apostolicity has many strands."[26] This general approach was then formally approved when the 1982 General Convention adopted a resolution on "Principles of Unity" which reaffirmed the Chicago-Lambeth Quadrilateral and in explication thereof broadened the fourth point to embrace the concept of apostolicity:

> Apostolicity is evidenced in continuity with the teaching, the ministry, and the mission of the apostles. Apostolic teaching must, under the guidance of the Holy Spirit, be founded upon the Holy Scriptures and the ancient fathers and creeds, making its proclamation of Jesus Christ and his Gospel for each new age consistent with those sources, not merely reproducing them in a transmission of verbal identity. Apostolic ministry exists to promote, safeguard and serve apostolic teaching. All Christians are called to this ministry by their Baptism. In order to serve, lead and enable this ministry, some are set apart and ordained in the historic orders of Bishop, Presbyter, and Deacon. We understand the historic episcopate as central to this apostolic ministry and essential to the reunion of the Church, even as we acknowledge "the spiritual reality of the ministries of those Communions which do not possess the Episcopate" (Lambeth Appeal 1920, Section 7). Apostolic mission is itself a succession of apostolic teaching and ministry inherited from

---

[26] See Chapter II, Paragraph 19, above for the full text of this section of the report.

the past and carried into the present and future. Bishops in apostolic succession are, therefore, the focus and personal symbols of this inheritance and mission as they preach and teach the Gospel and summon the people of God to their mission of worship and service.[27]

The 1985 General Convention directed Episcopal participants in Lutheran-Episcopal Dialogue III to advocate paragraph 53(a) of *Baptism, Eucharist and Ministry* as "a way forward" toward the mutual recognition of the ordained ministries of our respective churches:

> Churches which have preserved the episcopal succession are asked to recognize both the apostolic content of the ordained ministry which exists in churches which have not maintained such succession and also the existence in these churches of a ministry of *episkope* in various forms.

D. The Prayer Book Teaching on the Episcopate

This review of the ministry of the historic episcopate in the Episcopal Church as a Province of the Anglican Communion may conclude with statements on the meaning of the episcopate taken from the Book of Common Prayer (U.S.A., 1979). "An Outline of the Faith," after identifying the ministers of the Church as "lay persons, bishops, priests, and deacons," each of whom represents Christ in a particular way within the unity of the one Body, describes the ministry of the bishop:

> The ministry of a bishop is to represent Christ and his Church, particularly as apostle, chief priest, and pastor of a diocese; to guard the faith, unity, and discipline of the whole Church; to pro-

---

[27] *Journal of the General Convention 1982*, pp. C-56–C-57. On the Anglican understanding of apostolicity, see also *Anglican-Orthodox Dialogue: The Dublin Agreed Statement 1984* (St. Vladimir's Seminary Press, 1985), pp. 13-14.

claim the Word of God; to act in Christ's name for the reconciliation of the world and the building up of the Church; and to ordain others to continue Christ's ministry.[28]

In the rite for "The Ordination of a Bishop" the presiding bishop addresses the bishop-elect with this description of the episcopal office during the examination before the consecration:

> ...The people have chosen you and have affirmed their trust in you by acclaiming your election. A bishop in God's holy Church is called to be one with the apostles in proclaiming Christ's resurrection and interpreting the Gospel, and to testify to Christ's sovereignty as Lord of lords and King of kings.
>
> You are called to guard the faith, unity, and discipline of the Church; to celebrate and to provide for the administration of the sacraments of the New Covenant; to ordain priests and deacons and to join in ordaining bishops; and to be in all things a faithful pastor and wholesome example for the entire flock of Christ.
>
> With your fellow bishops you will share in the leadership of the Church throughout the world. Your heritage is the faith of patriarchs, prophets, apostles, and martyrs, and those of every generation who have looked to God in hope. Your joy will be to follow him who came, not to be served, but to serve, and to give his life a ransom for many.[29]

During the Prayer of Consecration the presiding bishop and

---

[28] Book of Common Prayer (U.S.A., 1979), p. 855 ("An Outline of the Faith").

[29] *Ibid.*, p. 517. In the emphases of Irenaeus, Ignatius, and Cyprian, respectively, each of these three paragraphs is mirrored in the writings of the early church.

other bishops lay their hands upon the head of the bishop-elect and say together:

> Therefore, Father, make *N.* a bishop in your Church. Pour out upon *him* the power of your princely Spirit, whom you bestowed upon your beloved Son Jesus Christ, with whom he endowed the apostles, and by whom your Church is built up in every place, to the glory and unceasing praise of your Name.[30]

The "Preface to the Ordination Rites" states the intention and purpose of this church to maintain and continue the threefold ministry:

> The Holy Scriptures and ancient Christian writers make it clear that from the apostles' time, there have been different ministries within the Church. In particular, since the time of the New Testament, three distinct orders of ordained ministers have been characteristic of Christ's holy catholic Church. First, there is the order of bishops who carry on the apostolic work of leading, supervising, and uniting the Church. Secondly, associated with them are the presbyters, or ordained elders, in subsequent times generally known as priests. Together with the bishops, they take part in the governance of the Church, in the carrying out of its missionary and pastoral work, and in the preaching of the Word of God and administering his holy Sacraments. Thirdly, there are deacons who assist bishops and priests in all of this work. It is also a special responsibility of dea-

---

[30] *Ibid.*, p. 521. Much of this wording is paraphrased from the earliest prayer for the ordination of a bishop, *The Apostolic Tradition* of Hippolytus, dating from the early third century.

cons to minister in Christ's name to the poor, the sick, the suffering, and the helpless.

The persons who are chosen and recognized by the Church as being called by God to the ordained ministry are admitted to these sacred orders by solemn prayer and the laying on of episcopal hands. It has been, and is, the intention and purpose of this Church to maintain and continue these three orders; and for this purpose these services of ordination and consecration are appointed. No persons are allowed to exercise the offices of bishop, priest, or deacon in this Church unless they are so ordained, or have already received such ordination with the laying on of hands by bishops who are themselves duly qualified to confer Holy Orders.

It is also recognized and affirmed that the threefold ministry is not the exclusive property of this portion of Christ's catholic Church, but is a gift from God for the nurture of his people and the proclamation of his Gospel everywhere. Accordingly, the manner of ordaining in this Church is to be such as has been, and is, most generally recognized by Christian people as suitable for the conferring of the sacred orders of bishop, priest, and deacon.[31]

---

[31] *Ibid*, p. 510.

II

Sixth Paper

The Practice of Episcopal Ministry in the Episcopal Church from a Bishop's Point of View

by The Rt. Rev. Roger J. White
Bishop of Milwaukee

The Ordinal of the Episcopal Church—U.S.A. is found as a part of the 1979 Book of Common Prayer (BCP) and will be the basis of these personal reflections on the practice of episcopal ministry. More specifically, these observations are rooted in the Prayer Book Service entitled, "The Ordination of a Bishop" (BCP, p. 512, 1979 edition) and will focus on what the "Preface to the Ordination Rites" describes as follows: "First, there is the order of bishops who carry on the apostolic work of leading, supervising, and uniting the Church" (BCP, p. 510). These personal reflections come out of eight years' experience as a bishop and only one year as a Provincial President with fourteen dioceses in that provincial jurisdiction.

Although much of what bishops do in practice is taken for granted and is at best only "soft data," these observations will stem from my own evaluative process of the practice of episcopal ministry, taking seven clearly discernable areas of accountability from the ordinal for the Ordination of a Bishop, and is thus based on specific promises and understandings established at the time of ordination.

In the examination of a bishop (BCP, p. 517) the bishop-elect is reminded that he or she is "called to be one with the apostles in proclaiming Christ's resurrection and in interpreting the Gospel, and to testify to Christ's sovereignty as Lord of lords and King of kings," a calling shared by all the baptized. More specifically, the examination calls upon the bishop-elect as a bishop to do the following: "to guard the faith, unity, and discipline of the Church; to celebrate and to provide for the administration of the sacraments of the New Covenant; to ordain priests and deacons and to join in ordaining bishops; and to be in all things a faithful pastor and wholesome example for the entire flock of Christ. With your fellow bishops, you will share in the leadership of the Church throughout the world." In all of this awesome responsibility the bishop-elect is reminded that such tasks are not performed alone, but that their heritage is "the faith of patriarchs, prophets, apostles, and martyrs, and those of every generation who have looked to God in hope. Your joy will be to follow him who came, not to be served, but to serve, and to give his life a ransom for many." The bishop-elect, being so persuaded of the call, responds affirmatively to a list of questions from other bishops present at the ordination, which are based on the summary of responsibilities, outlined in this service and already described.

In the polity of the Episcopal Church—U.S.A., a bishop is elected by the clergy and the elected lay representative from all parishes in the electing diocese, who come to a concurrence in both orders as to who should serve them as bishop. The hope in this process is that the diocese—represented by its clergy and lay delegates—may with the guidance of the Holy Spirit discern and call out one to be their spiritual leader.

The bishop is seen in practice as being the head of a diocese which is made up of people in all orders, laity, bishops, priests and deacons in a local geographical area. The "local church" is that clustering of parishes and institutions and their members who form a diocese of which the bishop is "chief priest and pastor."

As we examine the pastoral role and actual responsibilities of a bishop in the Episcopal Church, it soon becomes abundantly clear that we as bishops have failed to address these roles with consistency and have tended to depend on local custom, the personal style and charisma of the individual called and elected to this order, and what has become acceptable by way of the practice of episcopal ministry in the local church, the diocese.

The reality of this failure to address the specifics of the calling has brought about not only confusion of role but, in many cases, unacceptable stress on individual bishops. Such lack of clarity finds bishops wrestling with priorities for the focus of their ministry. "Am I a bishop of the whole Church, international (Catholic) or of this Province of the Church, or of this diocese?" "Am I a community leader in the wider community and not just the ecclesiastical community and, if so, what is that role?" "Am I priest and pastor first and foremost to the clergy of the diocese or 'shepherd' to the whole diocese—clergy and laity?" "Am I chief of a diocesan staff or administrator of a whole diocese?" "How can I be mediator, pastor, liturgical president, teacher, conflict manager and also judge?" Such unresolved questions often lead to confusion and poor performance and cry out for clarification and some specific focus for the various areas of responsibility.

In a very real sense, bishops exercise a catholic role, which they soon sense as they gather with all other Anglican bishops every ten years for the Lambeth Conference. Bishops also act as liaisons with other churches as they work for the unity of the whole Church. Most bishops are called upon to chair or to be members of several national Church committees, giving them opportunities to be bishops "of the whole Church." There is also a sense in which bishops are called upon to lead in their local communities as they attempt to proclaim the Gospel in cities in their own states, that there may be leadership for the Church, as it seeks to serve Christ in service to others and as it strives for justice and reconciliation. The bishop often becomes the focus of official statements and is looked to for leadership in addressing community issues.

For most bishops of our Church, the end result is the narrowing of these concerns into three very general and somewhat vague areas:
- Administration
- Policy making and implementation
- Addressing crises with clergy and parishes or both

A particular diocese is led to ask what do they want their bishop to do and to be—and to set priorities for the bishop's time based on the general areas just described. As we put such priorities together with the different local traditions and the bishop's gifts, interests, and personality, we begin to determine a local style of practice for the episcopate, of a particular bishop and diocese. This practical approach does not ignore, but takes into account, what may be described as "the deep and weighty traditions about the meaning of the office of bishop" which are inherited from the tradition of the Church catholic down the ages. Amazingly, out of what may appear to be an unclear basis, even out of such confusion, emerges much outstanding episcopal leadership both locally, in the Province, and throughout the Anglican Communion of Churches.

In attempting to reflect on the practical aspects of the episcopate, I am going to utilize an outline of a bishop's functions and responsibilities derived from the Ordinal which enables this paper to be much more specific and focused than the three general areas of administration, policy making and implementation, and crisis intervention, which have already been outlined.

These specific areas of responsibility and, therefore, accountability are described in the following seven descriptions.

i) Example, model, standard setter—"icon"

> "To be in all things a faithful pastor and wholesome example for the entire flock of Christ"; (BCP, p. 517) to "be faithful in prayer, and in the study of Holy Scriptures that you may have the mind of Christ." (BCP, p. 518)

As example, model or setter of the standard—"icon," we find ourselves describing the bishop's personal and spiritual life style. The call is for the bishop, who stands as president of every diocesan Eucharist, to be "a wholesome example to the entire flock"— an awesome responsibility. But a call followed, as the bishop is anchored in the presence of God through faithfulness in prayer and the study of scripture, that the bishop may indeed have the mind of Christ and truly be a spiritual leader for all the people whom the bishop is called to serve as pastor and priest. Frequently today this practice of prayer and study of scripture takes place, not only privately but also when bishops gather together in community or when bishops meet with clergy in the diocese, specifically for this mutual scriptural reflection and prayer. The expectation is that the bishop will work earnestly toward becoming a person of deep personal faith and commitment; a person of integrity of faith; one who lives with hope in God's promises and has a love and respect for all of God's creation.

ii) Teacher, preacher and visionary

To "boldly proclaim and interpret the Gospel of Christ, enlightening the minds and stirring up the conscience of your people." (BCP, p.518)

As a visionary who teaches and preaches, being bold in proclamations, an enlightener of people's minds and the stirrer up of conscience, we look for a bishop whose people are perceived to be increasingly inclined to wrestle with the theological dimensions of the issues of the day, and can attribute this partly to the witness of their bishop.

If the bishop is attempting to wrestle with this particular aspect of his or her role, religious perspectives on ethical or moral issues will be sought from the bishop by the people of the diocese, but also from the wider community, including its media. The bishop becomes recognized as a religious leader by the political, judicial and commercial interests in the wider community encompassed by the diocese. At the same time, the bishop is held in high esteem as a theologian and prophet in the diocese and the wider Christian fellowship. Ideally, the bishop would be one who is perceived to be creating the climate within which people are inspired toward life-changing witness and growth in Christ as they deepen and expand their understanding of the Gospel.

The Catechism of the Church, in answering what the ministry of a bishop is, responds in part that a bishop is "to act in Christ's name for the reconciliation of the world and the building up of the Church" (BCP, p. 855). This role of reconciler, negotiator, and "builder" of the body is frequently exercised in bringing con-flicted parties together in parishes, in the diocese and, when called upon, between parties within the Church nationally. This ministry of the bishop seeks to avoid schism in the Body of Christ, moving us to reconciliation and a refocusing on what our mission is to be, as those called by God to be one in seeking to do His will. The bishop finds his ministry as healer to be vital for the unity and health of the Church—local, diocesan and national—and even in the worldwide body of the followers of Christ, who may find themselves radically opposed to their brothers and sis-ters on some issues of faith and practice.

"The bishop does not need to do everything personally, but to see that every necessary thing does happen. The bishop must hold up the vision, articulate the basic theology, and help pro-vide the institutional structures by which it can occur." (House of Bishops' draft pastoral, "The Ministry of Bishops," p. 28, sec-tion 34.)

iii) Supporter of the Total Ministry of the Church

To "encourage and support all baptized people in their gifts and ministries" through nurture, prayer and sacraments. (BCP, p. 518)

As the bishop identifies and pursues an important role as the one who encourages all the baptized in ministry, the diocese becomes "a community in ministry" rather than a "community gathered around a minister." The diocese becomes a place where the concept of the ministry of all the baptized (total ministry) is evident in all aspects of diocesan and parish life and ministry. Such leadership by the bishop evolves toward a visible increase in the number of clergy who see their work as supporting and enabling lay leaders and the ministries of all baptized people, rather than feeling that they must do all the ministry themselves. All of this participation in the ministry of the Church is support-ed through nurture, prayer, sacrament and the strong and enthu-siastic encouragement of the bishop.

iv) Leader

To "guard the faith, unity and discipline of the Church." (BCP, p. 518)

As guardian of the faith, unity and discipline of the Church, the bishop is seen as "the first citizen" in the diocese with these very specific responsibilities. The practical manifestations of this important role emerge as the diocese is seen in the whole Church as a place where the local church is deeply rooted in Anglican tradition and is a clear advocate of unity and dialogue even in the face of controversy over contemporary issues.

The bishop is also perceived as a person who is consistent and fair in dealing with the disciplinary treatment of both clergy and laity and not judgmental or condescending. As guardian of the faith the bishop is welcome at the time of visitation to a parish and high value is placed on this opportunity to meet and greet the bishop. Confused as the bishop's role may be as pastor and on occasion judge, the clergy and their families avail themselves of the bishop's pastoral and crisis skills, or those of his or her staff, thus enabling the bishop to be pastor and guardian of the faith, unity, and above all, the discipline of the Church as such need arises.

v) General Church Management

To "share with your fellow bishops in the government of the whole Church." (BCP, p. 518)

This responsibility involves the need to share in the councils of the whole Church and to be an effective administrator. The fulfilling of this broad area of accountability is seen in very practical terms as the diocesan bishop is recognized by peers in the House of Bishops as a person of integrity, principle, and often solid common sense. Diocesan bishops are called upon to represent the Primate both within the life of the Church and in liaison with other churches. Bishops also join together in the governance of the local Province of the Church, in the House of Bishops, in the General Convention of the Episcopal Church, and in the

Lambeth Conference. They do indeed exercise that ministry of participating in the councils of the Church and in relating to partner churches at home and abroad.

On a very practical level, in the diocese, the bishop oversees the deployment of volunteers in various diocesan units, so that they perceive that the Church is making effective use of their time and talents. As administrator of the diocese, the bishop or the bishop's staff should be seen as contributing to the future welfare of parishes as new clergy are selected, as personnel practices of hiring and conditions of employment are set in accord with top standards in our society. The bishop's office should be seen as a warm, friendly environment which is efficient and serves the parishes and people of the diocese. In its fiscal responsibility the diocesan office needs to be exemplary, exceeding all pertinent Church standards so that the bishop and his staff may be above reproach and fully accountable to the diocese whom they serve.

vi) Team Leader

> To "sustain" and "take counsel with" other presbyters, to "guide and strengthen the deacons and all others who minister in the Church." (BCP, p. 518)

In the role of team leader, the bishop is seen in what is described in our culture as "the coach." It is the role of encouraging high morale among the clergy, the inspirer of a positive and creative team spirit among presbyters, deacons and all the leaders in the diocese. Such team leadership is on track when diocesan meetings attract good attendance and have as part of their make-up opportunity for participants to be creative, to have fun, to grow in Christian faith, and to build close community with one another, while at the same time being the place for new ideas, progress, and projects which can be seeded at the grass roots of the diocese.

If the bishop is an effective team leader in practice, the diocese will become a place where clergy will desire to minister, where others will be attracted from other dioceses, where both clergy and laity will sense that they have contributions to make to the life of the diocese and are pleased and proud to be a part with their bishop of the diocesan team.

vii) Servanthood in the World

> To "be merciful to all, show compassion to the poor and strangers, and defend those who have no helper." (BCP, p. 518)

As the example of servanthood and the advocate, or defender, of the outcast, the bishop has an overwhelming task in today's society. But the practical aspects of this particular portion of the bishop's calling give great opportunity for the bishop to follow our Lord in ministry.

Such ministry shows itself in the life of the bishop's diocese as it becomes well understood that, in this diocese, the Christian Church has a bias on the side of the poor, the disenfranchised, and the downtrodden. That the diocese involves itself under the leadership of the bishop in community and neighborhood outreach ministries which continue to expand, supported by money and volunteers from throughout the diocese. That the diocese is a place which is aware of the need for worldwide relief and willingly responds. That Episcopalians standing with their bishop stand tall in the public eye as champions of the poor, the hungry and the victims of society's malfunctions or alienations, thus showing together compassion and following in the footsteps of Jesus Christ.

"The episcopate is a unique, distinct and different but not 'superior' order in the Church, functioning both individually and collegially, calling each parish or congregation beyond itself to those wider obligations and responsibilities that transcend what could otherwise become a parochialism or congregationalism that might be inward-looking and narrowly based. A proper doctrine of the Church, or ecclesiology, thus depends upon a proper ministry of the episcopate." (House of Bishops' draft pastoral, "The Ministry of Bishops," p. 29, section 36.)

This attempt to be descriptive of a bishop's practical exercise of ministry based on these seven areas distilled from the Ordinal is not fully comprehensive, which leads us to conclude that the "job description" is variable, vast, and somewhat overwhelming!

Presidency of the Eucharist

All of these practical manifestations of a bishop's work are to be anchored in the bishop's role as president of the Eucharist. For a bishop is not simply a corporate executive with an ecclesiastical veneer, he or she does not preside over a corporation, but over "a people" to which the bishop also belongs. This is a relationship of bishop as "principal icon" or "first citizen" of a called people rather than an imported manager. This relationship is embodied in the bishop's presiding at the Eucharistic meal and at the Rites of Initiation when the church family gathers for such celebrations. This role "sets the bishop *within* the community, standing *with* the laity, the presbyters, and the deacons in the action by which the whole assembly enacts its common identity in Christ." (House of Bishops' draft pastoral, "The Ministry of Bishops," p. 30, section 38.)

"Thus the bishop's presidency at the Eucharist intimates and symbolizes the proper *form* of episcopal government—it is essentially collegial and conciliar in character, whether within or beyond the local Church." (House of Bishops' draft pastoral, "The Ministry of Bishops," p. 31.)

And so within the context of Eucharistic celebration, we see the bishop's role evolve—to preside, lead and to oversee the people, not necessarily being a direct participant alongside every baptized person in every area of the Church work and ministry, for such is totally impractical. But rather, to provide through priestly ministry the sacraments of the Church, through the teaching ministry of the bishop to provide an example and vision for formation of adults and children through the ministry of a multitude of teachers exercising their God-given gifts in ministry. As leader, to share with others in leadership of the Church throughout the world and to sustain and take counsel with the presbyters and to guide and strengthen the deacons and others. (BCP, p. 518) Thus fulfilling the call of the bishop, together in ministry with all God's called and baptized people, "to preside, lead and oversee," grounded and sustained by the Holy Spirit, the daily prayer of the Church and the support of the fellowship of Christ's body, the Church. With such broad oversight perhaps Ignatius of Antioch gave us wise guidance in Trallians 2:2, "Do nothing without the bishop." Advice which may also be helpful in reverse—'let bishops do nothing without the whole Church'!

There cannot be in the experience of the Episcopal Church a prescription for a set style of episcopacy that will be acceptable or workable in every local church. However, the Ordinal of the Book of Common Prayer gives us sufficient pegs on which to hang the basic characteristics of episcopal ministry as it is practiced with creative individuality in the dioceses of this Church. All of this ministry is being experienced with the premise that it can be carried out only as we turn to the Lord for help, support and guidance.

Postscript for Discussion: Affirmations and Problems

This postscript can be a mechanism for directing some discussion on the practical implications of the exercise of episcopal ministry.

There are many portions of episcopal ministry which are *affirming* and as such, they need to be highlighted.

i) There is often a real sense of being a part of the wider church community, of being a bishop of God's church.

ii) The support of clergy and laity is immensely affirming. Especially is that true as biblical study, reflection and prayer is shared.

iii) Support is also found in the establishment of close ecumenical relations with peers in one's own diocese and in other parts of the world and in other church communities, such as this relationship of the Episcopal Church with the Russian Orthodox Church.

iv) In a surprising way, being "first citizen" does afford many opportunities to be a pastor to both clergy and laity. To become close to people in their journey of faith.

v) There appears to be a never-ending procession of creative ways by which we can apply the Gospel and proclaim the good news; such is always a joy and privilege.

vi) To be seen as "principal icon," especially as president of the Eucharist, whether in a small parish gathering or when the whole diocese gathers to celebrate at its annual Convention.

vii) There is continual joy and a sense of achievement as we exercise our ministry as chief evangelists, encouraging others to follow Christ and to follow in the steps of Him who came to serve.

viii) As community leader there is a sense of support from one's people as we try to live out what we say we believe in the communities where God has placed us.

The other side of the coin presents some *problems* in the practice of being a bishop and these issues are now raised for discussion.

A) The uncertainty created by the lack of clarity and expectations of the role of bishop.

B) The above issue is especially problematic with the issues of authority in the life of the whole Church and how to exercise such authority in this episcopal ministry.

C) Clarity is also lacking in expectations of a bishop as he or she exercises ministry. Who teaches bishops, who deals with stress created by unclear—and at times impossible—expectations?

D) The administrative aspects of the role seem to continue to escalate, leading to frustration because of time management and the desire to balance the practice of episcopal ministry with other aspects of the calling.

E) There is a growing demand on bishops to be directly involved in intervening in clergy crises, lay and clergy disputes; conflict within the life of a parish, and single issue groups who focus only on winning and not on dialogue and negotiations.

F) A bishop's schedule and the lack of regular routine are not conducive to a stable and developing spiritual life.

G) There is little time to seek and offer the vision—to be anchored in God's presence and to discern God's will.

H) Many aspects of the ministry lead to isolation and a sense of loneliness.

I) Attempting to be open and fair to a widening cross-section of theological viewpoints becomes more difficult. The bishop as "guardian of the faith" finds such tension most difficult to hold together.

J) Being "guardian of the faith, unity and discipline of the Church" in a society focused on "self" is the cause of misunderstanding, and thus stress.

K) The loss of status in society and in the local community is a growing issue. Bishops are less frequently called upon to give counsel, advice, theological perspective, or opinions on moral and ethical issues in communities of their jurisdiction.

L) Family pressures of the bishop's spouse and family for a fair share of quality time when demands on a bishop's time seem to continue to grow.

M) Finally, attempts to be the advocate for the poor and outcast in our society and in the world are overwhelming and a continuous drain on the ability of bishops to solicit the support of volunteers and resources to address these growing maladies.

Such are some of the positive aspects of this episcopal ministry, with offsetting problems, which no doubt will remain with us as we call upon God to be with us as we attempt to serve as bishops.

12

Seventh Paper

And Who Is My Bishop? A Priest's Response to Bishop White

by The Rev. Kortright Davis
Rector of Holy Comforter Church
Diocese of Washington
and Professor of Theology, Howard University School of Divinity

The basic premise on which Bishop White's paper seeks to examine the practice of ministry among bishops is that the service of "Ordination of a Bishop" in The Book of Common Prayer signifies the beginning of a bishop's ministry; and that the "seven clearly discernable areas of accountability from the ordinal" provide the grid on which the episcopal office is to be understood and assessed. While this premise may be tenable for a bishop, it is hardly tenable for one who is not; for there are many factors involved in the stages leading up to the service of ordination which are carried over into the episcopal career.

The service of ordination is not a liturgical expression of discontinuity with one's past, nor even a creation of a radically new beginning in one's personal development. The service of ordination is the canonical culmination of an ecclesiastical process of selection, usually fraught with many searches and searchings of heart, and generally accepted as a victory for the successful candidate's lobby-group, or as an affirmation of the bishop-elect's career and known public and ecclesial character thus far. (The ecclesiastical color purple, or crimson, sometimes has a way of doing strange things to the characters and personalities of those ordained souls who have been accustomed to wearing black most of their lives! Perhaps that is why Roman Catholic Bishops use it more sparingly than their Anglican counterparts in non-liturgical settings.)

There is no probationary period, no episcopal novitiate, no post-ordination caveat. Ordination cannot be undone. Both church and newly ordained are stuck with each other for life; many entrances, but no exits. Furthermore, in spite of the multiplicity of prayers to the Holy Spirit before and during an episcopal election, it is clear that "the best" candidates do not always win, and the political process *in urbe* often finds a faithful ally in the electoral process *in ecclesia*. This should never be thought of as surprising, since it would be ludicrous to expect that the ecclesial mind and the political mind operate at cross-purposes in the same individual. For even if it has been often said that the Church of England is virtually the Conservative Party at prayer, I have never heard it said that the Episcopal Church is reminiscent of a political party at play; but the electoral process for bishops often seems to come very close.

It must, therefore, be fully acknowledged that the practice of episcopal ministry in the Episcopal Church is basically dependent less on the principles of the Ordinal and more on the predilections of the diocesan conventions, the aspirations of crypto-applicants, nominees and candidates, the expectations of the Ecclesio-Political Action Committees (EPAC's) which lobby successfully, and the pilgrimage of vocational and denominational formation through which candidates reach for the rochet, or try on the miter. The emergence of bishops in the Episcopal process is generally the result of getting the bishop you negotiate and not necessarily the bishop you need. This is why many persons at electoral conventions are cynical about the prayer for the guidance of the Holy Spirit, on the second and third ballots, when voters have already made up their minds, or candidates have already caucused. It seems to me, therefore, that the full scenario of how bishops are made must be taken into account before we analyze how they function. For even if it may be said of the ordained ministry as a whole that "many are called but few are chosen," the present danger in the Episcopal Church is that our electoral process is driving our critics to say that "many are chosen but few are called."

It is important to make this point early, for Bishop White has chosen to concentrate on the liturgical and institutional forms of episcopacy, while those of us who are not bishops, who have to work closely with them, and under their guidance, must be eternally vigilant about where bishops come from and how they ascend their thrones. Clearly, persons are not born to be bishops, nor do they simply achieve bishop's status; but it cannot be that the office is thrust on them either. The centrality of the episcopal office for the life and tradition of the Catholic Faith is far more important than that. Bishop White's paper rightly insists that a bishop is much more than the seven aspects outlined in the Ordination Service of the BCP. He does so by pointing to a number of "affirmations" and "problems" of ministry at the conclusion of his paper, which actually constitute the most helpful and interesting section of his whole discussion. This is not to suggest that the seven areas are not to be taken seriously. Indeed, bishops are expected to be Examples, Teachers, Supports, Leaders, Managers, Team-persons, Servants, but there is surely much more to the episcopal office than this. But before we look at some of these other factors, let us comment on some of the points raised by Bishop White.

Ripples from the White Paper

What may seem a small point to some is not so small to others; this has to do with language. A bishop has to watch the language being used. This was most poignantly driven home to me whenever I heard the late Bishop John Walker (of Washington) refrain from using the word "tall" as a metaphor for greatness or rectitude. This was presumably because he was somewhat less than a six-footer, and was always sensitive to others who lacked height. Whenever Bishop Walker came across that word in a liturgical setting, or elsewhere in public proclamation, he would find a more acceptable and comprehensive word to substitute. Bishop

White's use of it in the phrase "that Episcopalians standing with their bishop stand tall in the public eye…" is, therefore, less than fortunate, especially for those who lack physical height. I am not sure what is the term used for those who are discriminated against because they are not tall, but I know most assuredly that the use of language which even unwittingly oppresses those whom God has made in a particular way—race, gender, height, age, physiognomy—falls below the level of pastoral acceptability. My concern here is not to put Bishop White on the spot; it is simply to point to a critical area of a bishop's life, namely, episcopal utterances. The words of bishops have far more currency throughout the church than those from any other source. Such is the nature of the episcopal ethos. When the bishop speaks, everybody listens! So the bishop has to be careful to speak with everybody in mind.

There are several other areas in White's paper which require brief comments, and I shall proceed to offer them before discussing some of the broader issues which presbyters like myself hold up in answer to the question: "And who is my Bishop?"

1. Bishop White must have had it in mind, but it certainly did not show up in his paper: the basic question of the mission of God for the Church. His only reference to "mission" is to "our mission," as being synonymous with "agenda," or "job description." There is no evidence of an underlying concept of the Church as being constantly on God's mission, trying to discover what that true mission really is. White follows the Draft Pastoral *The Ministry of Bishops* in placing emphasis on "the vision." He quotes thus: "The bishop must hold up the vision, articulate the basic theology, and help provide the institutional structures by which it can occur." Yet towards the end of his paper he suggests: "There is little time to seek and offer the vision—to be anchored in God's presence and to discern God's will." There can hardly be any doubt that the bishop is called to be the leader in a missionary movement called "church," more than one who is called to be a visionary of the divine will. Episcopal ordination does not create a special hotline to the heavenly courts.

It is precisely because the bishop is a person on mission that the dynamics of uncertainty about the will of God overwhelm the politics of certainty in the static institutionalism of the church. For ministry that is fired by the faithful response to God's constant call to mission in, through, and beyond the church, can never be held hostage to the predilections of those who would make bold to define and shape God's vision in and for the Church. The bishop is called to be the chief "icon" of this fact, and the staff (crozier), as the symbol of episcopal office, is a tool for mission and movement forward and not a crutch for standing still, or steady. Bishop White is so obviously consumed by the pressures of the institution in the local church (diocese) that he neglects to focus on the primacy of being sent by God, first through baptism, and three times over through ordination. As an "icon" of God's mission, then, the bishop shares in the vision that is being shaped by God continuously, but the bishop must never seek to shape it nor even to service it. God does not take so big a risk with our human frailty by leaving the servicing or the shaping of God's vision for Re-Creation (Creation redeemed) up to us; we are simply called to be a part of it, and we often "mess up." In any event, it is the missional character of the episcopal office by which it is rooted firmly in what we call the Apostolic Succession. You cannot claim to be a successor to the Apostles if you are not willing to make *mission* (the fact of being sent by God) your fundamentally existential character.

2. While it is evident that Bishop White lays great stress on the bishop as a leader in various spheres of life in the Church, it is not so obvious where he stands on the question of power. How much power does an Episcopal bishop really have? What are the limits to that power? Who shares that power? Or, worse yet, from whom is it really derived? It is fashionable to speak about the moral authority which bishops possess, and this is often mentioned with the presumed force of canonical jurisprudence lurking somewhere in the background. But the basic question of power still raises its head time and again in the life and function of the bishop. I suppose that one way to arrive at a working answer is to observe how few bishops are willing to continue to function as bishops after they have demitted office. There is something which drives them from lingering around after they have decided to move on, or move out; so that matters of failing health or polity usually take precedence over any residual urges to continue to serve indefinitely as bishops in the Episcopal Church. It should, therefore, come as no surprise to hear Episcopal bishops lament to their counterparts in the African Methodist Episcopal Church, for example, about how much power the latter exercise in comparison with the former.

The power issue comes more sharply into focus if we insist on retaining the image of the bishop as a "prince of the Church." The prince is a ruler in a specific domain (diocese?) and, therefore, is expected to function with a certain amount of authority. But times have changed: principles of democracy and human entitlement have swept over the terrain; attitudes towards litigation have become the dominant ethos for putting legal might over moral right; church business has taken on the excitement of imitating corporate business; those who vote bishops into office often expect bishops to remember them favorably and respect them highly. Given all these realities, how much authority is any bishop expected to exercise under such conditions? How much power does the bishop have left?

Bishop White refers to the bishop as "the first citizen" in the diocese, but it is necessary to recognize that such primacy has more to do with traditional places of honor (liturgical processions, church functions, and the like) than with the primacy of power to decide, implement, and evaluate results. It is an abiding paradox in the Episcopal Church that a church which takes episcopacy so seriously as to put it into its very title has to live with the centers of power located more in the congregation than in the episcopate. The harsh reality is that the Episcopal Church is far more congregationalist in behavior and impulsion than we are often prepared to admit. Episcopal bishops know this only too well. Bishop White rightly admits to the bishop's role as pastor and "on occasion judge" as being confused. It seems to me that the confusion revolves around the question of power and authority in the church, compounded by the universal quest of bishops to become all things to all people, as a facet of their pastoral motif. In the final analysis, it is not so much a question of how much power bishops really have, but rather a question of how much power they really need, and what they need it for. One would hope that the answer would lie somewhere in the direction of bishops needing as much power as is necessary for them to minister as effective enablers of Christian freedom, but not as agents of sacred coercion. It is very unlikely that the Episcopal Church, in its present climate, will be able to arrive anywhere near a consensus on such an issue, which is nevertheless so centrifugal to its life and witness.

3. My Christocentric soul instinctively cringes when there appears to be no accountability to the meaning of the person and work of Jesus Christ as a paradigm for mission and ministry, whether ordained or not. It is true that Bishop White expects that the bishop "may indeed have the mind of Christ," and that the bishop may also encourage "others to follow Christ and to follow in the steps of Him who came to serve." But this is hardly a sufficient basis for the self-understanding of what the office and work of the bishop is all about. Not even in the section on the Eucharist does Bishop White make any attempt to establish an ontological identity between the mystical personhood of Christ and the sacerdotal personhood of the bishop as "president" of the Eucharist. One must also point out that the bishop is offering (or presiding at) the Eucharist not so much because of an episcopal character, but because of the sacerdotal character. The bishop is already the priest, who has been offering the sacrifice of the Eucharist on behalf of the faithful before episcopal ordination. We need to be very careful that we never lead ourselves into suggesting that when the priest offers up the Eucharist there is something about its validity and efficacy that is lacking because the priest is not also a bishop.

The Christological issue is still not settled in Bishop White's paper, for he missed a good opportunity to exegete the answers which the candidate makes in the Examination in the Ordinal. In the eight answers which the Bishop-elect makes, four of them are directly related to Jesus Christ. For example: (Question) "Will you accept this call and fulfill this trust in obedience to Christ?" (Answer) "I will obey Christ, and will serve in his name." Or again: (Question) "Will you be faithful in prayer, and in the study of Holy Scripture, that you may have the mind of Christ?" (Answer) "I will, for he is my help." The significance of such answers is far more critical to the self-understanding of the bishop's character than the insistence on the sovereignty of Jesus as Lord of lords and King of kings.

Those who met the Carpenter of Nazareth in person over-whelmingly agreed that he tried his best to steer clear of such imperial claims, or at least to deflect them into the meaning of self-emptying service. It was as if he were pre-warning "their lordships" (the bishops) not to use his Lordship as a pretext for their own pretensions. "He that wants to be chief among you," he said, "let him be as the servant." No, the Christological challenge for bishops everywhere is to demonstrate as faithfully as possible what is involved in being conspicuous "fools for Christ"; for when they do it well, those whom they lead are less embarrassed or hesitant to give it a try. It really works!

4. It is not without significance that, as a bishop in the richest church in the richest country in the world, Bishop White is fairly explicit in his bias towards the poor, while he omits any mention of the rich. This is particularly interesting since it is a well-known secret that the Episcopal Church as a whole has never mastered the social graces in the art of dealing with the poor. Indeed there are some who speak of Episcopalianism as an expensive social pasttime (not everyone can afford it), especially as the Episcopal Church has been commonly regarded as a refuge for the upwardly mobile in American socio-cultural habits. Thus, although it is true that the Christian Church as a whole "has a bias on the side of the poor, the disenfranchised, and the down-trodden," Bishop White must surely be aware of the insurmountable difficulties which the Episcopal Church, as the church of the rich, must encounter in trying to be "champions of the poor." The simplest test for this encounter is to observe how rich Episcopalians (black and white) behave in the Lord's House when poor, black, downtrodden souls wander into their services of worship. Champions of the poor do not try to escape from them, but Episcopalians sometimes do. The rich are always welcome.

Nothing in the foregoing paragraph should be taken to mean that bishops in a rich church cannot be genuinely and passionately committed to "be merciful and show compassion for the poor and strangers and to defend those who have no helper" (BCP, p. 518). Yet we have to take very seriously the confession which Bishop White makes when he says that "attempts to be the advocate for the poor and outcast in our society and in the world are overwhelming and a continuous drain on the ability of bishops to solicit the support of volunteers and resources to address these growing maladies." For therein lies the rub—how long must bishops, as champions of the poor, be expected to remain as rich beggars, Robin Hoods with budgets and membership in corporate circles? If Jesus is still right about having the poor with us always (or "growing maladies" according to White), then bishops have no time-out in this matter. So that when the rich come knocking on the bishops' door seeking affirmation, there is no alternative but to tell them to go, sell, give, and then come again. But our bishops could not survive if they did this too often. So we have the continuing irony in hearing the Gospel raise the awkward question, "what shall we do with the rich?" while we Episcopalians are troubled with the question, "what shall we do with the poor?" It is only in the emergence of the Poor Church that such ironies begin to find just resolution.

5. We turn next to the question of the "local church" as an area of theological concern. What exactly is a diocese in the context of the whole church? Throughout his paper, Bishop White often defines various roles and functions for the diocese as a unit—the "clustering of parishes and institutions and their members" with the bishop as "chief priest and pastor." Yet it appears as if Bishop White expects the diocese to have a competitive edge based on the effectiveness of the bishop. He writes: "If the bishop is an effective team leader in practice, the diocese will become a place where clergy will desire to minister, where others will be attracted from other dioceses, where both clergy and laity will sense that they have contributions to make to the life of the diocese and are pleased and proud to be a part with their bishop of the diocesan team." Such an assertion begs many questions, too many to articulate here. But does Bishop White make such an assertion *in the light of* episcopal collegiality, or is it *in spite of*? What happens to the flock when bishops compete in attracting members from other "local" churches?

It seems to me that the major determination for bishops has to be whether they are bishops *in* the church first, and then bishops *of* dioceses second, or the other way around. If the shared episcopate does not transcend the jurisdictional deployment, then the presumed unity of the church is in jeopardy, and the very notion of a Presiding Bishop goes out of the window. I, therefore, hold to the view that the "local church" is nothing more than the "local congregation," and that the diocese is not a local church but an association of local churches struggling under one bishop to become the family of God in a particular way. Furthermore, the relationships between local congregations often give comfort to the contention that there are many "dioceses" within a diocese.

To his great credit, Bishop White does indeed point us to some basic questions about bishops' priorities and self-understanding. He says: "Such unresolved questions often lead to confusion and poor performance and cry out for clarification..." Yet clarification will be postponed until the complex issue of "diocese" vis-a-vis "local church" is comprehensively addressed and resolved. For example, is the diocesan office *in service of*, or *in control of*, the local church (congregations)? Or again, who is to answer this question: What kind of diocese do you want? Is it the bishop, or the congregations? There are no easy answers to these problems.

6. How prophetic is a bishop expected to be? Where must the prophetic invective be proclaimed? To whom must it be addressed? When Jesus was probing his friends about John the

Baptist, he asked them, "Whom did you think you were going out into the wilderness to see?" "If you were looking for a man dressed in cope, miter, and golden ring, you should have gone into the bishop's palace (or court, or thorp, or manse, or penthouse)." Or words to that effect! Prophets do not dress like bishops. The prophet stands over against the institution, even if the prophet might be committed to the highest ideals to which the institution also ought to be committed. Bishop White contends that "the bishop is held in high esteem as a theologian and prophet in the diocese and the wider Christian fellowship." But I do not see how the prophetic character can be institutionalized or the prophetic ideal routinized; and I do not see how the bishop can be otherwise identified than with the institution (diocese) which he/she is leading. Who minds the store when the prophet is in the wilderness? Bishop White laments: "The loss of status in society and in the local community is a growing issue. Bishops are less frequently called upon to give counsel, advice, theological perspective, or opinions on moral and ethical issues in communities of their jurisdiction." If this is true (and I have no reason so to doubt) what is left of the prophetic portfolio, when there is often an equally discernable level of contempt within the bishop's own diocesan jurisdiction?

One can well imagine that there is often a temptation for bishops to demonstrate that they are not merely guardians of the faith but also champions of the faith on the frontiers. Bishops may well be tempted to "speak out" even for the sake of sharpening the image of the office they hold. But is this really the meaning of being prophetic? It may well be that the gift of prophecy is still widely distributed, but that many of us are not aware that we possess it. It may also be the case that forms of modern prophecy in the Christian dispensation are to be understood as being vastly different from the ancient forms scattered throughout the Old Testament. Let no one deny that God still calls men and women to make prophetic utterances in the light of the divine self-disclosures. But surely it must not be thought that a prophetic utterance or two can turn one into a prophet.

We need to retain the highest level of qualification for such a person and to recognize that the prophet is indeed one who is so seized by the word of God in the fullness of being, that there is no discontinuity or dichotomy between the prophet's existence and the prophet's utterance. Thus while it is traditional for bishops to hold forth on the triple paradigm of Jesus as Prophet, Priest, and King, it is also traditional for bishops to concentrate on the kingly and priestly spheres, and to admire the prophetic from a distance. In the wider community, prophets would have a hearing if God's just demands and pervasive presence were commonly acknowledged. But in a society which thrives mainly because it separates religion from livelihood, or church from state, how can a religious leader expect to be a prophet? Martin Luther King Jr. tried it for a little while, but alas, they killed him; in true prophetic style. O Jerusalem, Jerusalem!! (Matt. 23:37)

Rumblings From Below

Now that we have waded through some of the ripples which have been generated from a careful reading of the White Paper, it is necessary for us to go on to offer some reflections on some relevant factors which seem to me to be integral to a comprehensive answer to our question: "And who is my Bishop?" Bishop White wrote out of the crucible of his experience as a bishop in the Episcopal Church for the past eight years; and his reflections leave us in no doubt about what we already know, namely, that it is not easy to be a bishop. I once remember being told by a bishop that soon after he was ordained he was warned that he would always be sure of three things: He would never be out of work; he would never be out of a meal; and his clergy would not always tell him the truth. He went on to state that he had already found that to be true. Other bishops have offered similar testimony.

It is not easy to be a bishop. I have never had any cause to disagree with my Grammar School Chaplain, Father Brown, who once declared in the pulpit of St. John's Cathedral, Antigua: "I am sure that My Lord would agree with me that no one in his right mind would ever want to be a bishop." He was uttering this in the presence of the Bishop of the Diocese of Antigua, Donald Rowland Knowles, to whom I shall refer in greater detail later on. A remark like that of Father Brown points to the sometimes uncomfortable factor of being the bishop of some clergy; they put you on the spot when you least expect it, and you have no course for redress or escape! Further, it is sometimes difficult for a bishop to minister to clergy who are virtually impermeable to any pastoral beneficence. Bishops often feel themselves hostage to situations involving their clergy, particularly when they know that they are likely to be the losers in not disclosing all that they know, or all that they have done towards a more wholesome outcome. No wonder then that many bishops regard their pastoral leadership of the laity as the more refreshing and compensatory aspect of their difficult ministry.

This is the context, I believe, out of which we find Bishop White referring more than once to the stress involved in being a bishop. We hear him say: "Many aspects of the ministry lead to isolation and a sense of loneliness." He also speaks of family pressures. To paraphrase a sigh of Paul: Who is weak and bishops are not weak? Apart from other things, there is the daily pressure upon bishops of their anxiety for all the churches (2 Cor. 11:29).

It is this reality of stress, pressures, anxiety, and loneliness, which combines to make bishops truly human. *The humanity of bishops* is the first rumbling from below, that is, from the ranks of the clergy. Bishops must be seen and known to be truly human, not only in understanding suffering, but also sharing in it; becoming ever familiar with the imperfections involved in trying to lead lives of perfection, and other to perfection; continuing to be the living embodiment of the fact that, in the church, human error and mistakes are both a part of life and the prelude to new life. God's strength is made perfect in weakness, the weakness of earthen vessels bearing, as they do, that heavenly treasure. Bishops must be truly earthy people, truly rooted in the earthiness (*humus* = soil) of human creatureliness, and helping others to move forward and upward, in spite of the common inclinations not to do so.

It is virtually impossible to overstate the significance of this issue of the humanity of bishops, for this alone makes it natural for those who are being led to recognize that their bishop is truly a "Father-in-God" (or "Mother-in-God"). This is an ancient liturgical phrase by which bishops have been addressed over the years. It has always had a special ring to it; it has generated feelings of oneness in an ecclesial context, notions of the church as the family of God, and expressions of filial relationships which transcend the ordinary connections between subordinates and their superior.

This *ecclesial parenting* which bishops are expected to assume represents our **second rumbling from below**. We need someone who can re-present for us something of the common parenthood which we understand to be inherent in the fellowship of the Church. Although we are to call no one our Father on Earth, Jesus still expects us to acknowledge the special place which those who are entrusted with the charge of feeding his sheep must occupy in the midst of the flock. Further, it is the capacity of the bishops to identify, as unconditionally as possible, with those whom they have been called to lead which constitutes the existential character of being "fathers/mothers-in-God."

Our **third rumbling from below** follows on from what we have just been discussing. For not only are bishops accorded the place of ecclesial parents, but in a very unique way they are also expected to be *pastores pastorum*, pastors of pastors. There is hardly a priest who would not want to look for such a factor in the character of their bishop. Ministers need to be ministered to. Pastors need to be pastored. Priests need to know that there is someone to whom they can readily turn. The nature of the priesthood is such that very often there is no one to whom the priest can turn with issues, problems, choices and decisions, but the bishop. This requires in the bishop substantial integrity and trustworthiness, for so much of the innermost secrets and fears of one's life is put out on the line, there to be guarded and handled with delicacy, sensitivity, and personal care. Some priests would venture to say that this should perhaps be the most desirable element in the character of their bishop. The inevitable tensions which arise between a bishop and his/her clergy may at times make this episcopal character somewhat obscure; but it is the mark of a good and spiritually mature bishop not to allow such tensions to discourage the pursuit of the highest pastoral ideals.

The clergy are entitled to the pastoral care and attention of their bishops, but so are the laity. The relationship between bishops and the laity are often strained (or even controlled) because of the nature of the parochial system. Parish priests, or rectors, can sometimes be guilty of converting pastorship into proprietorship (the this-is-my-parish syndrome), and such attitudes can create unfavorable connections between the bishop on the throne and the person in the pew. Our **fourth rumbling from below** points to the need for the bishop to be in many respects a *congregational enabler*, a spiritual *provocateur*, a radical *animateur* of that which is inherent in the challenge of the Gospel. Bishops are sometimes known to adopt devious means of getting around their clergy in an effort to establish and maintain direct linkages with the laity. However effective this strategy might be in the short run, it is often counter productive in the long run.

Congregational enablement is a collective ministry, and the parish priests should be encouraged to work closely with the bishop in exploring continuously such new ways of becoming more like Christ in this sinful and naughty modern world. As a congregational enabler, the bishop can become a major resource person in endorsing and proclaiming such values, virtues, lessons, and admonitions which the parish priest has been attempting to proclaim continuously, but with less effect. The lack of congregational effectiveness on the part of the priest is often due to the universal trait of familiarity-breeding-contempt. The same thing sounds new, fresh, exciting, and dynamic, from the lips of a stranger, especially when that stranger speaks with an acknowledged voice of authority.

Fifth, just as the bishop is expected to be the enabler of the congregation in the task of being a living and dynamic witness to

Christ in the community, so too is the bishop called by God to be the *chief advocate of the church* in society. What kind of advocacy do we envisage here? How does this measure up to the multiplicity of advocates with which our modern society is encumbered? Who chooses the causes for the bishops? When should bishops speak out? Who is expected to listen to them, especially in light of Bishop White's admission that bishops' pronouncements are not taken that seriously these days? It seems to me that the advocacy of bishops in society should have a threefold effect. First, it should represent the collective voice of the church in that area. Second, it should teach the faithful about how to reach decisions on issues affecting the life of the Christian in society, while not necessarily telling them *what* to think. Third, it should bear witness to the wider community that there are levels of accountability in the human condition that transcend the normal bounds of political or economic dominance. Nevertheless, none of this should be taken to mean that the voice of the bishop, unlike that of Caesar, is the voice of God.

Our **sixth** and final rumbling from below deals with issues of diversity. Bishop White makes much of the role of the bishop as guardian of the faith, unity, and discipline of the church. This spells continuity as well as conformity. This conformity does not often reinforce the unity which is already given to us by the Holy Spirit. Indeed, it tends to produce the opposite effect, especially as the realities of power render it difficult for those who would define and control the church community to deal graciously and responsibly with the varieties of gifts which the Spirit also makes available. Yet, if bishops are to be guardians of unity they are also called by God to be *guardians of diversity* in the Church. They must so conduct themselves, order their affairs, make their decisions, arrange their priorities in such a way that the diversity in the Church becomes not a threat to ecclesial unity but enriches its very essence. For example, they must leave no stone unturned to encourage the appointment of black rectors in predominantly white congregations, just as they are hardly ever reluctant to

encourage the appointment of white rectors in black congregations. As guardians of diversity in the church, bishops are further
expected to take the lead on the frontiers of genuine ecumenical
relationships among Christian bodies, and even between groups
of differing faiths.

They should be in the forefront of helping to establish the ecumenical priorities not only for their respective dioceses, but also
for the local congregations within their dioceses. Ecumenical
obligations are too important to be left to the occasional
predilections of a few parish priests, who may not accord them a
status higher than an optional extra in the life of their congregations. Bishops must take the lead, and stay in the lead. If bishops
are truly symbols of unity, the boundaries of that unity do not
end at the borders of their diocese; for God has never created a
diocese, and has no intentions of creating one either. God's *oik-
oumene* is entirely non-diocesan, and bishops are called by God,
not created by the diocese. There is a unity-in-diversity and a
diversity-in-unity which must always be held in creative tension
in the Church, even if it is difficult in this competitive world. Our
bishops must continue to be the living embodiments of that tension, and must be shepherds of all the sheep. God forbid that
they should ever capitulate to the dominant cultural belief and
practice that to be different means to be inferior.

Brighter Rays On High

As we come to the final section of this essay, let us briefly
address some of the conditions under which bishops in the
Episcopal Church should be recruited, prepared, nurtured, and
sustained, even beyond their official episcopate. Thereafter, we
will finally pay tribute to two outstanding episcopal servants of
God, now deceased, who still worship their Lord in the realms on
high, where there is no diocese. They still shine like rays on high.
Once a bishop, eternally a bishop.

The other contributors of this collection of essays have offered
some very interesting insights on the whole question of bishops
in the historical and theological tradition of the Church. It would

certainly be beyond the scope of this essay to comment on many of them, but there are a few which seem to me to add some dimension to what we will be discussing in this final section.

Professor Wright has very carefully outlined for us the three traditional roles of the bishop in the early Church: Eucharistic President, Chief Teacher, and Administrative Leader. He finally leaves us with these questions: "Are there other functions of bishops today more important than any of the three...? What are, and what should be, the major emphases or functions in episcopal ministry today?" It seems to me that to look for episcopal functions more important than any of these three, or to establish new "major emphases" in our expectations of bishops, is to create some bishops as specialists and others generalists among the members of the episcopal ministry; it is to constitute a culture of professionalism and expertise for bishops, which would seem to me to be antithetical to what our chief pastors are truly called to become for the whole church of God. The only duty of the bishop is *to be the bishop*, and only God has an adequate definition of what that fully entails. But God is no respecter of persons, nor suppliant to any specialists.

While Professor Norris offers the profound thought that "God can, of course, dispense with bishops, and perhaps does so more frequently than we know," Bishop Dyer is convinced that "the bishop is called by God to be transfigured by this Mystery of God, the Blessed Trinity, and to serve and preserve this mystery for the people of God." Both comments perhaps tell us more about their respective authors than about bishops, since neither would claim the ability to comprehend the incomprehensible. What the comments tell us, however, is that bishops mean different things to different people; for some there is a transcendentalist doctrine of episcopacy, for others there is an immanentist doctrine of the same. The fact is that bishops are called to minister and take the lead in a pervasive context of theological pluralism, ethical complexity, and pastoral uncertainties. Who is sufficient for these things?

There is also a very significant comment offered by Professor

Price. He says that bishops "are our chief teachers and chief evangelists, and are in a good position to encourage and enable the other orders of ministers, especially the laity, to teach and evangelize the world." Price reminds us of the significance of the bishops' position in the church; not only is it strategic for leading the church in evangelism, it is also centrifugal for ecclesial edification. Evangelism and Edification go together as inherent among the divinely ordered tasks of the Church, and the role of bishops in enabling the corporate and personal pursuit of such tasks should never be taken lightly.

It is in this context that the following words of the Black Episcopal Bishops in their 1990 Pastoral Letter, *But We See Jesus*, shed more light on some bishops' own understanding of their function: "We strongly desire that this work (of the Episcopal Commission for Black Ministries) should be further strengthened in every way, so that our cultural and spiritual endowments may more clearly be offered to the greater glory of God, and in the wider Church...As your bishops, we are grateful to you all for the matchless support which you have given us, for the warmth and love you have shared, and for the immeasurable joy you have afforded us in serving you as your chief pastors.... Let us continue to bring warmth, and compassion, and humanity, and feeling to American cultures."[1] If the experience at the annual conventions of the Union of Black Episcopalians is anything to go by, then the high esteem and the universally deep affection which Black bishops are accorded at these gatherings attest to the fact that they certainly occupy "a good position" in the daily life of the church. There is nothing comparable in the life of the Episcopal Church.

If the foregoing discussion suggests a slight glimmer of how Episcopalians treat their bishops, we might also make bold to suggest a few considerations about how Episcopalians should create their bishops, and provide sustained enrichment for their ministry. These considerations emerge out of a prolonged process

---

[1] *But We See Jesus*, 1990, p. 25.

of dealing with the episcopal office in various contexts, and after many years of support for those who strive to carry out their episcopal duties gallantly and faithfully. For not only is it a lonely office, it is also for many a very thankless office; but that is not surprising to anyone who remembers that the church as an organization is perhaps the most exploitative community which Christians know. Yet it is also the Body of Christ, the Family of God, and those who take the lead within it, particularly in the Episcopal Church, should be carefully selected. The following considerations suggest some new ways of doing so.

1. The Episcopal Church should establish a national pool of candidates for episcopal office from which the diocesan search processes would draw their selectees. Such candidates would be properly screened, provided with suitable training, and given opportunities to explore the life and work of the episcopal office, even before they are selected. If bishops are bishops for the whole church, then the whole church needs to be involved earlier in the process of selection, long before diocesan standing committees are asked to sign off like rubber-stamps.

2. Diocesan search committees for bishops should always include some members who are not a part of the diocese that is in the search. The inclusion of suitable fellow-Episcopalians from the wider church family would certainly remove, or neutralize, some of the political factors by which many search processes are often affected.

3. Given the realities of today's social pressures, and the tremendous burdens which bishops are often called upon to bear, I would strongly urge that the minimum age of bishops be increased to at least 45 years. My constant amazement at the number of newly ordained, or newly converted, who offer themselves for episcopal election drives me also to suggest that no one be considered a candidate before his/her tenth anniversary of ordination to the priesthood. I would even venture to suggest a maximum period of cumulative service in episcopal office.

4. Although bishops take the lead in the constitutional governance of the Church, they are often perplexed by their being caught between the letter and the spirit. Compassion and pastoral wisdom often clash with bureaucratic accountability. This problem could be helped by the establishment of a Council of Bishops (Council of the Elders), other than the House of Bishops in General Convention. This Council would be guided by pastoral priorities for all aspects of the life of the church, and would serve more in an advisory capacity to the dioceses and congregations than in a juridical or administrative sphere.

5. The contributions of bishops should be more systematically recognized by the wider church, and they should be appropriately honored for their selfless labors. Too often our bishops are put out to pasture soon after they retire, and much of what they have attempted to accomplish for and on behalf of the Church is very quickly forgotten. Ecclesiastical structures should not become so oppressive that those who preside over them are eventually made victims of neglect and lack of compassion by those very structures.

I am under no illusion that any of the foregoing considerations would ever be taken very seriously in any sector of the Episcopal Church; for they suggest such a radical discontinuity with the way we choose and care for our bishops, that we would not really know where to begin. Nevertheless, the considerations only represent the responses of one individual priest of the Church to some of the infelicities with which our present system is now encumbered.

The title of this essay asked the question: "And Who Is My Bishop?" The answer must in the final analysis relate to a personal acquaintance with one's own bishop. However, when one has had a life-long connection with bishops, there is inevitably an episcopal paradigm, a historical (if not living) embodiment of the episcopal office by which one tends to relate to all other bishops. We look for the incarnation of our paradigm in any bishop we meet; we expect certain things from others because these were obvious in our own paradigm. There are two persons, now deceased, whose contributions and witness to the episcopal ministry in *Ecclesia Anglicana* have left an indelible impression on my mind. One is Bishop John Robinson, late Bishop of Woolwich (England) whom I never met, and the other is Bishop Donald Knowles, late

Bishop of Antigua (West Indies), who was in many ways my Father-in-God. The former was a pastorly scholar, and the latter was a scholarly pastor of pastors. Some brief comments on these two "brighter rays on high" will bring our discussion to a close.

In spite of his controversial notoriety for defending D.H. Lawrence's novel *Lady Chatterley's Lover*, and his authorship of the seminal best-seller *Honest To God*, John Robinson, as a Cambridge academic and a bishop in South London, exercised the full extent of his mind and his heart on the frontiers of the church's witness. He saw himself as a bishop who was called to "represent the wholeness of the catholic Church to its divided parts, to be the creative force of its coming unity."[2] Archbishop Michael Ramsey wrote to Robinson in these words: "I feel full of thankfulness for your 'Woolwich' time—in what you have given to so many, both clergy and others in your shepherding of them so lovingly, in what you have given to us in the central discussions of our church, and in your pioneering in the theological tasks before us. I reproach myself with having been rather 'slow' in understanding, but I have found myself increasingly learning from you and increasingly being grateful."[3] I had always held Michael Ramsey in very high regard, and I knew him personally. I, therefore, take comfort in his assessment of Robinson.

Bishop Robinson was a scholar-bishop who produced no fewer than twenty-nine books, apart from lectures, articles and chapters. He was not only an original thinker in New Testament scholarship, but he kept himself on the frontiers of Christian social thought, often assuming a truly prophetic role without ever realizing that he was doing so. It is difficult to match the prophetic profundity of these words: "The pervasive influence of Christianity is not promised to the strength of a self-contained ecclesiastical organization, but to leaven and salt mixed and dissolved in the lump of the world's life. Movements and groupings there must be, clusters of action and sanctity and thinking, and

---

[2] Eric James, *Bishop John A.T. Robinson*, London, Collins, 1988, p. 85.
[3] *Ibid.*, p. 168.

these must be structured if they are to penetrate effectively. But basically the attractive power of love and hope, integrity and justice—and these are the signs of the Kingdom at work—do not depend on institutional orthodoxies and establishments. Ours is an age in which these things have ceased to carry their own authentication."[4]

In the end, Robinson came to be regarded as a son of the Church who was clearly ahead of his time. After his death in 1984, the Church of England was for a time exercised with qualms of conscience about how he had been treated. Should he have been appointed a diocesan bishop? Who interfered with the Crown appointments to make such a possibility unachievable? Had his Diocesan at Southwark, Bishop Stockwood, done enough to defend him at the height of controversy around him? Who exactly was John Robinson? One who knew him well had this to say: "His tragedy was, as is the nature of tragedy, that the greatest strengths of his nature had a 'kick back' from which he was the greatest sufferer...What he lacked was what most of us have studiously developed—the self-regard which enables us to cover up the less socially attractive traits of our human nature."[5] For many people then, although he did not become a diocesan bishop, he was still a bishop of bishops who used all his gifts and pain in the full service of the whole church.

Finally, we look at the bishop who nurtured my vocation to the priesthood, and who ordained me, and officiated at our wedding. Bishop Donald Knowles was a native of the Bahamas who had distinguished himself in the Diocese of Nassau and the Bahamas as an outstanding parish priest and Archdeacon. He was consecrated Bishop of Antigua on January 25, 1953, and immediately immersed himself in the leadership of a Caribbean diocese of some fourteen scattered islands in the Leewards, Windwards and Dutch Antilles. Because of my reluctance to be more autobio-

---

[4] *Ibid.*, p. 194.
[5] *Ibid.*, p. 326.

graphical than I have already been in the essay, it will suffice it to say that Bishop Knowles enfleshed for us in the diocese, over the sixteen years of his episcopate, the selflessness and humility, the humanity and compassion, the pastoral care and suffering concern, the priestly sharing and the brotherly love far in excess of any other bishop in my experience. He literally wept with those who wept, and rejoiced with those who rejoiced. He was all things to all people. Thus when he preached the Commemoration Day Sermon at Codrington College, Barbados, in 1965, it was not a proud boast of his when he declared: "I have never asked any of my clergy to undertake any assignment or mission that I was not prepared to undertake myself."

Bishop Donald Knowles remains for me the model of bishops. I assess every bishop I meet in the light of his episcopal characteristics, not in search of carbon copies, but in an effort to perceive what they themselves understand about their episcopal vocation. Bishop Knowles made it possible for me to love and respect the office and work of the bishop, and to accord each holder of such office the respect and acceptance which he so richly deserved from me. This is why bishops have always been my "hobby"; they bring a radiance and meaning to the life and texture of the Church which is not transferable to any other type of personage. Bishops are special to the life of the church and to my own response to the fullness, the *plene esse*, of the Church. They always require the full support and respect of those whom they are called to lead; and we should always be prepared to provide that respect and support in all things lawful, honest, and reasonable.

I, therefore, conclude that as long as bishops represent the unity, the diversity, the vitality, and the continuity of the Church; as long as they continue to take the lead in helping us to break new ground in rolling back the borders of evil, ignorance and rabid individualism; as long as they inspire us to give full expression to all that the Gospel demands of us towards becoming fully human; as long as they selflessly seek to defend that freedom which has already been won for us in Jesus Christ; they will continue to deserve my unstinted admiration, loyalty and support.

13

Fifth Supplement

"Bishops in the Orthodox and Oriental Orthodox Churches"*

The Orthodox[1] would claim to have maintained the episcopal office without a break in tradition, from the early patristic era. The role of the bishop has been invested with a great deal of theological significance in Orthodox thinking. Certain concepts stand out:

    i. the bishop as bearer of the Apostolic tradition

    ii. the bishop as head and president of the eucharistic community

    iii. the bishop as head and representative of a local community

    iv. the bishop as link between Christian communities

To these may be added a further area, concerning the perception of the bishop and the way in which he embodies his ministry.

i. The Bishop as Bearer of the Apostolic Tradition

The bishop is teacher and transmitter of the faith of the Apostles. The Orthodox emphasis in the matter of apostolic suc-

---

* From *Episcopal Ministry: The Report of the Archbishops' Group on the Episcopate* (London, Church House Publishing, 1990, pp. 39-45).

[1] There are differences in the episcopal office in the Churches of the 'Byzantine' (those Churches in communion with Constantinople) and 'Oriental' (among them the Armenian, Syrian, Coptic, Ethiopian and Indian Churches) families. The separation of the non-Chalcedonian Churches from the fifth century has led to a certain amount of separate development. We speak here chiefly of the 'Byzantine' Orthodox tradition.

cession is primarily on the succession of communities in Orthodox faith. The tactile succession is regarded by the Orthodox as essential primarily because it serves this end, and provides a demonstrable line with the authority of the apostolic communities. But the early succession lists of (for example) Irenaeus and Hegisippus are more concerned to list the orderly succession of bishops in a see than the actual 'consecrators.'[2]

As well as being part of an apostolic community, the bishop must be *teaching* the apostolic faith to be in the apostolic succession. Most Eastern episcopal consecration rites include an examination of the candidate's faith far more rigorous than that of the Anglican rites. There is a clear aim of preserving doctrinal purity. A bishop who departs from this will not only be recognized to have done so, but may be rejected by his people.

ii. The Bishop as Head and President of the Eucharistic Community

For the Orthodox, the bishop is the center of the community and 'guarantees' its life and its sacraments. Membership of the Church depends on being in relation to the bishop—who, of course, in earlier centuries was not a remote but a familiar locally known figure. Liturgical expression of this survives today in Orthodoxy in the formal bow to the bishop's stall or throne by a presbyter before he begins to celebrate the Eucharist. He is mentioned by name in prayers and bowed to if present. The *fermentum* of the bishops of Rome—the practice whereby the Pope sent fragments of Bread from the Eucharist at which he presided to the presbyters presiding over the Eucharist at the other parish

---

[2] Cf. para. 87. Ware underlines the importance of this link of the succession with a local community very strongly:

'The act of consecration, even when correctly performed by other validly consecrated bishops, is not by itself sufficient; it is also required that the new bishop shall be consecrated for a specific local church. Unless he succeeds legitimately to a throne, he has no true share in the grace of apostolic succession, but is merely a pseudo-bishop' (*Bishops: But What Kind?*, p. 13).

churches of the City of Rome—gave expression to the same understanding.[3]

A further dimension of the concept of the bishop as the center of the eucharistic community is that he is also its representative. Although it is true that some of the Eastern Churches have a long tradition of lay theologians and lay participation in decision-making, it still remains the case that ecclesiologically the Orthodox would answer the question 'who represents the laity?' by 'the bishop, of course.' The bishop is the local representative of the *laos*—the people of God. This must be appreciated in order to understand what sometimes seems to Western eyes a lack of enthusiasm among the Orthodox for lay representation and participation in synods. It is also relevant to the issue of the 'representation' of women in the episcopate. The principle is that the bishop is not simply exercising a function among the many as a personal 'right'; he focuses and represents the whole body of men and women among whom he serves.

The impression must not be given, however, that the bishop can act in isolation. The classic images show him in a network of *relationships*—with deacons at his side, and surrounded by his presbyters and people. The modern Anglican concept of a synod (with three 'houses' which can veto each other's decisions) has not developed in Orthodoxy; but in many parts of the Orthodox diaspora there are assemblies with both clerical and lay representation. In addition, the Bishop's Council—a relatively small group of senior clergy and laity who advise the bishop—has manifested itself in various forms. In situations such as that which is found in modern Greece, the gathering of all the clergy of a diocese is not unknown.

---

[3] This link between the local Eucharist and the bishop has been largely lost in Anglicanism. The 1662 Book of Common Prayer does not mention the Diocesan Bishop by name in the Prayer for the Church Militant and until recently Confirmations—an occasion when parishes did see their bishop—were not held in a Eucharistic context. The provision for the mention of the bishop's name in the ASB Rite A Eucharist has gone some way to rediscovering the link between bishop and parish Eucharist. Cf. ORC, Munich, 47.

In Russia the Holy Synod—*Sobor*—has included laity and clergy since 1917. The *Sobor* for the celebration of the Millennium of the baptism of Russia in 1988 continued to exemplify this tradition. In June 1990, the *Sobor* which elected Patriarch Alesky II was composed of all the diocesan bishops, the heads of the monastic houses, and one clerical and one lay representative elected from each diocese. Each had an equal vote in the secret ballots.

The relationship between the laity and the bishop was strengthened, in many parts of the Orthodox and Oriental Orthodox world, by the *milet* system imposed by Arab and Turkish Muslim conquerors. Each non-Muslim ethnic or religious grouping was treated as a separate entity within the Muslim state, enjoying (within certain limits) the right to maintain its traditions and organize its internal affairs. With the disappearance of a Christian civil power at local and national level, the bishop became the head of the whole Christian community in relation to all aspects of its life. He was thus resorted to by senior lay leaders and looked up to by the whole Christian populace as their father and protector to whom they could come for help and advice. Something of the approachability and (in the right sense) dependence that this experience helped to foster, can still be found in many parts of the Orthodox world.

iii. The Bishop as Head and Representative of a Local Community

Orthodoxy sees the bishop as part of the structure of a local expression of the universal Church and not the bearer of a *potestas* or even a charism *in vacuo*, as it were. Liturgically this is expressed in the consecrating of a man *for a named see*. He is the father of the community and 'the one through whom all charismatic manifestations of the Church must pass, so that they may be manifestations not of individualism but of the *Koinonia* of the Spirit and of the community created by it.'[4] On such a view a bishop without a community is a nonsense.[5]

---

[4] J. Zizioulas, *Being as Communion* (London, 1985), p. 199.
[5] The link between bishops and a named see seems weaker among the Oriental

This is in keeping with the fact that frequently—probably normally in the earliest centuries—a bishop was chosen from *within* the community that he was consecrated to serve and, therefore, already shared in its 'apostolic tradition.' He was chosen from and by the *laos* (clergy and laity together)—originally by election. In practice this ideal has been lost in most of Orthodoxy, and candidates for the episcopate are usually selected by the Governing Synod of the Church—itself usually made up exclusively of bishops. The Moscow Council of 1917-18 laid down that henceforth bishops in the Russian Church should be elected by the clergy and laity. Political conditions have hitherto made the application of this rule impossible within the Soviet Union and Diocesan Bishops are appointed directly by the Patriarchate.[6] In the changing situation it is not impossible that the 1917/1918 regulations will soon be implemented.

iv. The Bishop as the Link Between the Christian Communities

The bishop is the bond between the local Church and the Church Universal in a way that no other minister can ever be. The local Church does not have to find representation to meet with representatives from other Churches; the *bishop* is its representative.[7] Central to this idea is the concept of 'the charismatic

---

[5] (continued) Orthodox (where there are some interesting parallels with early Celtic monastery-based bishops). Thus, in the modern Coptic Church there can be found a 'Bishop for Social and Public Affairs' and 'Bishops General' with no dioceses. In India until the last century there do not appear to have been any defined diocesan structures in the ancient Syrian community, even when there was more than one bishop in the country.

[6] T. Ware, *The Orthodox Church* (London, 1963), p. 299.

[7] 'Collectively the shepherds of the Church, whether apostles or bishops, speak with an authority which none of them possess individually...together the members of the episcopate become something more than they are as scattered individuals, and this "something more" is precisely the presence of Christ and the Holy Spirit in their midst...the "common mind" which the assembled bishops reach under the Spirit's guidance is not merely their mind but Christ's.' T. Ware, in *Bishops: But What Kind?*, p. 16.

equality of bishops.' *Each* bishop is the icon of Christ and the channel through which the plenitude of the Spirit's gifts flows into his community. In this respect there is no difference between a patriarchal see and a small rural one. The historical fact of having been founded by an Apostle, or the size and dignity of a city, may afford honor and even a degree of jurisdiction to a particular see, but it does not make its bishop more a bishop than any other. 'In the Orthodox Church such sees...have never been distinguished from the rest of the episcopal sees from the point of view of the essential apostolic continuity in which both the historical and the eschatological perspectives merge into a synthesis.'[8]

Nevertheless, it is manifestly true that Orthodoxy does afford a particular role to certain sees, especially in relation to gatherings of bishops. The primatial role of the Patriarch is an important one: he can summon the bishops in a given area, and it is generally through him that the decisions of the gathering are expressed and executed. Historically such an office has been attached to certain sees for reasons already noted, and especially to Constantinople.

The autocephalous metropolitan areas of Orthodoxy are one of its distinguishing features. Zizioulas begins a defence of regional authorities, in terms of the necessity to preserve (on an incarnational basis) cultural and historical diversity:

> Different cultures mean different ways of approaching the faith and expressing it. It also means differing creeds and liturgical customs. All this can be achieved and served through regional synods united with each other in a universal communion of Churches. These regional synods should have authority on all matters, including doctrine, for it is mainly in matters of doctrine that expression of cultural diversity is evident and necessary. As in the early Church, baptismal

---

[8] Zizioulas, *Being as Communion*, pp. 203 ff.

creeds can be local. The movement towards ecumenical expressions of the faith in the early church has been mistaken as a tendency to subject the local level to the universal level of Church unity, whereas the proper way of understanding it is that of mutual sharing of the churches' experiences and problems so that by common consent they might remain different without betraying the fundamental principles of faith.[9]

The existence of the patriarchates does not obscure the fact that Orthodox bishops attend local Synods or 'international' Councils as the heads of their communities—a fact reflected in the ruling that classically only *diocesan* bishops may vote. The decisions which they articulate must be in line with the faith of those communities and must be *received* by those communities in order to have any lasting authority.

It is thus incumbent on bishops to listen to the bishops of the rest of the Universal Church. 'Keeping in line' is not a stifling restriction, but is designed to enable the whole Church to speak and advance together, and, therefore, with authority. A bishop who finds himself 'out on a limb' should question his own position before the collective mind of the episcopate.[10] This sense of group solidarity, as least within each autocephalous Church, is much stronger in the Orthodox Churches than in the more individualistic West. Nevertheless, it has the same roots as the

---

[9] Zizioulas, 'The Institution of Episcopal Conferences: An Orthodox Reflection,' in *The Jurist 48* (1988): 1.

[10] At the same time the possibility of not reaching an agreement is faced by Fathers such as Cyprian—who 'considers that in the event of disagreement no compulsion should be brought to bear upon the dissident bishop or bishops. The Church, while still preserving unity, will be obliged to live for a time with the fact of this disagreement' (T. Ware, in *Bishops: But What Kind?*, p. 17). Cyprian's immediate context (*Letter 55*) is a discussion of the possibility of restoring the lapsed after a period of persecution. Cyprian would not have argued for toleration of diversity in all aspects of Christian belief and practice.

Western understanding of episcopal collegiality in the Roman Catholic Church and the developing sense of the solidarity of the House of Bishops within the Church of England.

v. The Perception of a Bishop

An important aspect of the Orthodox perception of a bishop in counties where the Orthodox Church is deeply rooted is his physical appearance. Beards and, increasingly, dress are simply matters of personal taste or fashion in the West. Not so in the East. The bishop has a *persona*. He is a *patriarch*, or image of the Father and the incarnate Son, and has a beard as an expression (with strong significance for the Orthodox) of the masculinity that goes with the concepts. Flowing robes, hat, veil, staff, all contribute to an overall image and create a kind of 'otherness' which does not necessarily mean distance or unapproachability in a Western sense. Indeed, traditionally, Eastern bishops are very approachable, holding court for all to present their pleas, as Ambrose of Milan did at the end of the fourth century in the West.[11]

Connected with the image of the bishop as Father or Patriarch is that of him as a Holy Man.[12] This is an elusive concept, but an important one. From the sixth century both Byzantine and Oriental bishops were chosen from monks and marked out by special head-gear. Archdeacons do the administration; bishops are praying, liturgical figures. Again this does not necessarily mean that they are remote; on the contrary, they are to be an image of the 'Holy One in your midst.' (In recent times both the Church of Ethiopia and the Coptic Church have elevated a monk directly to the Patriarchate.)

---

[11] But this has to be kept within bounds. Bernard of Clairvaux wrote the *De Consideratione* for Pope Eugenius III (1145-53) to encourage him to make himself rather less approachable, so that he might have time for prayer.

[12] *Bishops: But What Kind?*, p. 168.

14
Official Communiqué of 27 June 1992

Theological conversations between representatives of the Episcopal Church in the USA and the Russian Orthodox Church on the 'Episcopal Ministry in the Church' were held at St. Daniel's Monastery in Moscow from June 24 to 27, 1992.

Participating in the conversations on the part of the Episcopal Church were:

1. The Rt. Rev. Roger J. White, Bishop of Milwaukee—head of the delegation
2. The Rt. Rev. Richard Frank Grein, Bishop of New York
3. The Rt. Rev. Mark Dyer, Bishop of Bethlehem
4. The Rev. Dr. William A. Norgren, Ecumenical Officer, Episcopal Church
5. Dr. Suzanne Massie, Russian Research Center, Harvard University
6. The Rev. Professor Charles P. Price, Virginia Theological Seminary
7. The Rev. Canon Professor J. Robert Wright, The General Theological Seminary
8. The Rev. Canon Professor Richard A. Norris, Jr., Union Theological Seminary

Participating as observers were:

1. Ms. Marguerite Henninger, lay member of the Episcopal Church in the USA
2. The Rev. William Richard Kew, Executive Director, The Society for Promoting Christian Knowledge, Tennessee
3. The Rev. James C. McReynolds, Chairman, Board of Directors, The Teleios Foundation, New York State.

Participating in the conversations on the part of the Russian Orthodox Church were:

1. Metropolitan Juvenaly of Krutitsy and Kolomna, permanent member of the Holy Synod—head of the delegation
2. Archbishop Mikheil of Vologda and Veliky Ustiug, professor of the St. Petersburg Theological Academy
3. Archbishop Clement of Kaluga and Borovsk, deputy chairman of the Department for External Church Relations of the Moscow Patriarchate
4. Archimandrite Januarius (Ivliev), senior lecturer of the St. Petersburg Theological Academy
5. Archpriest Nikolay Gundyaev, professor of the St. Petersburg Theological Academy
6. Archpriest Vladimir Kucheriavy, clergyman of the Moscow Diocese
7. Deacon Maxim Kozlov, senior lecturer of the Moscow Theological Academy
8. Mr. Valery A. Chukalov, senior staff member of the Department for External Church Relations of the Moscow Patriarchate, head of the section for the relationship with the Protestant Churches
9. Ms. Helen S. Speranskaya, research assistant of the DECR section for the relationship with the Protestant Churches.

At the opening session, Metropolitan Juvenaly read out the Message of His Holiness Patriarch Aleksy II of Moscow and All Russia to the participants in the conversations.

Bishop Roger White passed the greetings from the Most Rev. Edmond Lee Browning, Presiding Bishop and Primate of the Episcopal Church in the USA.

Archbishop Clement read out a letter of welcome from Metropolitan Kirill of Smolensk and Kaliningrad, Chairman of the Department for External Church Relations.

Heard at the conversations were the following reports:

1. Theological and Historical Foundations of the Episcopal Ministry in the Church—by Prof. Archpriest Nikolay Gundyaev

2. The Origins of the Episcopate and Episcopal Ministry in the Early Church—by Canon Prof. J. Robert Wright
3. Bishops, Succession, and the Apostolicity of the Church—by Canon Prof. Richard A. Norris, Jr.
4. Theological Reflections on the Patristic Development—by Bishop Mark Dyer
5. Episcopal Consecration in the Orthodox Church—by Deacon Maxim Kozlov
6. Teachers and Evangelists for the Equipment of the Saints: Prayer Book Doctrine Concerning the Bishop as Teacher, Evangelizer, and Focus of Unity—by Prof. Charles P. Price
7. The Ministry of Bishops: A Study Document Authorized by the House of Bishops of the Episcopal Church—by Bishop Richard F. Grein of New York
8. The Practice of Episcopal Ministry in the Episcopal Church from A Bishop's Point of View—by Bishop Roger J. White of Milwaukee, and
9. The Practice of Episcopal Ministry in the Russian Orthodox Church Today—by Archbishop Mikhail of Vologda and Veliky Ustiug.

An extended discussion followed which was held in the atmosphere of mutual interest and openness, Christian love and fraternal understanding.

As a result of the discussion, a joint working document was adopted including summaries of the papers given and a review of the discussion following the presentations. The discussion led to new understandings for the participants, much mutual agreement in a variety of areas and the opportunity to share both ideas and experiences which gave them new information and thus was necessary and very useful.

A strong bond of fellowship was experienced during these days together for which we are grateful to Almighty God.

Representatives of the Russian Orthodox Church and the Episcopal Church in the USA considered the continuation of the bilateral theological dialogue useful and expressed their hope for its further development and improvement.

A copy of the Joint Summary Working Document is appended to this Communiqué.

On June 27, a reception was given in honor of the participants in the conversations on the occasion of their conclusion.

That same day the delegation of the Episcopal Church was received by His Holiness Patriarch Aleksy II of Moscow and all Russia.

✠ ROGER J. WHITE
BISHOP OF MILWAUKEE
HEAD OF DELEGATION
EPISCOPAL CHURCH IN THE USA

✠ JUVENALY
METROPOLITAN OF KRUTITSY AND KOLOMNA
HEAD OF DELEGATION
RUSSIAN ORTHODOX CHURCH

Moscow
27 June 1992

15

Joint Working Document:
Summary of the Moscow Papers and Review of the Discussions

The theme of the conversations was "Episcopal Ministry in the Church." Various aspects of this theme were discussed in nine presentations, summaries of which are given below.

I. Professor Archpriest Nikolay Gundyaev—"Theological and Historical Foundations of the Episcopal Ministry in the Church":

1. The apostolic ministry in the Church was first established by the Lord Jesus Christ Himself. Central in this ministry were teaching (Mt. 28:19-20), celebration of Baptism (Mt. 28:19) and Eucharist (Lk. 22:19), forgiveness of sins (Jn. 20:23), and the administrative authority in the Church (Mt. 18:18).

2. The apostolic ministry could not cease with the death of people performing it. It presupposes successors by its nature. While preaching the Gospel and founding Christian communities, the Apostles appointed their successors in them (Acts 14:23; Tit. 1:5), passing to them the threefold authority received by them from Christ Himself: preaching, celebration of sacraments and administration.

3. The conviction that the hierarchy in the Church was established by God Himself was alive in the consciousness of Christians (in the 1st-2nd centuries and further on) and found expression in the works of the Fathers of the Church, the Canons of the Councils, and in the liturgical books. As the hierarchy of the later time is linked with the first-established hierarchy through the continual succession, it has the same nature as the hierarchy of the apostolic age.

4. The continuity of the apostolic succession in teaching and ordination is an objective reality which cannot be replaced where it is absent. Destruction or rejection of this Church-wide tradition is a spiritual loss which distorts and impoverishes church life.

5. The hierarchial ministry is the only continual grace-filled ministry in the Church, which by its existence does not exclude manifestations of any unusual charisma.

II. The Rev. Canon Prof. J. Robert Wright—"The Origins of the Episcopate and Episcopal Ministry in the Early Church":

This paper describes three complementary, but not contradictory, models or emphases of episcopal ministry in the early Christian Church, in the writings of **1.** Sts. Ignatius of Antioch and Hippolytus of Rome, **2.** St. Irenaeus of Lyons, and **3.** St. Cyprian of Carthage. These three models emphasize the roles of the bishop as **1.** eucharistic president, **2.** chief teacher, and **3.** administrative leader. They also present three different models of church unity, each focused upon the bishop and again complementary rather than contradictory: **1.** eucharistic unity, **2.** doctrinal unity, and **3.** administrative unity. And, finally, they present three complementary pictures of the primary ministry of a bishop: **1.** one who presides over the eucharistic unity of each local church, **2.** the link in time between each local church and the teaching of the apostles, and **3.** the bond across space for the unity of each local church with all the others.

III. The Rev. Canon Prof. Richard A. Norris—"Bishops, Succession, and the Apostolicity of the Church":

This paper seeks to place the idea of an apostolic succession of bishops in the larger setting of the question of the apostolicity in the Church. Appealing to the so called '*Chicago-Lambeth Quadrilateral*,' it suggests that the apostolicity of the church's life and its unity with its own origins does not consist merely or solely in the succession of bishops but in the organic continuity of a 'concatenated set of institutions'—Scriptures, the Apostles' and Nicene Creeds, the two Gospel Sacraments, and Historic Episcopate which support each other and are mutually interrelated.

IV. The Rt. Rev. Mark Dyer, Bishop of Bethlehem— "Theological Reflections on the Patristic Development of Episcopal Ministry":

This theological reflection paper asks the question 'why' concerning the early patristic development of the episcopate. Why did God, the Father, the Son, and the Holy Spirit, give to the people of God, the Church, this specific ministry? Why did the Fathers see it to be essential to the life of the Church?

This paper treats only one aspect of the answer to the question 'why.' But it concerns the most essential gift of God to the Church. Why did the Blessed Trinity give to the people of God the ministry of the episcopate? Simply put: "for the sake of the Holy Life." That is, to serve, preserve and nurture the gift of *Koinonia* with God, the Father, the Son and the Holy Spirit that is the holy life of the baptized community. Because of the gift of the Holy Spirit the Christian is 'no longer a slave but a child, and if a child then also an heir of eternal life,' (Gal. 4:7). The bishop is called by God to serve this Mystery of Communion.

The guiding theological principle is what can be called the holiness of ministerial acts. The bishop is called by God to the ministry of Eucharistic presidency, chief teacher, and bond of unity between the local church and the church universal. It is precisely as he carries out these episcopal acts in fidelity that the bishop represents the Divine life of God. The bishop acts in the likeness of God and in doing so becomes like God, holy, and becomes a living link for the baptized. It is the ancient command of God to Moses: "Speak to all the congregation of the people of Israel and say to them: You shall be holy, for I the Lord your God am holy" (Leviticus 19:1-2).

The ministry of the episcopate is a series of sacred acts which God and the bishop have in common; they are acts in communion with God, a concelebration of the holy life. Fulfilling this ministry, as president of the Eucharistic assembly, teacher of the Word of God and the Holy Tradition, Sign of Unity in and for the Church, the bishop is absorbed, by the grace of the Holy Spirit, into a created participation in the Uncreated Holiness of God. Thus absorbed into the life of God the bishop leads the people of God in the holy life. The episcopate, faithfully exercised, is a sacred deed where heaven and earth encounter the holiness of God.

Essentially, the bishop is called by God to an unconditional loyalty to the holy to seek attachment daily to the holy God. this essay speaks to the life of prayer as central to the vocation of the bishop.

V. Deacon Maxim Kozlov, Docent—"Episcopal Consecration in the Orthodox Church":

Proceeding from the teachings of the Fathers of the first three centuries, excluding the conciliar period, the report states that
- The ordination of ministers (above all, bishops) is performed by bishops;
- Bishops have this right because of the succession in their ordinations coming from the apostles themselves;
- The grace of priesthood granted to a pastor at ordination can be taken away only if he has committed a grave crime against the Church;
- The episcopal consecration has a special grace-giving nature different from the grace of 'royal priesthood' given to all Christians;
- This special grace of holy orders is given to bishops in its fullness: the priesthood in the Church also has other, lower degrees, namely those of presbyters and deacons;
- Presbyters and deacons cannot perform ordinations. This right is exercised by bishops alone; therefore, the apostolic succession of ordinations in the Church is realized through bishops alone.

In the course of historical development of the Church some forms changed, new prayers were introduced and whole rites of pastoral ordinations were composed; but the dogmatic principle has stayed the same: apostolic succession in ordinations is realized only through the bishop. In this we see the full *consensus patrum*.

VI. The Rev. Professor Charles P. Price—"Teachers and Evangelists for the Equipment of the Saints: Prayer Book Doctrine Concerning the Bishop as Teacher, Evangelizer and Focus of Unity":

This paper first establishes the continuity of the threefold ministry of Bishops, Priests and Deacons in the American Episcopal Church with the apostolic ministry of the earliest days of the Church.

As teacher, the bishop has a special responsibility and opportunity to proclaim Christ's resurrection, to interpret the Gospel with the mind of Christ, and to testify to the lordship of Christ over the powers of this world.

As evangelist, the bishop is charged with the Gospel work of "presenting Christ Jesus in the power of the Holy Spirit, so that men may come to put their trust in God through Him as their Saviour" (*Towards the Conversion of England*, p. 1). This definition of evangelizer was accepted in a slightly revised form by the General Convention of the Episcopal Church in 1988.

As one elected by the clergy and people of a diocese, as one approved by the other bishops and dioceses of the Episcopal Church, as one then ordained and empowered by the Holy Spirit to preach and celebrate the sacraments, *the bishop is the focus of unity in the diocese*, who seeks to bring about a unity-in-diversity like the unity of the Father and the Son in the blessed and undivided Trinity.

VII. The Rt. Rev. Richard Frank Grein, Bishop of New York—"The Ministry of Bishops: A Study Document Authorized by the House of Bishops of the Episcopal Church":

In an effort to encourage theological discussion on the role of bishops, The House of Bishops of the Episcopal Church has issued a pastoral teaching: *The Ministry of Bishops: A Study Document*. This document is primarily focused on the rite for the

ordination of a bishop, which is itself rooted in the patristic theology of episcopacy. Thus the bishops' pastoral teaching calls the
Church to examine the origins of episcopacy while seeking to
understand the role of bishops in the present situation.

The Pastoral Teaching makes the following points: **(1)** Bishops
have three primary pastoral roles: teacher and preacher, celebrant
of sacraments, and conciliar leader. **(2)** These three pastoral roles
are not simply selected from a list of possibilities but were given
to us from the patristic age as it was in the process of formation.
They are thus part of a foundational theology of the Church. **(3)**
Each of these pastoral roles unites the Church in a different but
complementary way. **(4)** The bishop in council with other bishops unites the Church in the present. The bishop as teacher and
preacher of the Church's Tradition unites the Church to its past.
The bishop as the center of the eucharistic community connects
the Church to the future (eschatological dimension); thus the
bishop expresses the unity of the Church through time.

VIII. The Rt. Rev. Roger J. White, Bishop of Milwaukee— "The Practice of Episcopal Ministry in the Episcopal Church from a Bishop's Point of View":

These reflections are based on the Ordinal found in The Book
of Common Prayer of the Episcopal Church in the USA and on
the writer's practical experience.

The practice of episcopal ministry is shaped by various factors
including local practice and tradition, the personality of the bishop, and the accepted practice of the Episcopal Church.

There are seven discernable areas of accountability from the
service for 'The Ordination of a Bishop':

  i)   Example, Model, Standard-Setter, 'Icon.'
  ii) Teacher, Preacher and Visionary.
  iii) Supporter of the total ministry of the Church.
  iv) Leader, 'First Citizen,' Guardian of the Faith, Unity and
           Discipline of the Church.
  v)   General Manager and Administrator of a diocese who
           shares such responsibility in the larger Church.

vi) Team leader of priests and deacons, 'coach.'

vii) Servant of the poor, advocate of the outcast in the world.

All of these areas of practical ministry are to be seen within the context of the bishop's being President of the Eucharist and out of this context the bishop's ministry evolves.

As a postscript, some aspects of a bishop's life and ministry which are positive are noted as well as some problem areas.

Positive Aspects

    A. To be a part of the wider Church—being a bishop of God;

    B. To have the support of clergy and laity in prayer, and in sharing biblical reflections;

    C. Experience of ecumenical relations;

    D. To work as a pastor;

    E. To proclaim the Good News—as chief evangelist;

    F. To be 'principal icon' as Eucharistic president;

    G. Experience as community leader—living out our belief.

Some Problem Areas

    i) Lack of clarity in the role and expectation of a bishop;

    ii) Issues of authority and how to exercise such authority;

    iii) Who teaches bishops?

    iv) Growing administrative load;

    v) Clergy problems and issues of parish conflict;

    vi) Schedule that is not conducive to a healthy spiritual life;

    vii) Lack of time to 'vision';

    viii) Isolation and loneliness;

    ix) Being 'guardian of the faith, unity and discipline of the Church' in a self-centered society;

    x) Loss of status and influence in a secular society;

    xi) Pressures on family—lack of quality time with wife and children;

    xii) Difficulty in advocating for the poor as world-wide needs and demands grow.

In all of this practice of ministry bishops function with God's help and that is the central focus of their lives.

IX. Archbishop Mikhail of Vologda and Veliky Ustiug— "The Practice of Episcopal Ministry in the Russian Orthodox Church Today":

1. This paper gives information about the episcopal structure in the Russian Orthodox Church and about major areas of activity of a diocesan bishop.

2. The scope of activity of a bishop includes the celebration of sacraments, teaching, and administration. The last activity is the most labor-consuming and involves contacts with the external and non-ecclesiastical world, with individuals and officials and with organizations, including local administrative authorities.

3. The constant and principal objectives of the episcopal ministry coincide with those of the whole church—that is, to serve the salvation of people. This does not exclude but rather implies a flexibility with regard to the methodology used for a given place and time and especially with regard to those with whom the bishop comes into contact.

4. The bishop's fellowship with the people of God, the majority of whom are lay believers, occurs in prayer and in sacraments administered by him (especially the Eucharist), as well as through preaching, at diocesan meetings, during personal appointments as well as audiences and visitations, through messages and circular letters addressed to the flock.

5. For the most part the contacts a bishop has are those with the clergy, over whose activity the bishop supervises, either personally or through the deans. Such contacts are actualized through the concelebration of the Liturgy and other sacraments, through personal appointments and meetings on the diocesan and parish levels, through the assistance the clergy render to their bishop in the Diocesan council and within other diocesan bodies.

6. The diocesan bishop is the educator for the whole flock but, above all, to the clergy. In his capacity he must utilize not only reward but also discipline. The appointment of the clergy to parishes is a particular concern for the bishop.

7. The diocesan bishop is subject to the Patriarch and the Holy Synod acting under Patriarchal leadership.
8. The Patriarch and Synod exercise leadership by summoning bishops to the sessions of the Synod. They appoint, transfer, reward, and discipline bishops.
9. A bishop, as every member of the clergy, may be involved in the work of civic organizations.
10. A bishop has a special responsibility before God which is more weighty than that of any other in his flock.

As the central ecclesiastical person in his diocese, the bishop, in his spiritual life, especially in prayer, should give primary attention to the care of his flock and only after that to himself.

• • •

The following is the summary review of the main points of interest that emerged in discussion of the papers summarized above.

Discussion emphasized the essential nature of the patristic foundations of the historic episcopate that come from the theology of the early church. There was much discussion of the question, what weight should be given to developing patristic understanding of bishops in view of the rather sparse evidence that can be found in the New Testament, and on the question of whether the development was ever contradictory or actually continuous. (Example: Must bishops be always celibate or always married?) The representatives of both our churches affirmed a fundamental distinction of the episcopate from presbyterate as normative, and there was further discussion over the extent to which this is to be seen as irreversible. There was also discussion of the prescription of cumulative orders (the requirement that a priest must first be a deacon and that a bishop must already be both), a practice which both our churches follow.

The authors of papers from both churches highlighted the practice of "popular election" of bishops in the early church (Hippolytus: "chosen by all people"), and the ensuing conversation focused on alternative means of choosing, such as choice by secular rulers or choice by ordained ecclesiastical leaders only. The so-called "indelibility" of holy orders was raised, and in particular the life tenure of episcopal ordination, together with the related concepts of validity/invalidity and the related practices of suspension, deposition, and degradation and problems related thereto.

Attention was given to the various emphases or concepts of episcopal/apostolic succession that can be found in the patristic evidence, such as the eschatological emphasis of succession that has been found in St. Ignatius, the retrospective/linear/historical concept found in St. Clement of Rome, doctrinal succession emphasized by St. Irenaeus, ordinational succession (Tertullian and Hippolytus), and the authoritative/administrative emphasis found in St. Cyprian of Carthage. It was urged in our conversation that all these concepts of succession must be seen more as complementary than contradictory.

It was also pointed out that the episcopate should be seen as one very central ingredient in a "concatenated" set of institutions that developed side-by-side in the early church and are all to be seen as inter-related in their functions of continuing and safeguarding the apostolic inheritance: the canon of holy scriptures, the Gospel sacraments of Baptism and Eucharist, the Apostles' and Niceno-Constantinopolitan Creeds, and the historic episcopate. All this development was seen as part of God's providential ordering of the church from its very beginning, and thus was related ultimately to the mystery of God in the communion of the Holy Trinity.

Comments were also voiced about the need for an historical approach to the church's tradition, even to that of the early church, so that not all church writers of every age and of every school need to be seen as having the same validity or degree of importance. Questions were also raised as to the necessity of attributing divine origin or institution or foundation to every aspect of the episcopate and apostolic ministry.

Discussion also revealed that in the process of the consecration of bishops there are in both churches liturgical and terminological differences. However, both sides pointed out that the very process of episcopal consecration is inseparably linked to the Eucharist and in its essence conforms to the practice of the early church.

Challenges of the time and the missionary responsibilities of the church often lead to revision of both liturgical texts and praxis, as is witnessed by the appearance of a new Book of Common Prayer of the Episcopal Church in the U.S.A. in 1979. Faithfulness to the truth of the Gospel should be the criterion for any change or amendment to be introduced. To avoid misunderstanding, all liturgical changes should be introduced with utmost care and be accompanied with explanations.

There was discussion of the prophetic role of the bishop, and of the obstacles posed to such witness by the values of a 'consumer' society, especially in the United States.

Great interest was shown by the American participants in the present religious state of affairs in Russia. Of particular interest was the law of 1991 respecting religious freedom, which not only gave the church the status of a juridical person, but lifted restrictions on charitable activities and clergy gatherings, and removed the oppressive tax on clergy salaries. Equal interest was shown in the government policy which allowed the church to recover ownership and use of sequestered religious buildings—a policy which economic difficulties make it hard for the church to take advantage of.

Both sides in the dialogue evinced a desire to understand the canonical and organizational structures of the other, particularly in regard to the episcopate and its exercise of authority. On this subject several cordial exchanges took place.

Report on the Teaching Ministry of Bishops in the Church of England

by J. Robert Wright

[Prepared in the summer of 1992 from interviews with Dr. Mary Tanner and others in the Church of England]

Over the last five years in the Church of England there has been an increasing awareness of the historic responsibility of the House of Bishops to be guardians of the faith as well as leaders of the church in matters of doctrine, faith, and order, and this has at the same time coincided with a paralleled increasing awareness of the need for collegiality and better processes for consultation and common decision-making among the bishops themselves. All this has developed in the context of a church in change and also in response to an increased self-understanding of the functions of episcopal ministry that has come both from self-studies within the Church of England and from the discussions about bishops in ecumenical dialogues with other churches. In addition, there is a particular teaching responsibility vested collegially in the House of Bishops by Article 7 of the Synodical Government Measure of 1969, which provides that any motion or question "touching doctrinal formulae or the services or ceremonies of the Church of England or the administration of the Sacraments or sacred rites thereof shall, before it is finally approved by the General Synod, be referred to the House of Bishops and shall be submitted for such final approval [by the General Synod] in terms proposed by the House of Bishops and not otherwise." Thus, as is generally true in the church catholic throughout history, a particular responsibility for determining and teaching the apostolic faith of the church is placed upon the historic episcopate, acting collegially and in consultation with the whole church.

As a result of the increasing awareness of these responsibilities, in the last five years there have been three notable instances in which the bishops have sought to guide and give a lead in doctrinal matters facing the Church of England: **1)** On the question of the ordination of women, they have shaped and given to the General Synod a theological basis for any legislation that may eventually be passed. The preface of their report to the General Synod outlines the process they followed. It explains that their report is in three sections: "The first seeks to identify the principal theological issued concerned. The second section sets out the principles upon which the legislation should be based, and the third section sets out a more detailed framework for the legislation and for the safeguards." **2)** From the debate sparked by the Bishop of Durham on the Resurrection and the Virgin Birth, they produced an agreed six-point theological position statement, followed by a 39-page exposition, all published in a booklet as "The Nature of Christian Belief," of which the concluding section was entitled "The Individual and Collegial Responsibility of Bishops for the Faith of the Church." It states that, in teaching the Christian faith, "the bishops have a particular role and responsibility, but this is exercised in two ways: 'in council,' that is, in consultation with the whole people of God, and especially with their representatives in synod; and collegially, that is, seeking as one body the wisdom and insight that come from the grace of God's Holy Spirit in and through corporate prayer and reflection, and expressing to the rest of the Church and to the world the common mind given to them as a result." **3)** In the current debate on human sexuality, the bishops have also produced a position statement and report, now published and being discussed in the church.

Hence, in the three areas of church order, faith, and morals, the bishops over the last five years have collectively taken a lead in guiding the church, and in the cases of the ordination of women and "The Nature of Christian Belief", the work of the bishops has gone first to the General Synod and then to the dioceses for debate and discussion. The publication of the reports was paid for by the General Synod.

Nonetheless, there has been frustration with the lack of time and space for considering such questions. Even though the House of Bishops of the Church of England meets three times a year and consists only of 44 active diocesan bishops and nine elected suffragans (no other suffragans and no retired bishops at all), this composition is still regarded in England as inadequate to deal consultatively and collegially with the weight and complexity of matters doctrinal, theological, liturgical, and moral that come before the church and upon which the bishops are increasingly being asked to take a collective lead. During all this flurry of the last five years, the House of Bishops has become aware that if the bishops are to act collegially in such matters, they have need for an on-going "Theological Group" to give in-depth consideration and make initial recommendations, which has now been established on a standing basis to meet some 3-4 times a year. It is made up of the bishops who are chairs of the Doctrine Commission, the Liturgical Commission, the Faith and Order Advisory Group, the General Synod Board of Mission, the Council for Christian Unity of the General Synod, and also one or two other bishops deemed to have particular theological competence. Theologians, consultants, research persons, and other advisors are invited on an unpaid and ad-hoc basis for hearings on particular questions, either by correspondence or in person. This "Theological Group" has no initiatory authority, but only receives what is given to it, and its purpose is to take in-depth soundings and then produce papers of advice for the House of Bishops on key questions of a theological, doctrinal, liturgical, or moral nature that are referred to it (from such bodies as the Standing Committee of the General Synod, and, through the Standing Committee of the House of Bishops, the Council for Christian Unity, Anglican Consultative Council, etc.).

Thus far, some seven agenda items have come before this Theological Group: 1) What to do about the resolution from the Anglican Consultative Council on the *filioque* (which came via the

Faith and Order Advisory Group, from the Council for Christian Unity). 2) The question of whether the solemnization/blessing of marriage may be performed by Deacons. 3) Questions relating to the distribution of the Reserved Sacrament by Deacons. 4) The status and role of Suffragan Bishops. 5) Moral questions related to the phenomenon of assisted suicides. 6) The general subject of feminist theology, with its ramifications (referred by the General Synod). 7) Doctrinal matters relating to liturgical concelebration (referred by the General Synod). In the case of number 2 above, guidelines with extended notes have been produced and endorsed by the entire House of Bishops.

Thus, the Theological Group of the House of Bishops does seem a tentative way forward for the bishops of the Church of England in addressing the needs for episcopal consultation, collegiality, and doctrinal teaching, although it should also be noted that there are still other groups that do preparatory thinking for the House as well: 1) The Ecumenical Bishops Group, made up of all those bishops who have special responsibility for bilateral or multilateral dialogues; and 2) The Doctrine Commission and the Liturgical Commission, both of which report to the House of Bishops and each of which is chaired by a Bishop though their membership is not restricted to bishops.

The reality of the future is best struck by the concluding paragraph of the report on "Individual and Collegial Responsibility of Bishops" already mentioned: "To give this work the attention it requires may well call for a revision of the Church's expectations of a bishop's priorities. If bishops are to give more leadership and guidance in the sphere of teaching and belief they will need to redesign the patterns of their work together in order to give more time to this task, and to drawing on the resources of their various theological advisory bodies. We believe this would benefit the whole Church of England; but the effects would be widely felt, in that some things which bishops normally do at present would have to be done by others, and such a change could not, therefore, be carried out without the support and co-operation of the whole church community."